Adolescent Trauma:

Youth and the Mystery Wall

Phil Frampton, D.Phil (hc)

The International Federation of Social Workers

Artwork by Emily Mulenga
Published by IFSW

ISBN: 978-3-906820-27-9 (Paperback)
Edition 1 June 2022

Printed in Germany on 100% post-consumer recycled paper

Acknowledgements

I wish to heartily thank Dr Brian Apter, Andy Bevan, Dr Simon Claridge, Dr Liz Davies, Jo Eastop, Sidonie and Gail Frampton, Eleanor Hespe, James Honeybone, Brian and Glenys Ingham, Ann Kerrigan, Clemmie Leaver, Anne Peake, Dr Paulina Ramirez, Dr Annette Rimmer, John and Vicki Seddon, Ruth Stark and Kate Wright for all their assistance and advice with this work. In particular I would especially like to express my immense gratitude to Dr Simon Claridge for his invaluable suggestions, corrections, good humour and patience in helping me get this work over the line. I wish to commend Ruth Stark and Rory Truell at the International Federation of Social Workers for their fulsome encouragement and their support for promoting the voices of service users.

7th November 2021

Phil Frampton 2021 (and 1971)

Contents

Dedication

To those young people across the globe who have sacrificed their lives trying to make a better world for themselves, their peers and their families; and to the new generations of young activists who press forward in a never-ending stream of belief, hope and compassion for humankind.

Foreword

The UN Convention on the Rights of the Child was ratified on 2nd December 1990. 140 nation states have accepted that they have a responsibility to meet the 54 Articles of this international Treaty. and act on the obligations of the treaty. USA remains the one member of the UN that has yet to ratify.

Provision, Protection, Promotion and Participation were the headline principles to implementation. Much has been written and invested in the first three 'p's; but where is the world in terms of ***participation?***

I first met Phil around 20 years ago when the *IFSW Training Manual on Social Work and the Rights of the Child* was published in 2002. He was writing a column for one of the social work journals in the UK, *Community Care,* and was a founder member of the Care Leavers Association in England. Since then, we have met, debated, campaigned together and shared laughter and friendship. I have learnt more from the care experienced community family than from all the textbooks and research offered in training and post qualification development. The measured and patient honesty about our failings as professionals and members of our communities are there to be heard – we all must be better at listening to each other. When this happens, we all are empowered by each other to participate.

It is timely for IFSW to now publish this book as we co-build our vision of the 2020 Global Social Work Community conference into reality in our People's Global Summit Co-building a Sustainable Eco-social world. https://newecosocialworld.com/

Phil writes from the perspective of his experiences in England, but he sets them against wider international cultures and policies. He invites us to question some of the assumptions that we all make at different times and in different places. In the development of this publication, we too have had those conversations as we talked about the context of different demographic challenges of regions, be that predominance of older or younger people within different populations; we have debated different economic contexts and how change happens locally and globally. We have discussed how change happens - the sudden traumatic change from natural disasters or explosions and deaths when we have failed to ensure transportation of fuels. We have contrasted these with the slow changes, for example progress made in agricultural of industrial work producing the unintended consequences of climate change and the slow path to the death of the planet.

The unique perspective that Phil offers us is to 'read, mark, learn and in-wardly digest' is from reflecting on his lived experience, knowledge and learning and helping us to journey together to change our world for sus-tainable shared futures. Please join in and participate in our co-design and co-build of a balanced, sustainable eco-social world

Ruth Stark

Social Worker

President IFSW 2014-2018

Introduction

Adolescent Trauma: Youth and the Mystery Wall

Adolescent trauma and prolonged angst come at a huge cost to society as well as those who experience that trauma. This discourse explores an unidentified societal process which takes place in plain sight of parents, adolescents and the education system but which remains unacknowledged due to factors related to social conditioning. It places this feature within the collective context of the phrase: "it takes a whole village to raise a child" but references the overlooked collective role of the village children in raising that child.

It is argued that the young person's parented and formal academic worlds are based on property and power relations, which generate contradictory and polarised learning frameworks. During their teenage years, young people process these learning frameworks as separated by subconsciously erected walls. The result for many adolescents is that the existing formal (academic) and informal (parental) education system undermines their sense of wellbeing due to the contradictory messages and experiences emanating from these parallel worlds.

We consider the historical tendency to collectively raise children and how the emergence of capitalism saw a shift to the nuclear family, atomising child rearing and formalising children as the parental property. As industry developed, the increasing need for a literate, more educated and yet compliant workforce led to capitalism reintroducing a collective aspect of child rearing in the form of schooling. It is argued that as a result, modern childhood features two contrasting and often contradictory learning environments in the form of the atomised nuclear family and the corporate collective schools.

The exceptions to this development towards twin-track atomised collective children's education were the boarding schools rearing the offspring of the wealthy and the orphanages set up to house society's unwanted waifs. The author considers aspects in which the corporate residential environment may have some advantages over that of the nuclear family in facilitating peer empowerment and learning environments more akin to those in corporate academic establishments.

The young person's emergent perceptions of self-worth and personal and collective empowerment are discussed as key features of adolescent development and these are considered in the context of the prevailing property relations and the contrasting learning environments. It is contended that the societal siloing of the academic and parented worlds is mirrored by adolescents but creates an inferno of contradiction and uncertainty generating the trauma and angst that these teenagers experience in intensely personal ways.

To protect their empowered existence and sense of rationality, teenagers make the most of the societal siloing of the school and parental worlds, by using silence, lies, obfuscations and socially or digitally encrypted communication to strengthen the wall between the two worlds, so shutting out adult intervention; the latter to the chagrin of the parents.

This Mystery Wall is the cocoon in which adolescents' self-identity and self-esteem can emerge feeding off their peers and collective peer-empowered world as the lifeblood.

It is further contended that Western governments requiring a compliant workforce are wary of the unbridled collective insights, will and energy of young people. As a result, the ruling elites of modern societies have for decades taken advantage of adolescent trauma to deprecate and demonise their collectivity as a socially abhorrent physical and moral threat to the rest of society.

The ongoing Teen Year War, this battle to break in the young power-houses, the new workforce, brings many casualties not least society itself as the traumatic wounds suffered by parents and adolescents alike are often left unrecognised and unhealed.

Adult society tolerates the price of adolescent trauma rather than challenge the prevailing property and power relationships.

We conclude that for society to end this needless damage and become more open, honest and usefully productive requires discovering strategies to embrace the energy, collectivity, collective empowerment and societal emancipation of adolescents rather than continuing the repressive road of mistrust, atomisation and repression.

On Conventional Wisdoms

In this discourse, I expect that some may bridle at my challenging several of the conventional wisdoms about the family. If I challenge the actions or ideas of particular individuals or groups it is not to denigrate them. I hope that by continuing to read this book you may come to see different views and ways of considering the family and in particular the plight of young people and how we organise looking after them in our world primarily a result of the ever-present perspective for economic growth. I am not trying to convert or upset you, but I value the notion of offering hopefully new ideas and ways of looking at our world to complement and/or challenge the present status quo.

If society is to progress beyond the haze and demoralisation so evident in the global mistrust of our governments then we must focus on systemic facts that have developed for societal reasons. My arguments are centred on the observation that, as individuals, we largely operate within the societal narrative around which it generates social norms and influences.

I was born in a refuge for unmarried mothers-to-be and abandoned to the care system for the duration of my childhood. For the overwhelming majority of that time, I was in orphanages, spending more than ten years in one residence. I never knew my parents. I never experienced the love of adults but my childhood was not a loveless one. We children had each other. In doing our daily chores, traipsing to school, scrapping on the pitch, shoplifting in the town, bickering in the playroom, playing in the gardens and challenging the abusers, we learned to care for each other.

We were not the conventional wisdom. Black/Mixed Race, I was not the product of conventional wisdom. At 16, I was alone in my bedsit studying (unsuccessfully) for my Oxbridge University entrance exam in between running the school debating society and playing in the school's rugby 1st XV. At 17 I completed my A level exams then headed to work in a hotel so I had a roof over my head before attending Bristol University. When I arrived at the university, conventional wisdom said I was a compulsive liar and plagiarist because I could not get to university from being in an orphanage.

Conventional wisdom and its accompanying homilies never sat well with me. In studying economics at school, I had found and poured over J K Galbraith's celebrated critique of post-war America, The Affluent Society. In it he had coined the term conventional wisdom as commonly held tenets and beliefs, noting, especially in relation to economics that such wisdom often acted as an inert mass holding society back from progress. Strikingly, Marx had considered the flipside in relation to change. Marx asserted: "*theory also becomes a material force once it has gripped the masses*," highlighting how if conventional wisdoms can hold the world back, new wisdoms in the hands of the people can physically move society forward.

Conventional wisdoms, however, generally reflect the ruling ideology and are notably peddled out and brushed up as needs must. So, the English government when refusing the country's nurses a pay rise, declared: "There is no magic money tree!" but the tree miraculously appeared to provide for a deal with the same government's allies in Northern Ireland to prevent the government's collapse. After years of explaining away cuts in taxes with lines such as; "Human beings are ultimately selfish and must look after their own interests," the refrain during the COVID-19 pandemic switched to: "We're all in it together!" Sometimes, however, the 'taken-as-read' truth is doomed by the advance of science and understanding. The world is no longer flat and Napoleon Bonaparte was not short. The Bible can't be taken literally. The Sun does not revolve around the Earth and you do not have to eat for two during pregnancy.

At other times, as social movements pressed for change, political expediency opened the door to change, laying the basis for but not totally the undermining of the supposedly self-evident truths. Blacks could vote but they were still of lower intelligence. Women could vote but their brains were still too small or stuffed with homemaking to cope with politics. Nevertheless, the grounds were laid for major inroads to be made into those baseless truths.

Two decades and more of campaigning, lecturing, writing and broadcasting for just treatment of young people in care and careleavers and challenging societal prejudice and discrimination has involved me alongside other social care activists, almost on a daily basis, challenging the conventional wisdoms about young people in care and careleavers. What has become increasingly clear is that the prejudice and stigmatisation directed against young people in care has its roots not only in conventional wisdoms about the nuclear family but also in those regarding children and adolescents in particular.

I am sure all social workers would agree with the statement that we do not live in a child-centred society and most would also support the assertion that society does not take a child-centred approach even when dealing with issues relating to children. That approach is often left to the allocated social worker and child-focussed academic. The consequence is that in society as a whole, all manner of "conventional wisdoms" in relation to young people are allowed to fester despite the fact that, under scrutiny, they are revealed to show little basis in reality or logic. Yet these wisdoms, propagated as part of the dominant societal narrative, inevitably often inform those in the health and social care professions.

Many people will recognise the weaknesses in those conventional wisdoms as applied to their specific areas of interest. However, precisely because we are surrounded by them in the rest of our daily lives, we absorb many as self-evident truths, which is why establishment politicians and media celebrities are so happy to trot them out. Conventional wisdoms help us not to think matters through in detail. They conceal within them a writhing body of assumptions and contradictions and we use them for that very reason.

Those 'self-evident truths' that apply to the family carry particular additional weight to us because, in the midst of all the psychological complications and uncertainties of our closest personal relations, homilies and societal 'truths', they offer us a rope to cling to.

"Empowerment of the service user" has been a very prominent phrase in social work circles over the last 20 years and many will know that the phrase emanated from the works of Paulo Frere, the Liberation Psychologist. Frere also wrote that for people as a whole to progress it was necessary first to deconstruct society and its dominant narratives, inspecting each piece to assess its value for particular groups of individuals and communities; to challenge the narrative.

Challenging the arena and the co-ordinates in which we have grown comfortable to fight is a daunting prospect for all. How will we fare if the arena suddenly has no boundaries and the ground on which we stand turns to ocean? What will happen if we let the teenagers off the leash? If we let them stand together on a street or on a field?

I watched a group of lads playing football in a park and using their coats and sticks to mark the pitch. I wanted to bring the world to watch teenagers left to their own devices; playing, co-operating, arguing, niggling, risk-assessing and resolving conflicts. To refuse to challenge is to accept and deny what could be – a brighter future for families.

The pandemic has thrown a spotlight on our societies, their rulers and their rules, on our communities and our atomisation, our habits and our assumptions, our elderly and our youth, our present and our future. The adolescents are our future but they are also today's citizenship – this much they demonstrated in focussing the world on the urgent need to tackle climate change and racism. What better opportunity than now to seize the time, place under the microscope and review our approach to assisting young people to emerge safely and confidently into adulthood? However, if we are to travel down this road then we have to begin. Over 20 years ago, children's specialist, Professor Berry Mayall, may have been thinking of sitting in the dentist's chair when she used the word "extracting" to define the complexity and nerve-irritating nature of the first task, namely deconstructing childhood:

"The proper study of the social order has to include the social condition of childhood, and the contributions of children to it. The sociological project is to work initially on the task of extracting children theoretically from the family in order to study their social positioning as a social group. A next step is to replace children in reciprocal relations with adults, and childhood with adulthood." (The Sociology of Childhood in Relation to Children's Rights, Mayall, The International Journal of Children's Rights, 2000)

From deconstruction, Mayall argued, we can move on to reconstruction. In the same piece, Mayall was very hopeful, believing that society was moving forward:

"The sociology of childhood has begun to shift adult understandings of what it is to be a child, and how this varies across time and across societies. On the one hand, the work is leading to greater respect for children and childhood; on the other hand, it is leading to fuller understanding of the wrongs suffered by children." (ibid.)

However, two decades on and surveying the world of increased child exploitation and poverty, social control orders and teenage trauma, it is arguable that the position of adolescents in civil society has moved backwards rather than forwards.

Young people, as Mayall says, have agency; however, in her recognising the barriers to exercising that power for altering their collective status in society, she points to the solution:

"...it is hard for children to take the initiative and participate in social affairs, and it is hard for adults to permit them to, and very hard for children and adults to work together on anything like equal terms." (ibid.)
It is that togetherness and collectivity that may yet see the unfolding of a new world for young people. The starting point is that armies of academics and young people recognise the need for change. In the unprecedented youth-lead worldwide illegal strikes and demonstrations demanding action on climate change and racial injustice, teenagers denied social convention by asserting themselves as citizens even though they are denied citizens' rights. Adult society now applauds their stance. In considering adolescent trauma and the crises facing so many of our young people, the task now is to identify the causes and measures which will bring out change. That may mean defying social convention.

"It is not only the hostility of others that may prevent us from questioning the status quo. Our will to doubt can be just as powerfully sapped by an internal sense that societal conventions must have a sound basis, even if we are not sure exactly what this may be, because they have been adhered to by a great many people for a long time. It seems implausible that our society could be gravely mistaken in its beliefs, and at the same time, that we would be alone in noticing the fact." (The Consolations of Philosophy, De Botton, Hamish Hamilton, 2000)

'Youth Empowerment' or Youth Containment?

A decade ago, Archibald and Wilson highlighted the distortions of 'empowerment' discussions, pointing to the meaning of the word. which came to the fore in the 1970s as a term for emancipation and liberation from exploitation but has since been used as a fashionable cover to disguise any actions or tools of personal enhancement. In 2011, referring to the education sector, they wrote:

"The empowerment lexicon has grown over time. Yet the concept's ubiquity is troubling, largely because power has often ironically been omitted from discussions of empowerment. The theoretical concern is that the evolutionary lineage of empowerment as a concept has divaricated and been subtly waylaid, obfuscating its initial emancipatory import; the related practical concern is that educators and education researchers who use the concept may do so in ways which ignore (and could be complicit in perpetuating) underlying contentious power relations in the lives of purported beneficiaries."

(Rethinking Empowerment: Theories of Power and the Potential for Emancipatory Praxis, Archibald & Wilson, Cornell University 2011)

Archibald and Wilson may well have read the 1995 paper of Gutierrez, Maye, and DeLois which stated: *'Empowerment is the process of increasing personal, interpersonal or political power so that individuals, families, and communities can take action to improve their situations'.* (The organizational context of empowerment practice: Implications for social work administration. Social Work, Gutierrez, L., Maye, G. L., & DeLois, K. 1995)

The latter authors are some of many who focus on the process of acquisition of empowerment skills rather than empowerment being the arrival at a position of increased interpersonal or political power. Process-driven definitions may be suitable for some social work interventions but tells only half the story, losing sight of the result and focussing on the journey rather than reaching the destination. In this context it is worth noting that youth work history is littered with thousands of short-term youth projects that tick "skills development" boxes then abandon adolescents to their still societally disempowered fate.

Most worryingly, focussing empowerment studies on particularly marginalised cohorts of adolescents feeds into supporting both the establishment status quo, which requires disempowered adolescence, and the social narrative that glosses over adolescent trauma as an anti-social condition, colloquially referred to as "being a teenager".

In contrast, Robert Adams, referring to social work, described empowerment as: "...*the capacity of individuals, groups and/or communities to take control of their circumstances, exercise power and achieve their own goals, and the process by which, individually and collectively, they are able to help themselves and others to maximize the quality of their lives.*" (Adams, Robert. Empowerment, participation and social work. New York: Palgrave Macmillan, 2008, p.xvi)

The popular use of the English word, empowerment, is widely acknowledged to have only begun in the 1980s as a result of the emerging popularity amongst radical academic circles of Brazilian Marxist educator and philosopher, Paulo Freire's book, Pedagogy of the Oppressed, first published in 1968. The word empowerment (though Paulo Freire never used the exact word) was described as his key to the process of achieving social emancipation and liberation but the term has since been adopted by ruling elites across the world who have stripped it of its revolutionary content, and draped it over their shoulders to convey progressive intent. That multi-billionaire, Bill Gates, calls on leaders to "empower others" should be warning enough to academics and social work practitioners to consider whether "empowerment" and Paulo Freire have parted company.

The use and agreed meanings of the word can be ambiguous because it can refer to both status and the means or process by which it is achieved. In this discourse, I generally use the term empowerment to refer to attainment of levels of power at a level to successfully challenge adults and the term empowering to refer to the process.

Today, it is hard to read the mountains of writings purportedly on adolescence, (youth) empowerment and collective empowerment without considering that an army of academics has been employed simply to save the "adolescents who fall through the cracks". These scholars' benevolent standpoint appears to be that 'empowerment' (by which they mean increased self-efficacy) can be used to develop and integrate erring adolescents into society.

Their Labour of Sisyphus is against the background of prevailing societal political structures and countervailing approaches that are designed to disempower adolescents and subject them to the dictates of capitalism.

Western capitalism renders a social climate where unbridled collectives of adolescents are to be feared and society behaves as if the threshold for 'Original Sin' has been shifted whereby instead of beginning at birth it magically begins at 10 years of age and ends at the age of 19, if not 21.

Societal alarm at the sight of "youths on street corners" and media rants about "teenage yobs" is a more telling starting point for looking at adolescent empowerment than focussing on the young drop out. Adolescence is more usefully looked at as the stage for seizure of empowerment yet in the context that capital insists youth must be reined in to serve at its table.

What the academics and social researchers appear to overlook, which governments do not, is the actual empowerment that the adolescent is already achieving particularly through association with peers and peer groups. This collective power, which emerges particularly in adolescents' academic settings, significantly accelerates and increases their levels of empowerment. It develops at best out of sync with their limited empowerment in the nuclear family setting and at worst in volatile contradiction to parental fetters.

Being a teenager is a traumatic condition, reflected in prolonged periods of angst and, for many, mental turmoil. This is discussed in more detail in Chapter 5 of this work. Teenage trauma is a societally induced condition. On top of trying to make sense of their place in the world and manage the duality of their empowered and disempowered existences, they also face the unrelenting societal strains to disempower and atomise them as adolescents. Under this pressure many are spat out along the way. Government throws less and less resources at appearing to make attempts to salvage them for society and hands medals out to the social workers and academic researchers earnestly involved in the rescue attempts.

By stripping away the veil of autarchic benevolence we may yet discover means by which we can remove societal, if not governmental fear of adolescents, celebrate rather than denigrate their empowerment and so prevent the oft-irreparable damage and destruction caused to millions of young lives.

Youth work and youth studies that genuinely wish to assist young people will seek ways to enhance their collective empowerment in such a way as to accelerate their emancipation rather than subdue them. Societal emancipation is fundamental to empowerment and all else, if set within a framework of achieving less, is subjugation; at best akin to offering the disenfranchised a more comfortable bed.

Increased consideration needs to be given to whether teenage/adolescent trauma is more a product of property relations in society rather than of hormonal changes in the young person. As young people begin to grow in confidence in their ability to navigate their world they are increasingly faced with the many contradictions between their experience of life in their privately parented world of the nuclear family and the corporate world of their academic education. The young person is required to make sense of a multitude of contradictory experiences, degrees of empowerment, social structures and messages emerging from the two very different worlds.

Where most non-residential schooling is concerned, rather than attempt to make sense of these contradictions, parents, educators and pupils compartmentalise these two worlds. Unless the domestic situation is revealed to be incapable of delivering the child fit to be educated, a pupil's home life is a parked subject between parents, teachers and young people, if for different reasons.

The young people are left to internalise the contradictions which may seriously undermine their ability to develop their self-esteem and self-worth. Society is the loser, but puts on its blinkers for fear of upsetting parental property relations, which are key components of capitalist democratic societies.

Route Map

In Chapter 1 we discuss the background to the Mystery Wall discourse, a differing approach to childhood from the perspective of someone raised in orphanage care and how residential care as collective care has its roots in the predominant historic earlier form of care, engaging "the whole village to raise the child." We discuss how the societally dominant prejudices of careism and childism have distorted discussions on children away from being child-centred and consequently omitted the key part played by the village children in child-rearing and nurturing. The chapter includes a brief overview of adolescent academic education in the UK around much of which this discourse is centred.

In Chapter 2, we discuss the evolution of the social position of children and the emergence of the concept of adolescence as a unique life stage. We consider the legal and societal view of children as parental property. The predominant concepts of family, parental rights and responsibilities and the changing demands and role of the state in relation to children are discussed in the context of industrialisation and capitalism's growth to become the dominant global economic system. Capitalism's switch from seeing the child as a means of production into an investment for the future development and protection of production and markets is identified as the basis for the emergence of adolescence as a distinct period where children are excluded from the labour market. It is argued that the same processes have led to a rigid and stultifying standardisation of children's education, whereby children's contribution to their families and peer groups is overlooked and all focus is on adult-led academic education to the detriment of child development, families, education and intellectual capital as a whole.

We explore how, from the late 19th century, capitalism focussed on preparing adolescents to become part of the workforce by directing intensified propaganda and stigmatisation as to the social danger posed by adolescents in order to justify the use of repressive measures. We look at how the academic sciences were used to 'biologize' adolescence, justifying infantilisation and oppression of teenagers to the detriment of the family. Finally, this chapter looks at how capitalism is outgrowing and demanding the reshaping of adolescence as it was known in the 20th century.

Chapter 3 looks at the processes rooted in property relations that lead to the erection of the Mystery Wall. It argues that the Wall has its origins in property relations and arises from the state's division of spheres of responsibility between parents and corporate educational institutions. It contends that the corporate education process further commodifies and collectivises young people's transit through adolescence. We consider the impact on the adolescent of the parented/home world and the school world being respectively and contrastingly domains of private and corporate property.

Chapter 4 considers the functions and mechanisms of the adolescent's Mystery Wall, protecting the seeds of self-esteem and self-identity as they germinate in the fields of peer group collective empowerment. It argues that adolescents' rapidly developing self-efficacy is expanded within their collectively empowered peer groups; this in contrast to their disempowered atomised condition in the parental home. This sense of developing self-efficacy brings about a qualitative change in parental relationships necessitating a complex often dramatic period of negotiations which challenge both the self-esteem of the adolescent and the nurturing skills of the parent. The Wall acts to protect the adolescent's self-esteem by siloing the parental world. Adolescents bring in additional cement for the Wall by consciously and subconsciously developing communication barriers with specific functions for parents, teachers and peers. Parents nurturing aspirations are frustrated as they find themselves blocked off from large parts of their adolescents' peer empowered world.

Chapter 5 deals with government and media portrayals of adolescents and the impact they have on society. It then goes on to consider how this propaganda is perceived by adolescents and looks at how this might negatively impact on not only the collective self-esteem of adolescents but also their attitudes to other adolescents. It considers the levels of trauma faced by adolescents in today's Western societies and whether, by poisoning the well of collectivity and collective empowerment from which teenagers draw their self-esteem and self-identity, governments and their media are the primary cause for the rising tide of adolescent mental ill-health.

It has been argued that capitalism's development and capitalist property relations' growing contradictions with the needs of the modern nuclear family are a major contribution to adolescent trauma. Chapter 6 considers how taking young people out of the nuclear family settings impacts on their transition through adolescence. It looks at the peer collective empowerment in boarding school and orphanage/children's home environments and how this impacts on management practices. We discuss the removal of the many negotiation stages involved in the adolescent transition.

In Chapter 7 consideration is given as to moving forward regarding some of the issues raised by the Mystery Wall. Recognition of children's active role in the family and the benefits of parenting skills discussions for adolescents are raised for further debate and research. We highlight some of the issues raised for adults and adolescents to consider and also what teenage and adult action are required for meaningful collective empowerment of young people.

Background

Content

In this chapter, we discuss background to the Mystery Wall discourse, a differing approach to childhood from the perspective of someone raised in orphanage care and how residential care as collective care has its roots in the predominant historic earlier form of care, engaging "the whole village to raise the child." We discuss how the societally dominant prejudices of careism and childism have distorted discussions on children away from being child-centred and consequently omitted the key part played by the village children in child-rearing and nurturing. The chapter includes a brief overview of adolescent academic education in the UK around much of which this discourse is centred

Finding the Wall

As a lecturer, broadcaster and writer on issues facing social care and young people, I have had the benefit of being able to approach those issues through the lens of my eighteen years growing up in the English care system and mainly in mixed-gender orphanages for neglected, abandoned or abused children. I never knew my parents or blood siblings and spent only two brief periods in the care of a foster family. At an early stage, I was referred to in my care files as a "communal" child, which today might be translated into being a "corporate" child. They observed that I was content in corporate care settings.

As an adult, I became increasingly aware that I approached the compare and contrast assessments regarding parented and corporate parented childhoods from a very different perspective to most of the professionals involved with the care system. Care activists, such as Dr Mike Lindsay, over twenty years ago coined the term care-ism to articulate the underlying, often unconscious prejudices widely held and expressed by professionals and adults as a whole towards both young and old care-experienced individuals. The source of these prejudices care activists believed to be the deep-rooted psychological dependence of those adults on the notion of the supremacy of the nuclear family and with it the validity of their childhoods or their role as parents.

I set about penning an article for my old grammar school's alumni magazine because I had the opportunity to introduce my childhood autobiography, *The Golly in the Cupboard (2004)*, to hundreds of the school's former pupils. I was looking to see how, given only 2000 words, I could make it relevant to them and sufficiently interesting for this audience now comprising of lawyers, teachers, lecturers and senior managers, retired or otherwise. I was aware that taken in isolation, they might see what I wrote about my situation as a self-indulgent misery piece and so miss the opportunity both to reflect on why as teenagers we didn't discuss our domestic situations and to look back on their adolescent struggles to survive the swings, merry go rounds and big dippers of parenting.

Regarding the publication of The Golly, my most telling lesson was how much people absorb books through the prism of their own experience and that as my sentences chugged, sauntered and sometimes swerved and sped through readers' childhood experiences, the clauses and conjunctions passed into a bagatelle of emotions, emerging reshaped and moulded to fit my audience's world. Readers took my Golly and placed it in their world rather than mine. If they were outraged, they were upset for their world not mine. If they were moved to tears, they cried for their world not mine.

My primary intention in writing The Golly had been to argue for the validity of our childhood in care experience and strip away the crude horror and fantasy images created and sustained by "care-ism" – the sincerely held prejudices of those adults, professionals and "experts" who had no childhood care experience. When viewing our care world, at best, these people could only project and demonstrate their inability to process a childhood outside of the nuclear or extended family. Consequently, our care experiences and outcomes were put through the sieve of their psychological and societal attachment to the nuclear family. The Golly was in part an attempt to counteract this pool of prejudice.

By exposing our childhood to the readership, I invited them to consider comparisons with their own childhood. It was my intention. However, what I hadn't given real consideration to was that in doing so I was inviting them into that chaotic pin ball machine of their childhood and adolescent emotional chaos. With hindsight I might have made more of this aspect but I remain pleased that I opened up an avenue for reflection for others, even if their comprehension of the world of children in care only moved forward a few clauses and sentences.

As for my schooling; my single sex grammar school in Southport, a coastal town in the north west of England, was drawn primarily from the seaside resort's middle classes. What struck me most regarding my former school friends was their surprise not only at my revelations in The Golly but also their shock at not being aware of but the barest detail about my domestic situation, leading them to speculate on how different my life must have been.

The truth is that in our adolescent years, we, the totality of state school children, hardly ever shared or were interested in our peers' home lives. It was not simply because we were so geared up to our school lives and discussing the collective experiences that ensued. Nor can it be put down merely to children in two-parent families assuming that the variety of their experiences were the norm, in which case they may have had more reason to engage with others to seek and share empathy as they would commonly do as adults.

The Orphan World...A Perspective from the Other Side

For a long time, I also struggled to understand why parented individuals couldn't see either the possible benefits of my non-parented corporate collectivised upbringing or why my orphanage peers and I did not necessarily perceive ourselves as the damaged goods that the parented felt we must automatically be. They largely turned deaf ears to our "perspective from the other side."

The Village to Raise a Child

In pre-capitalist societies, children's welfare was perceived as the responsibility not only of the biological parents but also the local village or community, which often consisted of extended family. There is evidence that children were raised collectively by their local community *(Mothers and Others: The Evolutionary Origins of Mutual Understanding, by Sarah Blaffer Hrdy, ©2009)* and put to work at an early age, giving them added value in the village.

Today, in parts of Africa, the ubuntu phrase *"It takes a whole village to raise a child,"* still feeds into social work and childcare practices. There were and are very practical reasons for this. At the sharp end, this was necessitated by high maternal death rates. In Britain during the Middle Ages, it is believed that one in three women died during their child bearing years (https://www.tudorsociety.com/childbirth-in-medieval-and-tudor-times-by-sarah-bryson)

Short life expectancy, due to poverty, disease, violence and wars could often leave children without one or both of their biological parents or render their parents incapable of looking after them. Whether children were left as biological orphans or social orphans (where parents were unable or unwilling to care for them) was largely immaterial. They were orphans. They were the children of the community. The men, women and other children in the village looked after them as almost indistinguishable from their own biological kin.

25

The social importance of orphan care was reflected in the texts of the Abrahamic religions. Christianity, Islam and Judaism all extolled the need to look after orphans and the "fatherless". The Islamic prophet, Muhammed, was an orphan and the Bible states that Jesus Christ was not brought up by his birth father.

In Europe especially, the rise of mercantile capitalism, issuing in industrialisation and rapid urbanisation, made large inroads into the sense of community, atomising individuals and throwing them back onto the nuclear family for support. The extended family was increasingly split up in the search for survival, which meant employment wherever possible as wage labourers. As capitalism developed, the nuclear family became its bedrock, leaning on women as the domestic servants of the male dominated household.

Social science drifted in the same direction. In the 20th century, as capitalism triumphed over feudalism and battled socialist collectivism, Western governments focussed on individual rights as opposed to collective rights as highlighted in British Prime Minster, Margaret Thatcher's famous declaration: "

"And, you know, there's no such thing as society. There are individual men and women and there are families. And no government can do anything except through people, and people must look after themselves first. It is our duty to look after ourselves and then, also, to look after our neighbours." (Women's Own, 1987)

Social workers and those involved in the social sciences will be familiar with Maslow's "hierarchy of needs", the work of American psychologist, Abraham Maslow. (A Theory of Human Motivation, Psychological Review, Maslow, 1943)

Whilst Maslow, who positioned his work alongside Freud's, was one of the ten most quoted psychologists of the 20th century, few of those citing him were aware that his hierarchical presentation depicting individuals' needs was very similar to that of the more collectively focussed hierarchical presentation used by the Blackfoot Tribe whom he had engaged with five years previously in 1938.

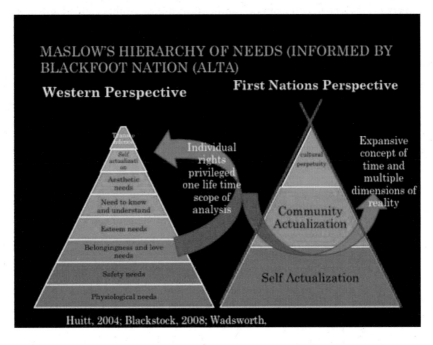

MASLOW'S HIERARCHY OF NEEDS (INFORMED BY BLACKFOOT NATION (ALTA)

Western Perspective   **First Nations Perspective**

Individual rights privileged one life time scope of analysis

Expansive concept of time and multiple dimensions of reality

Community Actualization

Self Actualization

Self actualisation
Aesthetic needs
Need to know and understand
Esteem needs
Belongingness and love needs
Safety needs
Physiological needs

cultural perpetuity

Huitt, 2004; Blackstock, 2008; Wadsworth.

Indeed, scholars from the North American tribe describe Maslow's hierarchical presentation as an unattributed "rip off" of theirs. (https://lincolnmichel.wordpress.com/2014/04/19/maslows-hierarchy-connected-to-blackfoot-beliefs)

The most striking aspect of Maslow's 'rework' of the Blackfoot hierarchy is his replacement of the role of the community as the provider of the basic needs of the individual. It has been suggested that Maslow unconsciously borrowed the tipi imagery used for the Blackfoot's hierarchy, particularly because it reflected the Q-sort methodology he used in his research.

Nevertheless, Maslow did reference other scientists in his work, so it is striking that he avoided reference to the Blackfoot Tribe. Had he done so, it could have usefully refocused debate on whether human actualisation is achieved via the atomised individual or the collective. The triumph in psychology, the social sciences and children and families social work of Maslow's individualistic focus certainly reflected the ideological needs of the Margaret Thatcher's of his era.

Reflecting the epoch, eight years after Maslow, British psychologist, John Bowlby's Maternal Care and Mental Health (1951) began to espouse his theories of maternal attachment focusing on the concept of children needing their mothers' care and attention in order to develop a 'balanced' personality. His adaptive theory, though it was open ended as to how attachments would emerge in different environments aside from the nuclear family, became the byword for justifying the middle-class mothering model and fundamental to most popular understandings of child development across the Western world. The model also arrived after the Second World War. With millions of men conscripted into the military machines, the war economy had created a key role for women in the workplace. Bowlby's focus on the maternal role conveniently arrived at a time when returning male troops needed to be pacified by employment, much of which was at the expense of female employees.

This model has come to be taken, as read, and to be scientifically sound enough for application to all of humanity – a biological, neuro-logical and child-centred fact. As with many theories and concepts, the elites of the Western world filleted out those bones that were considered inedible and presented the result, Bowlby-Light as the authentic essence.

However, the non-Westernised world still had and has communities where intense individual attachments are discouraged and replaced with multiple attachments, precisely for the benefit of the child in an uncertain world. There are societies such as the Cameroonian Nso community based on the principles of collective care which, according to Otto, believe maternal exclusivity is dangerous for the child, focus on collective caregiving and encouraging the child to trust and care for others in the community. (Culture-Specific Attachment Strategies in the Cameroonian Nso, Otto, 2008)

In his work, Otto tried to rescue what he believed to be the essential Bowlby. Similar evidence of communities highlighting the importance of children growing up with multiple attachments have been discovered across the non-Westernised world. But Otto's and other efforts still seem in vain and, besides, too late for the orphan world which has been scoured by Bowlby-Light as it scythed through sibling relationships, splitting up intensely attached brothers and sisters for the rest of their childhood, all in the name of hooking the beleaguered children to a parental attachment.

Residential Care as Collective Care

However, the ruling elite did not abandon the collective corporate raising of their own children. Focussed on accumulating, defending, managing and enjoying their wealth, the ruling classes employed bands of wet nurses, nannies, servants and tutors to raise their children. This system evolved into the creation of residential or boarding schools. These schools, in exchange for cash payments, freed wealthy parents from the tasks of raising and educating their children. The boarding schools became their "whole village to raise a child."

At the opposite end of the social spectrum, collective approaches were also employed to deal with destitute orphans. Whilst the landowners, merchants and industrialists accumulated more wealth, this was often at the expense of the rest of the population. Mass impoverishment threatened social upheaval. Social regulation was introduced in the form of rights and responsibilities for districts to look after their destitute. For orphans, community collective care was finally replaced with corporate care.

In much of Europe, these laws notably included orphans who, being fit and young would otherwise easily be taken into the employ of criminal gangs. In the cities this responsibility eventually became corporatised in the form of residential workhouses for adult destitutes and orphans alike. Eventually more farsighted local governors and philanthropists separated the orphans off from the adult destitutes. Scores and sometimes hundreds of children could then be housed together allowing the young males to be schooled to become apprentices and the young women to be domestic servants in the local workforce.

As technological developments increased the profitability of unskilled labour, child labour became ever more attractive and children were despatched from the orphanages and workhouses for the poor in their droves, working as child slaves in the mills and mines.

As with the boarding schools for the rich, wage labour was recruited to manage and educate the orphans, the main functional difference being that the orphans were forced more heavily into domestic service to assist the needs of the institution and its managers. Both the orphanages for impoverished waifs and the boarding schools for rich children, relied on "a whole village to raise a child," with management taking on ultimate pastoral responsibility.

Both were potent grounds for the growth of collectivity and youth empowerment. Consequently, both management systems heavily relied on rigid daily regimes and brutal repression. Significantly both also leaned heavily on the older more powerful youth to police their younger peers. Historical records show that physical, psychological and sexual abuse were common and more applauded than frowned upon.

In my dealings with the UK's Association of Boarding School Survivors, I noted that the main difference between we social orphans of the poor and the rich young boarders was that whilst we were abused and told it would help us understand that we were the lowest of the low, they were abused and told that their suffering would help them to be rulers of the world. Our final destinations were seen as very different but were intertwined. By the latter part of the 18th century, we were reared to become the commodities from which they would extract the profits to furnish their fine mansions, enrich their dining tables and enliven their already lavish balls.

INSET

As quoted in Marx's Das Kapital, "Honest" John Fielden, a 19th century Radical MP, Lancashire cotton mill owner and social reformer gave this account of the, often final, destinations awaiting the young children who entered the workhouses and orphanages:

"In the counties of Derbyshire, Nottinghamshire, and more particularly in Lancashire the newly-invented machinery was used in large factories built on the sides of streams capable of turning the water-wheel. Thousands of hands were suddenly required in these places, remote from towns; and Lancashire, in particular, being, till then, comparatively thinly populated and barren, a population was all that she now wanted. The small and nimble fingers of little children being by very far the most in request, the custom instantly sprang up of procuring apprentices from the different parish workhouses of London, Birmingham, and elsewhere.

"Many, many thousands of these little, hapless creatures were sent down into the north, being from the age of 7 to the age of 13 or 14 years old. The custom was for the master to clothe his apprentices and to feed and lodge them in an 'apprentice house' near the factory; overseers were appointed to see to the works, whose interest it was to work the children to the utmost, because their pay was in proportion to the quantity of work that they could exact.

"Cruelty was, of course, the consequence. ... In many of the manufacturing districts, but particularly, I am afraid, in the guilty county to which I belong [Lancashire], cruelties the most heart-rending were practised upon the unoffending and friendless creatures who were thus consigned to the charge of master-manufacturers; they were harassed to the brink of death by excess of labour ... were flogged, fettered and tortured in the most exquisite refinement of cruelty; ... they were in many cases starved to the bone while flogged to their work and ... even in some instances ... were driven to commit suicide....

"The beautiful and romantic valleys of Derbyshire, Nottinghamshire and Lancashire, secluded from the public eye, became the dismal solitudes of torture, and of many a murder. The profits of manufacturers were enormous; but this only whetted the appetite that it should have satisfied, and therefore the manufacturers had recourse to an expedient that seemed to secure to them those profits without any possibility of limit; they began

31

the practice of what is termed "night-working," that is, having tired one set of hands, by working them throughout the day, they had another set ready to go on working throughout the night; the day-set getting into the beds that the night-set had just quitted, and in their turn again, the night-set getting into the beds that the day-set quitted in the morning. It is a common tradition in Lancashire, that the beds never get cold." (The Curse of the Factory System: or a short account of the origin of factory cruelties, Fielden, 1836)

INSET ENDS

With management in both settings taking on the parental duty of care and the formal education of the child, there was little contradiction in either of the two learning spheres, especially compared to that facing most modern children forced to daily switch between the private atomised world of the nuclear family and the corporate collective world of their school.

The rich young boarders emerged from their schools, bruised but ready to be part of the collective ruling elite. They were groomed to understand that they were part of a resourceful class, from which they could personally benefit through collectively engaging. They joined their elite clubs and tossed each other government sinecures and company directorships. They defended their nuclear family as part of their property but also as a key prop to the system that kept them in wealth. Equally they defended their distorted but privileged collectivist upbringing as their right, if only through wealth and birth and thus not available or viable for the rest of humanity.

Meanwhile they had no interest in defending the orphanage collectivity but instead allowed the orphanages to be seen as dumping grounds for misfit children. The negative almost fearsome image of orphanages became a handy tool for keeping struggling working-class families in order by threatening the separation of children from their parents and vice versa. The pathologising of orphan children as "troubled" misfits also provided a perfect cover justifying poor outcomes for those who passed through the establishments and thus allowed for minimal expenditure on orphan care.

Modern Atomised Orphan Care

In the modern industrial era, with child labour no longer deemed so profitable, Western governments took over the running of the orphanages. Many began to resent the financial costs required for ensuring that salaried residential care staff safely met the needs of the orphan child. By lauding foster care in families as "more natural", governments could persuade the population that placing orphans in the hands of willing families, where women were used to performing as unpaid domestic servants, was preferable.

Even today, most foster parents across Europe are not recognised as professional workers and therefore outside the scope of employment legislation stipulating minimum wages and working conditions. Twenty years ago, UK government officials informed me that the opposition to professionalising foster care work was that under European Union conditions of work, children having 24-hour care would require paying for three carers per day.

The orphanage became seen as the home of the "unwanted" or "troubled" children, and the state was content not to challenge this notion. With racism widespread in 1960s England, this was graphically reflected in the high proportion of non-White children, such as my friends and I, who occupied the orphanages. Indeed, the proportion of "coloureds" in the children's homes became a problem for children's charities such as Barnardo's that the charity offered bonuses to adults prepared to foster non-White children.

Since the 1950s, the Western world has seen an establishment-led attack on orphanages as unsuitable for child-rearing. Instead, the fostering system handing children over to be cared for in individuals' homes has been lauded.

Society, as is discussed later, ignores the facts that fostering generally displays all the same fundamental poor management practices as residential care, in particular management practices centred primarily on adults' needs rather than those of the children. This permits governments to rest easy, using the societal veil cast across the nuclear family with its atomisation and disempowered condition of the child, which allows parents and foster carers to avoid close scrutiny.

Society is also asked to turn a blind eye to the modern history of families in Europe and across the capitalist commodified world, when free of state policing and inspection, using children placed in their care as no more than domestic servants and very cheap labour. When I first visited India in the 1990s, the anti-child slavery campaigner, Kailash Satyarthi told me how one in three urban upper middle class and rich families had a child as a domestic servant. The country currently has hundreds of thousands of children toiling away in family homes as the cheapest of labour but still Western-based global charities are demanding that the country's orphanages be closed. They point to all the failings of orphanages without seeing all the problems of foster care in the unregulated conditions of family. Sadly, the disempowered atomised orphans, have little effective means of giving voice to their mistreatment and exploitation.

Even so, today there are hundreds of thousands of young people across the globe still living in orphanages. These largely exist in impoverished parts of the world and, being hugely under resourced, are sitting ducks for Western criticism. Meanwhile some large well-managed orphanages still thrive in Germany, particularly where the young people are empowered by collective rights and representation (as in the East Berlin 'Kinderhaus' referenced below in Chapter 6).

In the 21st century there have been a few academic voices such as orphanage-raised Professor Richard B McKenzie still prepared to point to the relative benefits of collective residential care as opposed to atomised fostering care. *("The Best Thing About Orphanages". McKenzie, Richard B. 14 January 2010*
https://www.wsj.com/articles/SB10001424052748703510304574626080835477074).

Otherwise, the orphan voice is shut down either by straightforward social exclusion or the societal encouragement of a victim mentality, whereby the care leaver is overwhelmed by focusing on the injustices they suffered, so pathologising and nullifying their own voice.

Careism and Childism

Back, in 2003, the UK's Care Leavers' Association manifesto, reflecting on the experience of young people in care and the care experienced, outlined the extremes of societal prejudice and stigmatisation that they had to face up to.

"Government estimates show that Britain has over 1 million adults who have been through the care system as children. At least 500,000 spent substantial time in care as children. The time each of these care leavers spent in the care system varies tremendously from less than one year to the full 18 years of their pre-adult life. The effect of these years in care on the outlook of the care survivor is permanent. Most care leavers are acutely aware of a social stigma towards those who have been in care.

Care is seen as a place of repository for difficult or inadequate children. Those who have been in care are expected to have experienced a childhood of criminal activity. At root is the establishment attitude that children in its care are an unwanted financial burden and since these children have nobody to defend their interests, then it is justified to offer the children the poorest of existences.

*"All children are difficult to rear but children in care are treated as inherently criminal when they pass through difficult phases. Much of the care system is characterised by a penal/workhouse approach, designed to control the child **until** adulthood rather than to educate the child and prepare the survivor **for** adult life. This establishment stigmatisation of children in care as a natural part of the criminal fraternity is reflected in millions of homes across the country where young children are threatened by their parents: "If you keep making trouble, we will have to put you in care!" In turn millions of children grow up with the attitude that those in care are bad by nature.*

"The experience of this real stigmatisation leads many care leavers to attempt to bury the fact that they spent their childhood in the care system. Many are not prepared to tell even their closest friends and family about their childhood experience. For care leavers this social isolation is intensified by the fact that on leaving care they often are forced to drift around the country and lose contact with others who have been through the care system."(Care Leavers' Manifesto, Care Leavers Association, 2003)

This prejudice and stigmatisation had been defined by care leaver activists as 'careism', a term introduced into the care professionals' world in the 1998 paper by care leaver, Dr Mike Lindsay (Discrimination against young people in care: theory of careism, Lindsay, Childright, November 1998). The basis of careism, care leavers argued were threefold:

- Ideological: in the establishment's determination to protect the ideological sanctity of the nuclear family

- Material: in minimising the financial cost to society of orphans

- Psychological and prejudicial: reflecting the inability of those without significant care experience to hear or understand the psyche of those devoid of parental care/or significant childhood-long adult attachments.

As a consequence, virtually all the academic research into care, having been carried out by adults parented in childhood, was ridden with prejudicial lack of understanding. It was this careism that my The Golly in the Cupboard memoir (ibid.) was aiming to play a role in combatting.

Childism
Meanwhile modern capitalism was busy bringing its own agenda into the nuclear family, squeezing labour out of every adult. Today, with child labour for employers and contractors all but banned, parents' children are taken out of the employment market but in turn both parents are pressed into working as many hours, as possible, and this mainly away

36

from home, to ensure the household survives. This creates additional pressures for child-rearing.

The Danish socialist historian, Hendrick in his 2016 work "Narcissistic Parenting in an Insecure World", argues that under pressure modern society has shifted towards: *"'behavioural', punitive and managerial methods of child rearing today, made popular by 'tough love' experts, and by New Labour's parent education programmes."* (Narcissistic Parenting in an Insecure World: A History of Parenting Culture 1920s to Present, Hendrick, 2016)

Hendrick adds: *"...this trend is symptomatic of the sour, mean-spirited and vindictive social norms found throughout society today, which undermine the better instincts of parents and damage parent-child relations."*

He argues that during the last 30 years the process has intensified as modern society has shifted towards neo-liberalism, producing a situation in which: *"...much of contemporary child rearing conceals a guilt-ridden malevolence, fearful and insecure, fuelled by an unacknowledged and deeply repressed childism that is just as pernicious as sexism, racism, homophobia and any other disabling and discriminatory prejudice."*

Hendrick defines childism, as a prejudice that has: *"children as a 'target group', that is one 'whose members share characteristics and conditions that those prejudiced against them seize on and distort for their own purposes.... a malign force in human affairs, quietly and unobtrusively polluting our relations with those we have brought into the world."*

In this regard Hendrick is on the same page as psychotherapist, Elizabeth Young-Bruehl who identified childism: *"... as a belief system that constructs its target group, 'the child', as an immature being, produced and owned by adults who use it to serve their own needs and fantasies."* (Childism: Confronting Prejudice Against Children, Young-Bruehl, 2012)

In the same work, Young-Bruehl contended that this belief system or prejudice was harmful to young people and their development:

"...one of the key reasons for the prejudice against them not to be recognized as such or its being so easily rationalized. Adults who argue that children do not and should not have rights, for example, base their arguments on children's natural dependency, making assertions about their lack of agency or capacity for choice, expression of interest, or reason. But such arguments are prejudicial against children's development; by declaring that children do not have these capacities, the arguments are really contributing to the difficulties children have in developing the capacities."

If one agrees with the notion that prejudice against others is generally based on ignorance leading to false notions about others, one might question how an adult who has per se experienced childhood can be prejudiced against the child and other children. To paraphrase Aristotle, how can I be prejudiced towards my own seed? In the area of racism, we see how Black people can become prejudiced against other Black people in general through the weight of social propaganda, atomisation and alienation.

With regard to children there is a particular difficulty to escape the psychological uniqueness of one's own childhood and especially the traumatic experiences of adolescence. The alienation is completed in the young person's transition from existence as property to the emancipation of adulthood and sanctioned property owner. Young adolescents have traditionally faced enormous social pressure to bury their 'childish' selves and act 'adult', inducing self-loathing; one of the aspects which can make negotiations with parents so traumatic.

Looking at Britain, in 2010 the UK government passed the Equality Act outlawing age discrimination and declaring:

"...you must not be discriminated against because:

you are (or are not) a certain age or in a certain age group

- *someone thinks you are (or are not) a specific age or age group, this is known as discrimination by perception*

- *you are connected to someone of a specific age or age group, this is known as discrimination by association"*

Regarding the implementation of the act, it was clarified that: *"Age groups can be quite wide (for example, 'people under 50' or 'under 18s'). They can also be quite specific (for example, 'people in their mid-40s'). Terms such as 'young person' and 'youthful' or 'elderly' and 'pensioner' can also indicate an age group* (www.equalityhumanrights.com/en/advice-and-guidance/age-discrimination, Equality & Human Rights Commission, 2021)

However, Harriet Harman, Labour's Women and Equality Minister, in her explanation as to why children were excluded from protection in this regard by the law, effectively sanctioned age discrimination against children:

"The provisions will not cover people under 18. It is right to treat children and young people differently, for example through age limits on alcohol consumption, and there is little evidence of harmful age discrimination against young people. Harmful age discrimination is basically against older people." (Harriet Harman, Minister for Women and Equality, statement in the House of Commons, 26 June 2008: Hansard)

The Equality Act allowed for children to be protected against racism, sexism and disability discrimination but discrimination on age grounds was considered acceptable; this despite 43% of under 18s and the majority of teenagers surveyed by the Department for Children, Schools & Families having reported that they had suffered from age discrimination. (Meeting the Obligations of the Convention on the Rights of the Child in England. Children and Young People's Messages to Government. DCSF, Willow, Franklin and Shaw, 2007)

Hendrick identifies three disturbing aspects in which childism manifests itself in modern society: *"i) the child is an unharmonious presence, disruptive of cohesion, and the cause of apprehension and frustration, ii) the growth of a deeply felt parental desire to exercise a form of 'managerial' control over children, subjecting them to a kind of neoliberal contractual status, and iii) displaying an impatience with their little ways of being."*

The result, he contends, is that adults are losing sight of the joys of parenting and children have become the butt of parental frustrations: *"...parents are much more inclined to regard children as a nuisance, a hindrance, a burden..."* (Narcissistic Parenting in an Insecure World: A History of Parenting Culture 1920s to Present, Hendrick 2016)

However, an important aspect overlooked by Hendrick is how childism in utterly devalued children's role in child-rearing and the more collective role they often play in nurturing and developing their peers. Childism is easily accommodated by asserting that it: "...takes a whole village to raise a child," but for this one has to forget that the village children also have critical agency. As much as one asserts the collective role of adults in child-rearing one also has to include the collective role of young people, and this especially in regard to teenagers.

At the cornerstone of discrimination against children, as ironically embodied in the Labour government's Equality Act is this denial of young people's agency. In her insightful paper, The Sociology of Childhood in Relation to Children's Rights, in 2000, Professor Berry Mayall, sympathetically laid bare the basis and consequences regarding the overlooking of children's agency in the adult's developmental narrative:

"Adult visions of adult-child relations are built from the long history of developmentalism, intersecting with ideologies and policies which stress adult socialisation duties and responsibility for protection and provision; adult input rather than child agency are at the forefront of these visions. All these combine to foster adult suspicion of children – to disbelieve them, to blame them, to suspect their moral competence, to assign moral responsibility to adults rather than to children." (The Sociology of Childhood in Relation to Children's Rights, Mayall, The International Journal of Children's Rights, 2000)

Basing herself on many years of researching young people and "interacting with them as people," Mayall called for a repositioning of children as competent agents as a pre-requisite for society moving forward:

"Taking children seriously as people leads to shifts in thinking. First, children move from being objects of adult work, to being competent, contributing social actors. Secondly, at a broader level, when facing the age-old debates about agency and structure, we have to consider the extent to which children may be regarded as agents intersecting with the structures surrounding their lives. This can mean, considering how far children reproduce and transform such structures; and how far, therefore, they are effective in altering the conditions of their own childhoods. Thirdly, the idea that adult views are sufficient for defining children's needs has to give way to the understanding that children's own wishes and expressed needs are relevant to the construction and implementation of social policies and practices." (ibid.)

Childism, as Hendrick defines it, preceded modern neo-liberalism by many centuries. Careism may be much younger but sits comfortably as a subset of childism in so much as it is the commodification of children that facilitates their exploitation and suppression. Hendrick's observations are additionally important because they once more highlight how society has moved in complete opposition to the modern plethora of youth charters, declaration of rights of children and academic youth empowerment studies. Bearing the brunt of childism and these latest trends in adult society are those most sensitive to their commodification, the adolescents. The most sceptical will rightly ask whether all the latter affirmations of young people's rightful place in society is more a reflection of the collective adult guilt than a meaningful attempt to enhance the life and prospects of their children.

On another front, a growing army of sociologists point to the weakness of the nuclear family model as applied to dual-employed parents who, if boarding schools are financially out of reach or seen as undesirable, raise their children by relying on a posse of paid carers, friends, relatives and personal tutors.

(Not-So-Nuclear Families: Class, Gender, and Networks of Care 2004 Karen V. Hansen).

To this we should add that the practice of having children later in life has brought a greater ability to use retired and semi-retired grandparents as free and often very willing childcare assistants.

Philosopher, Anca Gheaus and many neo-republicans go further, suggesting that collective parenting needs to be developed as an effective solution for families today. (Multi-parenting: What Would It Take for It to Work? Anca Gheaus 2019)

Western society was blinded to any of the benefits of the collectivist care practised by the boarding schools and orphanages in its midst. This blindfold is kept on despite the increasing dysfunctionality of modern society. This is largely because governments rely, on the one hand on the super-exploitation of the majority of women as both domestic servants and wage labourers, and on the other on the disempowerment of young people as a means to prevent them from collectively challenging a socially damaging system. It is notable that the academic vanguard arguing for the viability of collective parenting is largely led by women such as Anca Gheaus.

In this paper I argue that the pain of parenting dysfunctionality is largely born by the innocent adolescent and, as much as collective parenting has a role, so too do collectives and empowered collectivity of and for young people.

Adolescent Education in the UK

In Europe and North America today, the prevailing educational model for most adolescents is that they are expected to attend school on a daily basis, at least until the age of 16. Schooling is provided by government out of taxes. Fee-paying schools are also available for the middle classes, as are fee-paying residential/boarding schools. The boarding schools are much more expensive and mainly the preserve of the wealthy. The residential schools act in loco parentis and, as such, have some functional, if not financial, similarity to the few orphanages that remain; especially those orphanages that have in-house schooling.

In the UK, academic education of adolescents is delivered corporately and with nationwide curricula so has little relevance to the particular needs or wishes of the local community.

As with academic education, the UK has a health and social services system that is funded mainly by the taxpayers and controlled at a national level by the government and managed by the local authorities. Health services and social work are also delivered corporately and focussed on enabling the individual or the nuclear family unit to survive and engage with society at what is seen nationally as a satisfactory level.

Neither involve the communities in their localities aside from the election of local political representatives to the empowered local government bodies which cover tens of thousands of people. Local community engagement in most cities is very low and overwhelmingly top-down. Teaching staff are only expected to liaise with social workers on an operational level when it is perceived that a pupil is unable to engage with their schooling or displaying signs of serious mental or physical harm. Social workers are then expected to engage with the pupil and the family.

The Mystery Wall

As related above, only through chance conversations decades later did I become aware that as adolescents, my school friends and I had never at the time discussed our domestic lives, our lives at home. As a result, they barely had any idea as to what living in an orphanage or as an orphan involved for me. Yet, I had never intentionally hidden my being in care from anyone. As far as I am aware, I had never seen the point or felt the need.

Those chance conversations led me to question whether, had I spoken more about my domestic situation to my school friends, my life at the time could have been different. There was the chance that, if my peers had become aware of the abuse being inflicted by the orphanage's manager on the children, my peers might have acted with me or I might have been more forthright in my acting against the abusive manager of the orphanage; the consequence of which may have been to save several children's lives from being blighted. On the other hand, my peers' involvement could have left me in such an exposed position vis a vis the abuser that I would have been carted off and incarcerated in an institution for young offenders (as would happen to at least two of the abuser's victims) and never have escaped the penal system.

At the time, I was 14 years old and sent a note of complaint to the regional headquarters of the charity running the orphanage but I backtracked when grilled. A few other children did complain but, like me, they were shunted off out of the home. Only later, when the children collectively organised a very public revolt, some refusing to end their sit-down protest on a local bus until the police were called, did they force an end to the abuse.

Yet almost a half century passed before I considered whether I had subconsciously drawn a veil over my life at the orphanage when discussing with my school friends. At the same time, I recalled that one of those former friends had written to me years ago revealing the terrible time (of which I was totally unaware) that he had suffered at the hands of his parents during his school days. So, I questioned a few of those former friends and it transpired that they too, as adolescents, never discussed their home lives with their peers. I questioned my children. I questioned teenagers fresh out of school and the answers were overwhelmingly the same. Widening my net further, I received the same response from 98% of those I quizzed: leading me to conclude that as adolescents we do not discuss our home lives with our peers, unless they are the very closest of friends, spending large amounts of time in one another's parental homes – like close siblings.

The barrier between our school lives and our home lives was harder to cross than the Cold War's Berlin Wall. It was a wall with its own No Man's Land. Parents, teachers and pupils all contributed to maintaining this wall, and this without ever discussing its existence. We placed our guards and gun turrets on the wall, posted look outs and hung barbed wire, as silently as ants building their nests. The construction and maintenance of the wall was such a mystery that none of us were aware of the part we played. Not one James Bond reincarnation could ever penetrate the construction site. It was a process so hidden in our consciousness that we might well have been sleep walking.

Yet, when our teenage years were over and we schoolchildren became adults, taking the keys to our own homes, doorways appeared in the wall. We felt enabled to discuss our home life with certain individuals in our social circles. Without ever realising that the doors were there, we passed through them, sometimes casually sometimes apprehensively when we wanted support or to assist our adult friends and colleagues. As adults, we passed through the wall to draw succour from the well which we denied ourselves as adolescents. What was the source of that denial?

Child Labour and Adolescence

Content

In this chapter, we discuss the evolution of the social position of children and the emergence of the concept of adolescence as a unique life stage. We consider the legal and societal view of children as parental property. The predominant concepts of family, parental rights and responsibilities and the changing demands and role of the state in relation to children are discussed in the context of Industrialisation and capitalism's growth to become the dominant global economic system. Capitalism's switch from seeing the child as a means of production into an investment for the future development and protection of production and markets is identified as the basis for the emergence of adolescence as a distinct period where children are excluded from the labour market. The same processes have led to a rigid and stultifying standardisation of children's education, whereby children's contribution to their families and peer groups is overlooked and all focus is on adult-led academic education to the detriment of child development, families, education and intellectual capital as a whole.

We explore how from the late 19th century capitalism focussed on preparing adolescents to become part of the workforce by directing intensified propaganda and stigmatisation as to the social danger posed by adolescents in order to justify the use of repressive measures. We look at how the academic sciences were used to 'biologize' adolescence, justifying infantilisation and oppression of teenagers to the detriment of the family. Finally, this chapter looks at how capitalism is outgrowing and demanding the reshaping of adolescence as it was known in the 20th century.

The Child as Parental Property
In the daily journey between school and home, the modern adolescent comes face to face with the contradictions between society's commitment to equal treatment and children's rights on the one hand and its positioning of the child as parental property on the other. Much of modern capitalism sees little profit in the employment of child labour and currently sits content with the laws restricting the child's working day. Certain industries still benefit from child labour and child slavery as utilised in some of the less economically developed countries, but this does not dent the Western message that children's labour is not considered to be a valid method of exploitation.

Such rights for children do not however amount to equality and emancipation and that is where adolescents find themselves confronted by the mist that surrounds their commodification as parental property.

For hundreds of years the West dominant civilisations overtly considered men's children to be their property and many gave men leeway to deal with this property as they saw fit. In 350BC, the Greek philosopher, Aristotle, famously offered the justification that, since the child was begat by the seed of the man (rather than the woman), so the child was part of him and therefore, just as he washed or cut his own hair, so he could wash or cut his child.

"The justice of a master and that of a father are not the same as the justice of citizens, though they are like it; for there can be no injustice in the unqualified sense towards things that are one's own, but a man's chattel,

and his child until it reaches a certain age and sets up for itself, are as it were part of himself, and no one chooses to hurt himself (for which reason there can be no injustice towards oneself). Therefore, the justice or injustice of citizens is not manifested in these relations;"

(Nicomachean Ethics, Book V, Aristotle)

In 1992, Woodhouse's critique on children being property summarised the legal position of children and fathers in Imperial Rome:

"Roman law treated children as chattels. The Roman Paterfamilias could not only sell his children at will, but also kill them. Women and children, in fact, may have represented the first accumulation of private property. Patriarchal theories of state and theories of domestic government were mutually reinforcing. Men, it was said, ruled over their families like sovereigns over their subjects - or kings like fathers over their families.

Paternal property rights grew naturally from a patriarchal account of procreation - fathers gave children material being through their seed."

(Who Owns the Child? Meyer and Pierce and the Child as Property, Barbara Bennett Woodhouse, 1992)

This notion of children as the property of their fathers, to be treated and disposed of at their will was maintained by the main Western European civilisations through the next 2000 years and more. The Christian church adopted the notion of Original Sin whereby children were said to be born as sinners and therefore only obedience to their fathers, the church and baptism could absolve them. Beatings and even infanticide were justified. In the Anglican Christian's theocratic 17th century Massachusetts Bay Colony, children could be put to death for disobeying their parents under laws based on the concept that children having been born sinners must always submit to parental authority. Yet such sanctions were not confined to fervent religious sects. In 1650, the renowned English philosopher, Thomas Hobbs commented that, with regard to their children, parents may: *"alienate them...pawn them for hostages, kill them for rebellion, or sacrifice them for peace."* (Hobbes, The Elements of Law, Natural and Politic, 1650).

Prior to the modern era of industrial imperialism, children played a role in the household as soon as they were able. Today some rural societies still see children as young as three carrying around babies on their backs and in the urban ghettoes and shanty towns, elder children often take on daytime childcare roles whilst their parents are out at work. The practice of children at five years of age being put to work in the fields and mines was a reflexion of families' daily battle for survival necessitated not only by class exploitation but also by the low level of the productive forces.

In the centuries preceding the imperialist era, life, as the English philosopher, Thomas Hobbes, commented, was "poor, nasty, brutish and short" (Leviathan, Hobbes, 1651). The average life expectancy for those surviving infancy was just 55.

The social philosopher, Max Roser, commenting on historic mortality rates portrayed how, across cultures and centuries, surviving into adulthood was a perilous experience with infant mortality at around 25% and half of all children dying before they reached puberty - a far cry from the late twentieth century. *"Every fourth newborn died in the first year of life. One out of two died in childhood.... The global infant mortality rate is now 2.9%. And 4.6% die before reaching the age of 15."* (Mortality in the Past – Around Half Died as Children. Max Roser, June, 2019 https://ourworldindata.org/child-mortality-in-the-past)

Children were a precious commodity enabling the family to survive meaning that laws allowed young men and women to be married off even before they completed puberty. Females as young as 12 and males at 14 could be legally married. Still today the tiny European country of Andorra allows some females to be married off at 14, as do the US states of North Carolina and Alaska and the countries of Colombia, Cuba, Brunei, Lebanon, Brunei, Sao Tome, whilst in Iran it is 13.

In practice, younger marital ages were more the province of the wealthy. Poverty meant that historically the average age of marriage for most young women was in their later teens and males often would wait until they were in their 20s.

An added factor was feudal rule whereby the peasants were often required to seek the local ruler's permission to marry and the lords of the manor had an eye on the impact on production. The young male was spared the concerns of fatherhood but only because he was needed to focus on the workplace. There was no social conception of adolescence (though the word comes from the Latin for growing up, adolescere). Children conceptually passed from childhood to adulthood in one fell swoop.

Meanwhile, with low level labour-intensive production, children were employable, and rapidly introduced to the collectivity of work first in the family and then in the productive process. The young people worked but their contribution to the family was the property of the family and they had no say in retention or distribution of any of the surplus they created. That was left to the patriarch. In effect, both mothers and children while contributing to the family were exploited by the patriarch who in turn was exploited by the local rulers. The young very quickly took their place on the treadmill of survival and exploitation. As such, they were introduced to their social and collective identity as labourers very quickly with hardly time to wait around and wander.

The life of a child was very much that of a family serf. Even the practice of sending one's seven-year-old sons to another household to act as apprentices to work and learn a trade was underlain by the harsh reality that it was more productive to set others' children to work than one's own and avoided the emotional complications of harshly exploiting them.

The Englishman's home was truly his castle. Since the King's Bench ruling of 1505, that: *"the house of one is to him his castle and his defence,"* generations of politicians, lawyers and academics have repeated this phrase upholding private property as the ruling elite's pact with its property-owning citizens. For hundreds of years that ruling also applied a blindfold to how a man treated his wife and those children who resided on the property. Only with the struggle for the emancipation of women has that blindfold been relaxed.

The declared legal intention of statements to the effect that the Englishmen's castles were inviolable, was to allow a man the legal right of self-defence when attacked in his own home. Patriarchal society took this further, using it to reassert that a property-owning man's wife and children also constituted his private property.

Nevertheless, this law was adjacent to other laws of political economy, most notably in those parts of the country still dominated by feudalism where the feudal lords often treated the children of those living in conditions of serfdom as their property to be disposed of at their pleasure. The same could be said in relation to chattel slavery where the slaves' children became the property of the slaveowner - like the eggs born to the owners' hens.

Other laws permitted debts to be paid by selling (indenturing) one's labour for a definite period to any individual. Since children were men's property. they could be used to settle debts and were commonly indentured (a form of slavery) for life. Indentured children were often sent to the colonial corners of empire to act as house or field slaves, whilst collecting orphans also proved a profitable practice, housing and indebting them before selling them off.

This societal commodification of children was exemplified in American law as carried down from days of British colonial rule which: "*treated children 'as assets of estates in which fathers had a vested right. . .. Their services, earnings, and the like became the property of their paternal masters in exchange for life and maintenance.'*"

(Michael Grossberg, Governing the Hearth: Law and The Family in 19th Century America, 1985)

Industrialisation, Imperialism and State Intervention

The completely laissez faire attitude towards how fathers dealt with their children in the household would be dealt a death knell by capitalism's development of industry, which required increasing proportions of skilled and literate labour. As capitalism took over the state machinery so it sought to advance its profits via increased production and markets. Fit and able young people were needed both for production and for the armed forces; the latter's role being to expand and protect production and markets at home and abroad. Young people now had a value to the state. The state intervened to assert a role for itself in children's development. Woodhouse identified this process of growing state intervention over matters of childhood in 19th century America:

"Modern historians generally depict American family law as having undergone a process of transformation, from the hierarchical, patriarchal model of the family of colonial times toward a more egalitarian model. Under the earlier patriarchal model, the father's power over his household, like that of a God or King, was absolute... Influential courts in the mid-1800's, however, began to articulate a theory that parental control was not an absolute power conferred by God, but a civic duty conferred and regulated by the state, in the interests of children and of the public." (Who Owns the Child? Meyer and Pierce and the Child as Property, Barbara Bennett Woodhouse, 1992)

In Western Europe, the state began to carve inroads into the realms of the gods and children, which also involved stepping into the family home, the Englishman's castle and the nuclear family. However, in the imperialist era of wage slavery, urbanisation and industrialisation, where children carried less value in the workplace, the state increasingly deemed it necessary to invest in children to protect and generate the future labour force and military machine.

At the same time, capitalism rested on the nuclear family, whereby the super-exploitation of women, often doubling up as wage earners and "homemakers" policed by their male patriarchs, lowered the cost of male labour to employers. As a consequence, the state placed itself in the middle of family relations, replacing the unquestioned supremacy of the patriarch with that of the state as protector of the male-dominated nuclear family and its offspring.

Children were left as the property of the family but now only on sufferance of the state. The state publicly venerated the institution of the family whilst developing the means to ensure that its offspring met the corporate world's needs.

As industries waxed and waned in their demands for labour, the nuclear family came into its own, with parents and their children driven to the four corners of the world in search of work resulting in the scattering and trimming down of extended family units.

Twenty first century governments and state laws treat children as the property of their parents, even if this is no longer explicit, because the state inserts itself as the child's corporate guardian. In a world where the state publicly at least recognises children as being more than commodities it nevertheless still leaves room for them being dealt with as such.

Meanwhile the nuclear family is being shaken to the core as a unit. In 1971, Juliet Mitchell was calling, in her treatise Women's Estate, for an end to the nuclear family as the *"only one legitimised form"* family institution and the need to fight for others to be recognised, but capitalism has almost achieved that of its own devices. Whilst Mitchell pointed to the "rigidity" of only recognising the legitimacy of the nuclear family, that has been outgrown:

"What," Mitchell wrote, *"we should seek for is not the abolition of the family, but the diversification of the socially acknowledged relationships which are today forcibly and rigidly compressed into it. This would mean a plural range of institutions - where the family is only one such institution, and its abolition implies none. Couples - of the same or of different sexes – living together or not living together, long-term unions with or without children, single parents – male or female – bringing up children, children socialized by conventional rather than biological parents, extended kin groups, etc."* (Women's Estate, Mitchell, 1971)

In the West, capitalism, through its ever-ongoing striving to raise profit margins by lowering the costs of production, replacing its labour forces with cheaper alternatives, has critically and almost fatally undermined the might of brawn and the might of men in gender relationships. Whole industries highly relied on and valued men for their heavy lifting but this work has been replaced through automation and the technological drive for less labour-intensive products.

As the manual jobs disappear, so capitalism undermines the position of male labour (the manual labour value of men) and hence the position and authority of males as the main wage earners in many households. Centuries of tradition of male dominance in the consciousness and decades of men's thought processes are being shredded.

The impact, not only on gender relations but also the family, is huge and places the adolescent in a maelstrom, trying to make sense of a world where mothers and fathers and other adults are struggling to cope with the new transitional realities.

Many people fail to understand that it is not "society" that provides the bells for ringing these changes but capitalism. Those most impacted rage against society as the Luddites railed against machinery. Capitalism offers no solution for the displaced males to restore their income levels and instead drives down the price of their labour. They especially act as the social Luddites of today clamouring for a return to the terrible life they had been worn down to accept as "the way things are". Meanwhile the adolescent is left to look on at their parents who cling to their understanding of a disappeared past, but a past which is made a mockery of by their present.

The Shrinking Nuclear Family

In addition, despite the shrill lauding of the family unit by establishment politicians, capitalism is less and less willing to offer parents the wages, conditions and social structures which are required for children to be raised and brought to the jobs' market. The erosion of living standards of young adults in particular has eroded their 'right' to earn sufficient to safely raise a family. Meanwhile, that a wealthy country like the UK has 700,000 children i.e. young carers, looking after not only themselves, but adults and often siblings says something about the realities of the family and the care system today. By any stretch of the imagination, young carers and their siblings are suffering, often unavoidably from parental neglect. Alongside their siblings and the 100,000 young people in care they make a vast 1 million children whose parents cannot give them the care that is considered basic for a young family. Society is starving itself of its oxygen.

With more women in work and the costs of rearing children rising, women have been delaying having children until a later age when they can be more confident of affording the costs. Additional delays are built in if they are looking for a stable male partner to share the burden because of the increasingly transitory nature of employment, encouraging adults to live for today rather than plan for tomorrow. Many delay and many others find it is almost too late to bear their own children and the proportion of women over 40 years of giving birth is increasing.

The OECD in 2019 reported that this trend to put off starting a family has been a developing international phenomenon in the last 50 years:

"In most OECD countries, the average age at which women give birth now stands at 30 or above ...Most OECD countries have seen the average age of women at childbirth increase in recent decades. Between 1970 and 2017, most OECD countries saw the mean age increase by somewhere between 2 and 5 years..." (OECD Family Database, 2019 www.oecd.org/els/family/database.htm)

Urbanised societies are seeing divorce rates and single parent households increasing whilst birth rates and the institution of marriage are on the decline. Single parent households now account for one quarter of households with young children in the USA, up to one third in Sweden and one in seven in the European Union where almost one in three households (30%) have no children at all. (https://ec.europa.eu/eurostat/web/products-eurostat-news/-/edn-20210601-2)
Women's delaying when they have a first child and society's ageing are together threatening the sustainability of the supply of labour and domestic demand in market economies.

Japan led the world in capital-intensive investment and industrial innovation and for many decades kept its doors closed to mass immigration. However, for the last five years the labour markets have been given free rein in recruiting several million interns and immigrants to make up for a declining workforce.

Western countries have for decades been sucking in surplus labour (and with it demand) from their former imperial colonies. In 1970, the United States had 132 million adults and 70 million children. In 2019, the same country, had 255 million adults and just 73 million children, meaning that in a couple of decades today children will be supporting a population twice as large as the 'class' of 1970.

Countries such as Japan which have shunned using immigrant labour find themselves with labour shortages and insufficient internal markets for their products. From fears about overpopulation, some states are now touting cash incentives specifically aimed at rewarding parents who have more children. Hungary and Russia have responded to their crises by offering large financial incentives for families to have three or more children.

China having recently abandoned its one-child stricture is now imploring its families to have three children. It may also be required to follow down the road of major financial incentives for women to have children. Otherwise, families that have adjusted their lifestyle to having one or no children by reducing their lifestyle either by cuts in spending or retirement savings per head or working for even longer hours. Hence China's relaxing of its draconian one-child rule has not yet resulted in the scale of baby-boost that the government had hoped for.

The Nuclear Family and the State
Later in this paper I argue that the pain of parenting dysfunctionality is largely born by the innocent adolescent and, as much as collective parenting has a role, so too do collectives and empowered collectivity of and for young people.

I have no doubt that often very well-meaning people will construe this discourse as 'anti-family' or 'demonising the family' because it highlights some of the weaknesses of the modern nuclear family. It points to the misappropriation and distortion of the institution of the family by capitalism before going on to propose the need for radical solutions.

There are some, especially in the field of child protection, who see society as an ongoing battle between the family and the state who may fear that any references to the incapacity of the nuclear family will be an excuse for the state to exert more control over parents and children. To them I reply that the state hardly needs an excuse in this regard. The state has shaped the family in its own interest and, without conscious mass opposition, will continue to do so.

Autocratic States, the Family and Adolescents

Examining the autocratic states of Hitler's Nazi Germany and Stalin's Soviet Union, it is clear that neither directed themselves against the nuclear family but leaned on it and attempted to shape it for their own needs. In China we see a similar situation with the Communist Party bureaucracy veering from encouraging parents to have as many children as they could manage, to the one child law, then the two children rule and now the desperate change to the three children law.

Fascism sought to prop up the capitalist notion of the family, intensifying women's oppression within the household. Nazis and their propagandists such as the self-anointed but popular "parenting" specialist, Joanna Haarer, wanted families to be breeding grounds for atomised individuals to follow the will of the ruling elite (The German Mother and Her First Child, Haarer, 1934). We shall later illustrate how this process is mirrored in what we see today with capitalism's economic demands driving the marketisation of children's education with its consequent impact on young people's available time for collective engagement and on their mental health.

Modern capitalism's drive is to shape and further discipline the workforce. Haarer's books on mothering aimed at weakening young children's attachments with parents and siblings and destroying empathy. This met the needs of a German ruling class which saw its only way forward as one of pitiless military wars and fierce subjugation of whole populations, as had laid the basis for the empires of the other imperialist powers.

Fascism sought the individualisation of adolescents to ensure they were susceptible to government control. Stalinism sought to draw adolescents into the government's autarchic control via the Communist Party youth organisation, the Komsomol, which was as top down as Stalin's Communist Party had become. Stalin's and Hitler's regimes likewise ruled through intense terror of the population as a whole, setting individuals in fear not only of the state but of one another. Their countries had been ravaged by war and civil war, leaving families living with death, crippling disabilities and searing psychological trauma. For many young people, the authority of their parents was compromised whilst the new strong state image offered hope of a brighter future.

In modern Western democratic societies, rather than being ranged against the state, families have accepted legislation permitting for the state to act as it sees fit "in the best interest of the child." The state will not consciously intervene against its best interests. The power over children has already been ceded to the state. For example, if it comes to war, we have seen how the state can impose conscription sending hundreds of thousands of adolescents to their death - in the best interest of the child.

The real duality is not between the family and the state but between atomisation and collective empowerment of the people. The rights of citizens, parents and children in the battle against the state are defended by an empowered population ready to defend its interests where they contrast with those of the state. Whilst the state is in the hands of a minority class or group it will always be drawn to moulding society in its own interests rather than that of the majority.

At present the Westernised states around the world are intensifying pressure on parents to increase surveillance and maintain the disempowerment of adolescents. It is argued here that families and adolescents resisting this move and shifting to a new paradigm will strengthen family bonds rather than weaken them.

Ideology and the Family

A society's prevailing ideology for the most part lags behind the economic realities and requirements for its survival. To paraphrase Goethe's Faust, 'the ideology is grey my friend, ever green is the glad golden tree of life'. Those living under the umbrella of the prevailing ideology are driven to seek happiness only beneath its shelter and are continually warned that leaving its protection will invoke calamity. Yet the ideology shaped by the ruling strata overwhelmingly consists of an eclectic mix of what ideas the new elite drew from the previous reigning strata and those ideas and concepts it developed to distinguish it from the old regime. Ideologies draw on the past to shape the basic needs of the future and the prevailing paradigms must reflect principally those demanded by the forces of production or survival. As a result, they lag behind the economic base and come into contradiction with it, requiring adjustments which may be relatively peaceful, transforming the treatises of a few ideologues into historical curiosities, or may result in wholesale societal upheaval.

For the capitalist class to triumph over Europe's feudal rulers and free capital to shape the political and social superstructure structure to meet its needs, it was required to push aside the intransigent old regimes. In this task of revolution, it needed to draw the exploited peasants and workers into the political arena and evoke the promise of democratic rule and declarations of "The Rights of Man," to give the vast majority of society an apparent stake in its governance. Ideology feeding off the discontent of the people played a key role. For decades, the threat of the feudal regime returning to power, either through national counter-revolution or foreign invasion, forced the new ruling class to continue leaning on the mass of the population and so too consolidate their ideological power base.

The prevailing ideology is shaped by past battles and the reshaping of the economic base. In contrast the economic base is shifting, and, as was seen in the feudal era, shifted so much that the "Divine Right of Kings" had to fall to "The Rights of Man".

Ruling elites sought ideological justification for their exploitation of others - first in God, then in logic and then in science. It is well documented how Western capitalist ideologues used the pseudo-scientific notions of race to validate the subjugation of Blacks to slavery. The "Rights of Man" and "Liberté, Égalité, Fraternité" sat uncomfortably alongside the super exploitation of women and Black slaves. The contradictions were further explained away once scientists were able to declare that an adult female brain weighed five ounces less than the male's and that an African's brain was smaller than a Scandinavian's. The fact that taller people tended to have larger brains but no more notable 'intelligence' was soon pointed out but it counted for nothing in the many decades that followed.

In tandem, all available evidence countering these pseudo-scientific theories such as the vast achievements of non-Western civilisations and female inventors, were brushed over. At each stage when the oppressed peoples of the colonies and the world's women pressed forward with their demands for emancipation, the ruling strata pushed their ideologues to centre stage to parrot how their oppression was for their own good. The same argument is advanced regarding adolescents who struggle for equality in modern society.

Women's Suffrage: An Attack on the Family?
It should not be forgotten that a century and more ago, women's fight for equal property rights and the right to vote were met with similar outcries. Women having the same right as men to decide on the government of their towns, cities and countries would, suffrage opponents declared, undermine and wreck the family.

Authors such as American professor, Suzanne Marilley, highlight how arguments rained down declaring that giving women the right to vote would threaten the family institution. (Woman Suffrage and the Origins of Liberal Feminism in the United States, 1820-1920, Marilley,1996)

In a notorious piece of text, the Chair of California's Democratic Party, J B Sanford, derided women's suffrage as a "home destroyer":

"Politics is no place for a woman consequently the privilege should not be granted to her. The mother's influence is needed in the home. She can do little good by gadding the streets and neglecting her children.... statistics go to show that in most equal suffrage states, Colorado particularly, that divorces have greatly increased since the adoption of the equal suffrage amendment, showing that it has been a home destroyer. Crime has also increased due to lack of the mothers in the home. Woman is woman. She cannot unsex herself or change her sphere. Let her be content with her lot and perform those high duties intended for her by the Great Creator... (Argument Against Women's Suffrage, J B Sanford, 1911)

The attack on women's suffrage took place over several fronts. Notably one other major front was the claim that women were not biologically suited to politics and other affairs considered to be in the male domain. The same angle is often used by those denying adolescents' adult rights.

Reviewing the arguments of woman's suffrage opponents, Marina Koren, in The Atlantic (USA) journal, highlighted in 2019 how even many US scientists expressed the opinion that women did not have the faculties for the politics of power, were biologically more suited to looking after the home and should be left to focus on Kinder, Küche and Kirche (children, kitchen and church). Koren quotes a British scientist writing in The Times (UK) whose words may meet with derision today and for that reason illustrate how far capitalist society has been forced to move on by struggles of women and the changing demands of the labour market:

"'For man the physiological psychology of woman is full of difficulties,' wrote the British immunologist Almroth Wright in a 1912 letter to The Times of London, which Sedgwick would later quote. 'He is not a little mystified when he encounters in her periodically recurring phases of hypersensitiveness, unreasonableness, and loss of the sense of proportion.' Even menopause made women ineligible to participate in elections, Wright said, because it gave rise to 'serious and long-continued mental disorders developing in connexion with the approaching extinction of a woman's reproductive faculty.'" (Why Men Thought Women Weren't Made to Vote, Koren, The Atlantic, July 2019)

Long after women in the Western world had won the vote, the calls for women's equal rights in other spheres was still met with the anti-family refrain. The 1980's push in the USA for the Women's' Economic Equity Act was countered by President Ronald Reagan's supporters claims that the act would undermine the family. A quarter of a century after the Act was finally passed under President Bill Clinton, right wing American conservatives are claiming just that – that the act has undermined US family life. The impact of the deterioration of workers' working conditions and real wages on life in the USA is minimised and instead the finger is pointed at measures for women's equality.

When immigration is not being blamed for cuts in working people's living standards then it is those fighting for women's equality who have seemingly wrecked the institution of marriage, bringing unemployment, job instability and mental health issues raining down on the heads of all those 'living in sin' in Sodom and Gomorrah:

"The sexual revolution has scythed through the institution of marriage, leaving millions of women without the love and emotional and financial security that they and their children so need... Diseases of despair — alcoholism, overdoses, suicide — have been rising among white, working-class Americans, the very population that has witnessed a steep decline in family stability over the past several decades." (Feminism has Destabilized the American Family, Mona Charen, New York Post July 7, 2018)

Meanwhile capitalism has had to move the discussion on. Once capitalism needed women in senior management, society began to take note. Those sexist brain theories coined as 'neuro-sexism' are being revoked by scientists. Nevertheless, because sexism is a handy tool for exploitation, the ruling elite will cling on to this venomous injection into the arteries and veins of the family and human interaction, just as they cling on to racism.

In 2018, neuro-scientist, Professor Gina Rippon, wrote this succinct take on the ideological battle:

"The very concept of a 'male' and 'female' brain has been found to be flawed. A recently reported study showed that every brain is actually a mosaic of different patterns, some more commonly found in men's brains and some in women's. But none could be described as fully male or fully female. Yet the old neuro-nonsense arguments have not gone away. Everyone loves a sex difference story, particularly one that can be illustrated with a brain image. Self-help books, adverts, newspaper articles and social media fasten on such stories – even those that are almost immediately challenged." (How 'Neurosexism' is Holding Back Gender Equality, Rippon, Oct 2018, theconversation.com)

The Evolving Family

We have considered how the same process is progressing in relation to the nuclear family, where the religious, pseudo-logical and scientific ideological props are increasingly crashing against the brutal economic realities of 21st century capitalism, which now denies the majority of its labour force the means by which to support the raising of a healthy nuclear family. Capitalism only survives in the West by sustaining intense poverty in large swathes of the world that traffics desperate armies of people into the industrialised economies to act as cheap labour.

Back in 1877, pointing to the evolution of the family over thousands of years, American anthropologist Lewis Morgan, argued that it would be forced by economic developments to change once again:

"When the fact is accepted that the family has passed through four successive forms, and is now in a fifth, the question at once arises whether this form can be permanent in the future. The only answer that can be given is, that it must advance as society advances, and change as society changes, even as it has done in the past. It is the culture of the social system, and will reflect its culture... Should the monogamian family in the distant future fail to answer the requirements of society, assuming the continuous progress of civilization, it is impossible to predict the nature of its successor." (Ancient Society, Lewis Morgan, 1877)

The fundamental contradiction between the family and capitalism is that capitalism treats each individual member of the family as a unit, calculates their value and sets them apart – even against each other. The father who is an operative at Volkswagen must compete against the daughter who is an operative down the road at Ford and the mother who is at Nissan. All the time, whether in the same or different industries they are pressurised by management, fighting to defend or expand their share of the market spend. The one's bonus may be the other's redundancy. Capitalism at its essence only values the family as a means of exploitation and control.

It is here contended that capitalism, in aiming to squeeze as much short term value-added out of the nuclear family, is not only destroying the capacity of families to survive as a unit but also, in atomising and automatising adults and adolescents, is undermining itself, and more importantly, society's future. Both societal and capitalism's needs are pressing the family to change. Whether the changes are beneficial or detrimental to family members will be determined by whether families join together to demand the changes they require rather than allowing themselves to be pushed down the road of further commodifying their children.

Rather than undermining families, the collective and individual empowerment and emancipation of teenagers will strengthen and enrich those social and emotional bonds that benefit the family.

Children as Property: Legality and Reality?

Godwin in 2015, whilst highlighting how children are excluded from the debate about democratic respect and rights for all, outlined the arguments of many who are critical of the legal position of children today and argue that the state continues to deal with children as property contrary to the spirit of equal rights.

"Relatively few in the political mainstream today speak of parents as the owners of their children, but the implied logic of parental rights suggests a type of ownership or quasi-property interest in children. In many regards, this allocation of powers to parents, functions as a sort of ownership, and

some (though not all) of the putative legal interests that parents have in their children can be compared to property interests.

"For example, that the religious education of a particular parent's child is purportedly a matter of that parent's freedom, but the religious education of someone else's child is not, makes sense only if one accepts that in some way children belong to their parents as possessions that the scope of their freedom extends over. The idea that parents can impose on their child what others cannot, because that child is their child and belongs to them, and not to others, amounts to a belief that parents are functionally related to their children as car owners are to their cars.

"This is of course not to say that quasi-ownership is the only dimension of how parents relate to children legally or socially, but that it is a significant element in the function and legitimacy of parent-child power dynamics." (Against Parental Rights, Samantha Godwin, 2015, Columbia Human Rights Law Review)

Indeed, Godwin points out that in the USA the legal term used to denote releasing a child from custody is the same as that used for the freeing of slaves i.e. emancipation.

From conception to marriage, she illustrates how the state often treats the children as property. This includes commercial surrogacy, where birth parents sell the foetus handing over all rights to control the child and satisfy whatever purpose they chose to make their purchase, indicating a property relationship:

"...parental rights include the right to control a child and to exclude others from accessing that child. In this regard, arguing that commercial surrogacy sells not children but parental rights makes little sense: selling parental rights is selling the legal right to control a child, just as selling chattel property is selling the legal right to control the chattel property." (Against Parental Rights, Samantha Godwin, 2015, Columbia Human Rights Law Review)

The author makes similar points in relation to adoption and custody procedures:

"Parents can 'give up a child' for adoption by an adult of their choice, demonstrating a right similar to the right to alienate property through a gift (though not a sale). Children have no parallel right to claim adoption by a preferred potential parent. Parents can even decide who should 'inherit' their children if they die while their children are minors by naming guardians in their wills, just as they can name beneficiaries." (Against Parental Rights, Samantha Godwin, 2015, Columbia Human Rights Law Review)

To this one can add the process whereby private adoption agencies exist by profiting from these transactions, often doing so as a result of relieving the parents of the financial burdens of child rearing. Moreover, the rise of large corporate foster care and residential care companies where children are taken in and passed on for profit and dividends, which are in turn passed on to private and corporate shareholders, is the sharpest indication of how children have been commodified.

We begin to see how children have an exchange value, which is also reflected in the black-market trading of child slaves and the financial incentives being touted by governments such as Russia and Hungary for women to bear more children.

Corporal punishment is another case in point. Only children face corporal punishment. For adults this is legally termed as assault or torture. Over 50 countries across the globe have now banned corporal punishment However many have followed the English legal example whereby whilst third party assaults on children are now illegal, parents still have the right to physically chastise i.e. smack or beat their children, so long as the assault is considered "reasonable" by the courts, and notably the determinations of other adults.

"Reasonable chastisement" nevertheless still includes an intent to cause harm to a child but only the parent has that right, no other adult. They have the right to do with their property as they reasonably see fit.

Even so, where serious abuse of the child is legally deemed to have taken place, it is the experience of most children that it is they who lose the right to the roof over their head rather than the abusive parents.

Further Godwin argues that the freeing of the child from parental custody often requires court satisfaction that the parent has abandoned the young person or consented to their marriage, demonstrating the parental autarchy.

Some will argue that parents' custodial role in law is one simply of conveyed guardianship and that the state is simply outlining the boundaries. However, a family pet such as a cat or dog is bought and considered property. The state also intervenes with laws outlining what are considered the civilised boundaries for treating the animal. It is property that can and is traded on the open market. The difference is in style not content.

Wonderfully aspirational, the 1989 United Nations Convention of the Child (https://www.unicef.org/child-rights-convention/convention-text) was a major step forward in the recognition of children in international law. Nevertheless, despite it being the most ratified treaty in history, the above examples show that, even in the wealthiest countries, its implementation still has far to go in improving the position of children. Indeed, with the treaty far from aimed at the emancipation of young people, its many caveats, particularly relating to parental rights and state laws allow governments to continue with their oppressive approaches.

Woodhouse pointed to how the United States, wrapped up as it is in the property-based concept of childhood, still had far to go in considering the rights of the child:

"Stamped on the reverse side of the coinage of family privacy and parental rights are the child's voicelessness, objectification, and isolation from the community... our attachment to this property-based notion of the private child cuts off a more fruitful consideration of the rights of all children to safety, nurture, and stability, to a voice, and to membership in the national family." (Who Owns the Child? Meyer and Pierce and the Child as Property, Barbara Bennett Woodhouse, 1992)

Those adults vociferously questioning the morality of parental rights can only too effectively highlight the contradictions with the rights of the child, as does Godwin in her 2015 Human Rights Law review article:

"Rather than parental rights deriving from protectionist necessity, the deference granted to parental autonomy in child rearing implies that children are still implicitly accorded a quasi-property like status in law and society. This status is incompatible with broadly shared commitments to human dignity and the equality of persons' moral worth. The legal rights granted to parents equally enable the use of power for paternalism and the use of power for self-interested or arbitrary purposes without distinction. Child protectionist arguments in favor of parental rights cannot explain why parents should be empowered to coerce their children in ways other than those useful for child protection." (Against Parental Rights, Samantha Godwin, 2015, Columbia Human Rights Law Review)

As regards to their labours, young people are left in a condition of serfdom. Legally, all those products that they secure for themselves are owned by their parents. From the earliest age, children can earn money e.g. from filming and modelling contracts, then later for their physical labour and progressing to adolescence when they can perform tasks often on a par with adults in the workforce. There are some restrictions, for example in England a 14-year-old is allowed to work no more than 25 hours a week. Nevertheless, by the laws of most Western countries, irrespective of all their endeavours the earnings of young children and adolescents are the property of the parents, as are the rest of their possessions. As property they cannot own property. They are objectified.

Modern Child Labour and the Family

Despite all the labour laws and global frowning on child labour in the workplace, UNICEF and the International Labour Organisation still estimate that 160 million children are employed in the labour markets around the world, and that this figure increased by 10% between 2016 and 2020 (Child Labour: Global Estimates 2020, Trends and the Road Forward, June 2021, UNICEF/ILO).

They also estimate that a quarter of all children in the poorest countries are in employment. A good proportion of these children will be employed as domestic servants, which begs the question of children's unacknowledged economic role in society.

Utilising a Marxist analysis of labour and surplus value, Indian economist, Anjan Chakrabarti, advances a useful explanation for the basis of the transformation towards attitudes to children's contribution to the home.

In his 2007 article, Children's Working World through the Lens of Class, the economist argues that modern capitalism deliberately ignores or downplays labour in the home that does not have a sufficient market value in an era when *"...economy procreating in the public space came to symbolise capitalism."* (Children's Working World through the Lens of Class, Anjan Chakrabarti, Journal of Social and Economic Development July - Dec. 2007)

This, he states, was down to a view of the economy which was both wage labour-centric and patriarchal and was evolved in the 20th century. The home ("the Englishman's castle") was declared to be conceptually outside of the economy and its laws pertained to a different world, that of the religiously sanctified family: *"...the moment of children's work within the household and traditional sectors that is rendered value-less by virtue of their belonging to a pre-supposed 'familial-non modern' space that is already de-valued in terms of (i) a modern capitalist economy that positions wage labour at the centre of its conception and (ii) by the socially constructed process of 'gender-seniority' that de-franchises 'household' work as feminine which in turn makes household work, including that performed by children, as non-economic or less economic."*

However, we should add that, as Juliet Mitchell commented in her 1971 treatise, Women's Estate, women's work in the household had been discounted long before the 20th century: *"Once woman was accorded the menial tasks involved in maintenance while man undertook conquest and creation, she became an aspect of the things preserved; private property and children."* (Women's Estate, Mitchell, 1971)

Suffice to say, for the male-dominated capitalist system labour in the home was considered to be an irrelevant constant.

"...the non-capitalist economic structures (including economic organisations consisting of unpaid labour or labour remunerated in kind)

are immediately subordinated in relation to capitalist class ones. Given this hierarchical relationship in which the centricity of capitalism is a pre-supposition, the private and the traditional ('third world') sectors that are overwhelmingly non capitalist in nature came to be judged as effeminate, rather valueless, that is, not the sites in which the maximum of wealth is created, not the site in which economic history is produced."

This outlook, as the reader will have concluded, meant completely overlooking the vast market for domestic labour-saving devices such as washing machines, vacuum cleaners and the market for domestic servants whose labour clearly possessed not only a use value but also an exchange value. The conceptual ignoring of the home as part of the market suited both patriarchal society (the state's pact with its property owners and parents to cede their children to corporate education) and capitalism's leaning on the nuclear family to exploit and doubly exploit homemakers, who are overwhelmingly female.

This is reflected in the UK government's financial support for those people aged over 16 who have primary responsibility for caring for someone in the household for reasons of incapacity. The government offers one carer in each household a weekly grant of £67.60 (in 2021) providing they can demonstrate that their care duty is for at least 35 hours in a week. This cash grant (which is distinct from that for state funded foster care) is equivalent to less than £2 per hour, less than a quarter of the same government's National Living Wage. As a result, the real market cost of replacing the unpaid carer with a paid carer would start at least five times greater and that assumes that the care hours involved will be no more than the government's level of just five hours per day.

To consider the value of women's domestic toils both as mothers and "homemakers", today we need look no further than the life insurance companies which will value the cost of professionally replacing these activities in the labour market and present a price to the courts. To their calculations we could also add the money spent on labour saving devices for the home and probably reach a figure near to £250,000 for just the 20 years involved in a modern child's upbringing. With this in mind, we can start approaching the issue of a child's contribution to the home, something which is acknowledged in histories and tales of pre-19th century society but overlooked in the present as part of the state's propagandist notion that children's childhood should be devoted to their academic education and the rest of the time left primarily to 'play'. To this end, state regulations often limit the hours that children can be hired for work but place no limit on the hours of education.

Chakrabarti points out that all children work in one form or other: *"Like all social actors, children work. Children work individually and in groups. In the working groups, a child sometimes works among the community of children and at other times he or she works alongside adults. However, much of the work children perform is not recognised as labour."*

The economist refers to Nieuwenhuys's observation that children's work can be divided into two spheres: child labour and child work (Children's Lifeworlds, Gender, Welfare and Labour in the Developing World, Nieuwenhuys, 1994, Routledge). Child labour as defined by Nieuwenhuys is that work which is performed in the public space for the market, whereas child work is outside the public space and largely in the home.

However, child work, because it mainly takes place in the 'sanctity' of the home, writes Chakrabarti is conceptually devalued, placed in the parent-child paradigm and dressed in notions of duty, responsibility, love, role play and care: *"The parents are supposed to show responsibility, care and love towards the children while the children must meet their obligation, fulfil their duties and have emotional attachments towards their parents. Children's work is thus not really labour in the sense of producing wealth but comes to be seen as part of a reciprocal obligation, duties and emotion that as they are activated help keep the seemingly naturalised parent-children moral paradigm in order and provide stability to the society at large."* (Children's Working World through the Lens of Class, Anjan Chakrabarti, Journal of Social and Economic Development July - Dec. 2007)

The result is that children's productive role and contribution to the family is airbrushed and children are marginalised. We will see, for example, how children's inputs are often ignored in the discussions about child-rearing. At a more mundane level, when at 15 I was shifted from my orphanage into a foster placement, the middle-class couple employed a young Danish live in au pair to look after their baby. I was rather disappointed when she was despatched on her way and at the same time, as many older siblings would recognise, I became the babysitter (my services were in effect funded by the state). As with many older siblings when they reach a certain age, my capacity to act as a babysitter saved the family considerable amounts of money.

To place children's material contribution in a formal situation, it is worth considering, the implications of the work as children we contributed to the household's welfare. In "The Golly in the Cupboard" I recorded some of the rostered duties we orphans were expected to perform in the children's homes as a matter of course and without reward. Our many chores included tidying and cleaning most of the rooms, preparing the large dining room for meals, washing and drying the dishes and kitchen pots and pans by hand, tidying the lawns and gardens and annually we were expected to perform to entertain the support committee composed of the town's dignitaries. The only regular reward for our labour came when the child who got up early to make the staff toast was rewarded with a slice of toast.

Outside of these formal duties, we voluntarily played a mainly pro-active role nurturing, caring, educating and protecting the younger children and each other. We also took responsibility for each other outside the home. Outside of school hours, we were largely left to play amongst ourselves. A mixed group of 20 to 40 boys and girls aged three to fifteen were left to their own devices and, sometimes in mixed age, sometimes in peer groups, we autonomously and largely unconsciously, as paediatricians and psychologists might recognise today, developed many of the fundamental skills required to set us up for life.

Whether we were in the playroom, or the gardens, on the pitch or in the parks we were busy playing, enhancing our executive function skills, our creative thinking, our decision-making skills and memory, our social flexibility and adaptability, empathy, communication techniques self-regulation self-control and self-discipline, muscle control, coordination, and reflexes – and didn't charge one penny.

All in all, were our combined contributions to be analysed by insurance companies, then they probably amounted to more than the cost of staffing the orphanage. Had that cost been borne by the state then it would have been drawn from taxes and part of the societal sum of surplus value. We created a surplus but had no say in its distribution.

Nor did we give this time and effort to one another begrudgingly. Like in many orphanages, left to our own devices we were not the renowned self-centred young savages of William Golding's Lord of the Flies. We were, as human beings, social animals and learned the value of caring for each other. Golding's young savages were no doubt modelled on tales, heard whilst growing up, of antics at the nearby Marlborough College, one of the country's elite public schools at the time. Those schools were to develop an elite ready to rule and exploit the world. We were at best being disciplined to be part of the exploited workforce.

Nevertheless, in British boarding schools, the children were also heavily relied on as a domestic labour force. This took the form of the notorious fagging system whereby the senior pupils directed the rest of the pupils to carry out most of the mundane chores. The senior pupils were rewarded with privileges including their own fags and encouraged to maintain their dominant position by fear, bribery and divide and rule – the tactics of empire. It was survival of the fittest and woe betide the weak or unsuspecting. The role of the public schools as prep schools for the country's militarised elite was highlighted by George Orwell in his 1941 novel, The Lion and the Unicorn, when he wrote: "*Probably the battle of Waterloo was won on the playing-fields of Eton, but the opening battles of all subsequent wars have been lost there.*"

If the fagging system proved defective in maintaining the Empire, it nevertheless paid off handsomely in reducing the labour costs of the schools and financially benefitted either the school's management or, if all or some of the savings were passed on, the parents.

A Progressive Aspect to Child Labour

Marx argued that there was a progressive element to child labour in so much as it introduced children to the world of production. Often children engage in labour as 'play'. Our enforced labours in the orphanage were not play but gave us a sense of a 'use value'. They additionally helped us learn basic skills including collectively working together. On the other hand, we generally construed our pro-active voluntary engagement in nurturing other children as play.

The point made by Chakrabarti (ibid) was not that most child work is wrong but that there is a failure to recognise young people's contribution to the family. This is particularly notable in regard to sibling nurturing and is linked to a failure to understand and research the key role of sibling attachments and their place within the family. One common abusive biproduct is the callous and psychologically damaging disregard shown in the practice of separating siblings when they enter the English care system.

The reaction to the widespread phenomenon of young carers, adolescents who act as primary carers for one or more of their households, is instructive. The children's charities, aiming at pulling adults' heartstrings, mainly focus on their missing out on the "play" and "learning" of childhood. For many of Britain's 700,000 young carers there are more pressing issues such as lack of support and isolation from social ties, which can have long term impact on mental health. However, there is another generally unacknowledged side to the young carer experience that is their significant capacity for taking on the assumed role of adults in the home. They are often featured as looking after older close relatives but, in many cases, they also take responsibility for young siblings.

Researchers Matzka and Nagl-Cupal make the point that: *"Young carers largely have the same repertoire of resources as other children and can use them specifically to respond to the care burden."* (Psychosocial Resources

74

Contributing to Resilience in Austrian Young Carers, Matzka, Nagl-Cupal, 30 October 2020, Research in Nursing & Health).

Their observation highlights the consciously responsible role that adolescents can and often do play within the household. This is not to downplay the difficulties faced by young carers, especially when caring alone for those with mental health and or chronic substance abuse issues. The extremes of their situation should not blind us to the capacities they display and that their often-lonely role in the household is one end of the spectrum of children's productive contribution to the family.

Equally it raises questions about the age of adult capacity of a young person, irrespective of the neuro-scientifically specified level of particular chemical compounds. We know that millions of children are still employed in workforces across the world as they were en masse in Europe prior to the 20th Century, performing many of the tasks that are reserved for adults today. In terms of young people's potential for contributing technologically and culturally to the world, it is notable that Blaise Pascal began his development of the hand-held mathematical calculator at 19. Louis Braille was just 15 when he presented what we now know as braille, the reading and writing system for the blind or visually impaired. In the classical arts, Mozart, Mendelssohn, Michelangelo and Pablo Picasso had all produced renowned works, and in battle, Joan of Arc and Alexander the Great had led troops in successful military campaigns before any of them reached 18 years of age. To top it all on the strategic side, the world has already witnessed 40 teenagers who attained the title of chess grandmaster before they were 15.

The Role of Children in Child-Rearing
The downplaying of the importance of women's role in the household and that of children in child work, by further marginalising children had another major detrimental impact in distorting social research into the family and child development.

Women's changing role on the labour market, the developing market for labour-saving household devices and women's advocacy has seen the beginning of a change in attitudes towards the contribution of work in the household and child-rearing, nevertheless the child's role remained a marginalised and overlooked one. Almost two thirds of the 20th century had passed by before American sociologist, Donald Irish, was moved to point out that: *"...little empirical research has been conducted regarding the interactions of siblings with each other."* and that logic, *"would lead one to conclude that parents rear their children one at a time—or in separate compartments."* (Sibling Interaction: A neglected aspect in family life research, Irish DP, Social Forces. 1964).

The impact of the research was to overlook not only the complexity of child-rearing that women were expected to carry out, but also the role of the children in that task. Irish was writing at a time when households had historically composed of many more children than today, when still an estimated 80% of people in the USA have grown up in multi-child households. It is also telling that despite it being a half century since Irish's call for more research on the matter, psychologists still refer to a dearth of sibling interactional research. In turn this academic shortfall reflects and reinforces the societal marginalisation of children's role in child-rearing.

A Dearth of Sibling Research
Human Development Professor, Susan McHale and her colleagues, Updegraff and Whiteman, in 2012 published their paper, Sibling Relationships and Influences in Childhood and Adolescence, and highlighted the minute proportion of citations regarding sibling interactions in academic texts:

"Our search of the 1990 – 2011 psychological and sociological abstracts for 'sibling and relation or relationships,' for example, yielded 741 citations. In contrast, the counts were 33,990 citations for 'parent or parenting, '8,685 citations for 'marriage or marital relationship or marital relation,' and 5,059 citations for 'peer relations or peer relationships or friend-ships.'" (Sibling Relationships and Influences in Childhood and Adolescence, McHale, Updegraff and Whiteman, 2012)

The paper also illustrated how this absence of consideration was reflected in America's major family journals:

"Drilling down to the abstracts of the major family journals between 1990 and 2011 and focusing on the neonatal through adolescent periods yielded citation counts of 41 articles in the Journal of Marriage and Family, 18 articles in Family Relations, 21 articles in the Journal of Family Issues and 131 articles in the Journal of Family Psychology with the term sibling in the abstract; only about one third of these articles, however, focused directly on sibling relationships." (ibid)

Parenting is discussed in even the most progressive of media channels as a singleton relationship, of the parental unit nurturing and protecting the child. As McHale et al, echoing Donald Irish, point out:

"Most family research has been conducted with the seeming assumption that studying one child in a family is sufficient for understanding how families operate and how they influence individual development and adjustment. Research on siblings has revealed, however, that two individuals from the same family are often as different as unrelated individuals (Plomin & Daniels, 1987), suggesting that, in failing to incorporate siblings in their investigations, family scholars may be missing important pieces of the family puzzle." (ibid)

There is little consideration of the roles, for example that we children in our orphanage played of educating, teaching, protecting, disputing with and advocating for one another. Nor is there comment on how these roles teach children nurturing and educational skills.

"'Come on Mark, tell us one of yer monster stories.'

"'All right,' Mark assented, 'but let me think of one first.'

"Mickey Thompson turned off his torch and put his comic down. Then we all lay down facing Mark's bed beside the window. Mark began: 'Once upon a time there was a big green 'ouse where lots of boys lived. They played football and soldiers all day an' ate sandwiches, strawberries and ice cream and jelly every day. They didn't 'ave to go to school because they

could read and write already.'" (The Golly in the Cupboard, Frampton, 2004)

In 2012 McHale also published a paper, The Third Rail of Family Systems, with Feinberg and Solmeyer, which pointed to the implications for paediatricians, care and family practitioners, in which they highlighted the time siblings spend together and the importance of the ensuing dynamics regarding development:

"Sibling relationships are an important context for development, but are often ignored in research and preventive interventions with youth and families. In childhood and adolescence siblings spend considerable time together, and siblings' characteristics and sibling dynamics substantially influence developmental trajectories and outcomes." (The Third Rail of Family Systems: Sibling Relationships, Mental and Behavioral Health, and Preventive Intervention in Childhood and Adolescence, Feinberg, Solmeyer and McHale, 2012)

As McHale, Feinberg and others point out, the absence of research on the role of siblings had left the void in the narrative of parenting to be filled with the negative perceptions of siblings, such as sibling rivalry, sibling squabbles and violence. The children were often out of sight, if not of mind, when as parents we ditched what we were doing to respond to the cries and shouts of our aggrieved children, as they fought or argued out their conflicts. Otherwise, we left them at play, but without hardly a thought given that they were busy developing their cognitive and emotional skills and that the violent incidents were part of their road to develop their relationship skills. It is how to deal with the conflicts that gets ingrained into our consciousness.

Feinberg, Solmeyer and McHale referenced several sources to point out the degree of violent interactions between young siblings that parents and carers record and debate in the USA:

"Indeed, our research suggests that the most frequent source of disagreements and arguments between parents and young adolescents is how siblings are getting along (McHale & Crouter, 1996). Observational research has documented the occurrence of sibling conflict at a rate of up

to 8 times per hour (Berndt & Bulleit, 1985; Dunn & Munn, 1986), and sibling aggression is common: 70% of families report physical violence between siblings, and over 40% of children were kicked, bitten, or punched by their siblings during a one-year period (Steinmetz, Straus, & Gelles, 1981). In fact, sibling violence occurs more frequently than other forms of child abuse, and is significantly related to substance use, delinquency, and aggression—even controlling for other forms of family violence." (ibid)

The religious texts abound with tales of fratricide. Cain and Abel star as the first act of violence in the Bible. The Egyptian god Osiris is dismembered by his brother Set. Rome was built by Romulus who had killed his brother, Remus, and the Hindu Ramayana narrates how Vali brutally subjugates his brother, Sugriv.

Sororicide is less common in our myths and historical tales but Cinderella is mistreated by her stepsisters, the Biblical Leah and Rachel fight over a man, the English Anne Boleyn beats her sister Mary to the throne only to be beheaded and the later English Queen Mary imprisoned her half-sister Elizabeth in the Tower of London.

At least Hansel and Gretel got along... didn't they?

Modern family journals do generally now point to potential development benefits of sibling altercations but seemingly more to assuage parents as opposed to focussing on the real benefits of sibling interactions. McHale, Updegraff and Whiteman's paper argued for the focus in the USA to be shifted onto the benefits:

"Sibling influences emerge not only in the context of siblings' frequent and often emotionally intense interactions but also by virtue of siblings' role in larger family system dynamics. Although siblings are building blocks of family structure and key players in family dynamics, their role has been relatively neglected by family scholars and by those who study close relationships. Incorporating study of siblings into family research provides novel insights into the operation of families as social and socializing systems." (Sibling Relationships and Influences in Childhood and Adolescence, McHale, Updegraff and Whiteman, 2012)

Feinberg, Solmeyer and McHale's research focussed on taking into account and utilising siblings' roles within the family for practical intervention in assisting young families. They emphasised the positive results of the programme but highlighted the need for much more research and discussion focussed not only on tackling family problems but also to unlock all the other benefits of recognising children's active role within the family.

"Studies suggest that siblings can have positive influences on outcomes including social competence (Stormshak, Bellanti, Bierman et al., 1996) and adaptive relationships skills (Updegraff et al., 2000), but the processes underlying these associations have not been articulated and documented. Research on the benefits of sibling relationships could inform sibling-focused interventions and help to expand their goals to promoting positive outcomes in addition to reducing harmful sibling conflict and subsequent problem behaviors.

"Given these questions and areas for future work, to what extent is our understanding of sibling relationships ready for translation into practice? We believe that there is sufficient evidence for clinicians to integrate a focus on siblings into child and family programs." (The Third Rail of Family Systems: Sibling Relationships, Mental and Behavioral Health, and Preventive Intervention in Childhood and Adolescence, Feinberg, Solmeyer and McHale, 2012)

Promoters of increased research into the workings and benefits of sibling relationships recognise some of the hurdles that especially quantitative research must overcome. These include the complexities and cost of sampling, which, apart from age, gender, accommodation type, location, socio-economic position and quantity of parents may also need to include quantity of siblings, age difference between siblings of different and same genders etc.

Overlaying these practical difficulties is the difficulty of securing funding for research which challenges the reigning ideological primacy of the parent-child and marital bonds in the family. Consequently, most funding is secured for research in solving acute family problems in the social welfare sector rather than directed at benefitting families as a whole.

"... an increasing focus in the past two decades has been on sibling influences on adolescents' risky behavior and adjustment problems. Sibling conflicts in childhood, for example, are associated with concurrent and later deviance, school problems, bullying, substance use, and internalizing symptoms." (Sibling Relationships and Influences in Childhood and Adolescence, McHale, Updegraff and Whiteman, 2012)

There is nevertheless, the additional issue that a great deal of sibling interactions take place in the form of unstructured play and interactions making the processes difficult to quantify but also taking them out of the sphere of adult micro-management. If anything, despite all the general promotion of the value of play, the age of neo-liberalism has seen a move away from incorporating play with parents pressured to increase the micro-management or digitalisation of their children with quantifiable activities and results that can meet the demand of the state and capitalism's commodification not only of children but also their educational development.

Education and Children's Collective Play
Testing children by getting them to write down what they have learnt regarding specific questions at an early age can be quantified. Quantitative data allows for comparative short-term data across hundreds of academic units which can they be used to convey 'value for money' to meet the needs of the 'parental market'. Parents can be pressurised to focus on their children achieving good 'marks' to help their offspring on their way to becoming attractive to the labour market. The parents are offered control of their children's pathway providing they ensure that they focus the child on what the state says the child needs to be able to show they know.

For the concerned parent, the focus is taken off their children's development and onto an exam. That is the education they must direct the children's time to. Studying and reading is primary, the rest of the time the children are left to their own devices – to play and converse with their siblings if any are available. In contrast play is largely out of the parents' control. Parents cannot sit down and order a child to play and be guaranteed a result that they consider to be play. Play is voluntary and involves engagement of the imagination. It requires an agency, which is out of their control.

This point is made very well in an instructive piece on play published by the American journal, Pediatrics in 2018, The Power of Play: A Pediatric Role in Enhancing Development in Young Children, which states that play: *"...is an activity that is intrinsically motivated, entails active engagement, and results in joyful discovery. Play is voluntary and often has no extrinsic goals; it is fun and often spontaneous... Play often creates an imaginative private reality, contains elements of make believe, and is nonliteral."* (The Power of Play: A Pediatric Role in Enhancing Development in Young Children, Yogman, Garner, Hutchinson, Hirsh-Pasek and Michnick Golinkoff, Pediatrics September 2018)

Fun and spontaneous it might be but, as paediatricians and child psychologists are well aware, it has huge benefits in child development. The Power of Play authors highlight: *"improvements in executive functioning, language, early math skills (numerosity and spatial concepts), social development, peer relations, physical development and health, and enhanced sense of agency."*

In all this, peer engagement (other children) is playing its part in preparing the child for future learning.

"Pretend play encourages self-regulation because children must collaborate on the imaginary environment and agree about pretending and conforming to roles, which improves their ability to reason about hypothetical events. Social–emotional skills are increasingly viewed as related to academic and economic success. Third-grade prosocial behavior correlated with eighth-grade reading and math better than with third-grade reading and math."

And developing children's engagement skills: *"Opportunities for peer engagement through play cultivate the ability to negotiate. Peer play usually involves problem solving about the rules of the game, which requires negotiation and cooperation. Through these encounters, children learn to use more sophisticated language when playing with peers."*

Play they argue is a critical learning block for 21st century skills, developing software and new technologies:

"Play is fundamentally important for learning 21st century skills, such as problem solving, collaboration, and creativity, which require the executive functioning skills that are critical for adult success... Some studies note that the new information economy, as opposed to the older industrial one demands more innovation and less imitation, more creativity and less conformity. Research on children's learning indicates that learning thrives when children are given some agency (control of their own actions) to play a role in their own learning."

British Educationalist, Sir Ken Robinson, made this same point in his 2008 lecture to the country's Royal Society of Arts, when he called for the abandonment of an education system that he argued was geared to meet the needs of the 19th century:

"We have to think differently about human capacity. We have to get over this old conception of academic, non-academic, abstract, theoretical, vocational... and see it for what it is, a myth. Second, you have to recognize that most great learning happens in groups, that collaboration is the stuff of growth. If you atomize people and separate them and judge them separately, we form a kind of disjunction between them and their natural learning environment. And thirdly, it's crucially about the culture of our institutions, the habits of institution and the habitats that they occupy."
(Changing Education Paradigms, Robinson, 2008
https://www.youtube.com/watch?v=zDZFcDGpL4U)

Robinson pointed to the societal importance of developing creativity amongst adolescents and how the school systems were failing – an issue that we will return to later. Developing creativity amongst children involves acknowledging the vital role that young people and their peers play in their own education but that defies the atomisation of children demanded by the modern education systems. That Robinson, for all the plaudits and honours he received, was unable to turn the tide demonstrates the immensity of the task.

Indeed, the World Economic Forum has declared that developing the Emotional Intelligence (EQ) skills of self-awareness, self-regulation, self-motivation, empathy and social skills will be critical in this new industrial and economic era. Psychologists recognise that these interpersonal skills are not developed by rote but in collective exchanges with one's peers and the more those exchanges are regulated the less effective they are. The uncertainty and relatively random nature of the inputs is critical but because academics cannot control the input it defies the accountants staring at their laptops in the marketisation bunker.

If adults have little control over the working of one child's imagination, they have next to none regarding the results of two children's imagination's interacting. Nor can they easily check the results by sticking a thermometer under their arm, telling the child to stick their tongue out or checking their online score.

Even if they could measure the results (and psychologists do get a rough picture) then there is little they could do to ensure a repeat of the interaction sufficient to secure the same results. And this process goes on through early childhood and adolescence. A huge amount of work is enacted as play but vital to the psyche. But because child's work is overlooked and play is partitioned off as a luxury, parents under pressure from the state and social pressure ditch play.

Children's Association Time
The authors point out that in the latter part of the 20th century social pressures cut American children's play by 12 hours per week, equivalent to a colossal 250 two-hour timeouts per year: *"From 1981 to 1997, children's playtime decreased by 25%. Children 3 to 11 years of age have lost 12 hours per week of free time. Because of increased academic pressure, 30% of US kindergarten children no longer have recess."*

They also add that the country's nationwide No Child Left Behind Act of 2001 placed even more pressure on professionals and parents to limit play in pursuit of measurable academic tests.

This process of eating into play was mirrored in England. In 2019, a study of over 1000 children's schools by University College London of children's in-school playtime revealed that school breaks had been dramatically cut between 1995 and 2017: *"At key stage 1 in primary school, where children are aged five to seven, pupils now have 45 minutes less break time per week than children of the same age in 1995. Meanwhile, pupils at key stage 3 and 4 (aged 11 to 16) have 65 minutes less than two decades ago."* (A follow up survey of break and lunch times in schools, Baines and Blatchford, University College London, 2019)

The survey revealed that the country's high school students were only receiving an average of one hour and three minutes of break time in a school day. It is worth noting that the UK's Prisons Inspectorate in 2007 stated that it expected adult prisoners to have, on top of eight hours study or work:

"...the opportunity for at least one hour of exercise in the open air every day,"

and have

"...the opportunity of at least one hour of association every day." (Time Out of Cell, HM Inspectorate of Prisons, 2007)

The Inspectorate's report went on to declare that this time was: *"critical to the mental health and wellbeing of prisoners."*

In this regard at least, Britain's criminals were treated with more care than its children. The University College London report argued that one of the major causes for the erosion of breaks was a lack of consideration regarding the value of play and children's association time. *"There is no statutory requirement for schools to provide children with a break in the school day and they hardly figure in government policy or in Ofsted inspection processes. When they are considered by schools it is often in the context of the problems that can arise and the practicalities of school management."*

"60% of primary and secondary schools said that children might miss a full break or lunch time. The main reasons given for this related to the management of misbehaviour or to help pupils catch up with schoolwork. Many schools indicated that this was part of a school policy."

Geoff Barton, General Secretary of the country's Association of School and College Leaders, placed the blame on government pressure to deliver academic results: *"School timetables are bursting at the seams because of the pressure to deliver a huge amount of learning and to prepare children for high-stakes tests and exams."* (Independent, 20th May, 2019)

The report's authors pointed to the young people, especially the adolescents stating that they wanted more, not less, break time: *" "A majority of pupils indicated that lunchbreaks were too short and should be made longer. Surprisingly, older students were more likely to express this view, possibly because of the relatively short lunch breaks that secondary pupils experience compared to primary pupils."*

The University also reported that by 2017 fewer pupils were meeting up with friends in person after school. In 2017, 31% of children reported that they seldom got to meet peers and friends, compared to 15% in 2006. We should not be surprised that the erosion of children's ability to interact face-to-face is fuelling young people's reliance on the internet for social contact. The relatively safe peer-dominated space of the school playground and the youth club is replaced by the barely regulated space of social media; a space with interactions far more easily hidden behind the Mystery Wall.

The authors concluded by pointing to the: *"... growing concern about children's mental health and personal and social development,"* and emphasising the need to recognise the valuable role of 'playtime', *"It is important, we believe, to acknowledge the valuable contributions that break times make to the social, emotional, mental and physical development of children and young people."*

A Danish study illustrated how, for adolescents, playtime and breaks were not only important to protect mental health but also to develop creativity. Danish educational psychologist, Professor Lene Tanggaard, in her 2014 paper, A Situated Model of Creative Learning, described how her passive observation of young apprentices' development revealed to her the importance of leisure time and breaks for young people developing their creative faculties.

The professor's observations helped her to conclude that, while creativity could not be forced or taught, it was best nurtured in conditions where young people had time free from structured teaching where they could freely consider issues and work on them, particularly with their peers:

"...as a researcher found out that the apprentices spent enormous amounts of time doing moonlighting, 'And I realised how much they learned from this and how creative they really were, when they were allowed to experiment with the materials within their domain.

"These experiments often happened in breaks or in zones and spaces in the workplace or at school when they had time to play relatively freely with materials and make their own projects and design-ideas work. The experiment as a basic concept is furthermore very closely aligned with the pragmatic assumption that creativity is a matter of curious and open-minded inquiry in situations requiring us to respond in new ways.

"The fooling around during moonlighting activities is something the apprentices do when they have something at hand that needs to be fixed. And it appeared that they actually took responsibility for their own learning, learning what was needed to be done and what needed to be fixed. Accordingly, doing so, the apprentices were moving, unrestrained, in the direction of the democratic, peer-based learning

"...There is potential innovation capital in the gaps between all of the intended attempts at promoting creativity in a school context. I argue that these 'gaps' are ideal places for experimenting with that which is taught during school. Breaks in teaching can represent a gap of this sort, as can spaces at school in which students may experiment with various tools and materials." (A Situated Model of Creative Learning, Tanggaard, February 2014, European Educational Research Journal 13)

Moreover, Tanggaard, in the same paper made the point that in a fast-changing technologized world with its fluid labour market, it was important that young people not only saw how the world around them could be changed but felt empowered to carry out that change, writing: "... *it is extremely important that pupils and students learn to recognise and see their own possibilities for acting in and quite literally manipulating their world.*"

Play is a very important part of early years child development and remains important through to adolescence and adulthood. Beyond play other nurturing skills begin to play a role with the passing on of knowledge, survival techniques and the protecting, caring for and entertaining of other siblings and peers. Some of this will be done voluntarily by children and some via adult request or orders. In the child or adolescent that begins to voluntarily organise others as enjoyment, look out for the social leaders and organisers of the future, the ones who lose the fear of falling over, see the power of the collective, gain its confidence and leadership experience through 'play'.

From organising their siblings' tea parties, or their mates' kick abouts in the park they go on to become the social and campaign organisers, the managers and union leaders – and all because of 'play'. (e.g. see The Benefits of a Long-Lens Approach to Leader Development: Understanding The Seeds Of Leadership, Murphy & Johnson, 2011, The Leadership Quarterly, 22(1))

The consequence of marginalising young children and adolescents and their role in the family is that, just when adolescents are developing their self-efficacy and can make a much more nuanced contribution to the family, the processes behind the creation of the Mystery Wall act as a barrier to them making a further contribution. They hide away in their rooms and are cut off from their other siblings as they try to progress their way through to the relative freedom and clean air of adulthood. Official society blames this on the adolescent's chemistry but meanwhile the same teenagers will often be making a full contribution to their peer groups. So, the psychologist can resort to calling upon Freud's Oedipus complex or point to the adolescent's smartphone.

The teenager could tidy his or her own room, they could do the laundry, wash the pots, clean the kitchen or even cook; they could walk the dog and take the younger siblings to the park or shopping. This much and more young carers do. They could also help younger siblings with their homework, play games with them, read with them, tell stories to them, advocate for them and help to protect them from harm thereby developing the nurturing skills that will benefit them should they bring up or work with children in the future. Yet society has been persuaded to forget all this because child work is not important and the adolescent's contribution is worthless compared to achieving high grades in this year's Mathematics and Physics exams.

The consequences of society downplaying all that is not capable of being standardised and easily commodified as a brick in the wall is palpable. By marginalising children and their role in their own and their peers' development, society is undermining the foundations not only of its future but the present.

Child Labour – The Unwelcome Reminder of Children's Exploitation
Many men still see housework as the natural work of women and children's work in the household is similarly devalued but much more heavily shrouded in ideas of nurturing and contributing to the family... but that is the point.

Often adults hide behind the idea of good child work and bad child labour. Both contribute to the family. Child work is seen as nurturing and instructive whereas child labour for non-family is seen as exploitative. Some argue that child labour is exploitative because children will learn very little from repetitive work, but what is washing the dishes or cleaning the floors?

The holier than thou attitude of Western society in condemning those countries where child labour is common has more than a touch of neurotic guilt. It is as if there is a desire to wipe the streets of child labour so not to be reminded of the child work that is sanctified in the home, and the reminder that children do not have equal rights.

We shall later discuss the twisted logic where orphanages are condemned as an affront to the sanctity of the nuclear family and so the children must be 'protected' by being thrown, like a sacrificial offering, into the hands of the family where they can be put to work for hours longer than the legal limits and exploited without any questions being asked because they are now in the care of a 'loving family'.

The "Adolescent" Child as Parental Property

It was no accident that the modern concept of adolescence was developed around the turn of the 19th century at a similar time to the growing notion of unproductive childhood.

The concept and experience of adolescence as we know it in the West today emerged as a biproduct of the age of industrial imperialism. The more developed economies in Europe and America not only required a more compliant and skilled labour force, through the bounty from Imperial rule they could also afford to extend the length of a young person's education and in doing so make giant steps along the road to abolishing commercial child labour, which was deemed as less productive than adult labour.

In enforcing education on a layer of young people until well into in their teenage years, capitalism had created a period in time where children were placed largely outside the labour market and therefore seen to be unproductive despite their rapidly developing self-efficacy. They were not bound to the labour market but were capable of many of the tasks of an adult, almost as capable (as encouraged by release for academic education) of abstract thought and often as strong. Capitalism had created a new youth and with it came the social construct of adolescence, a prolonged period of development to adulthood, to 'maturity'.

The life of teenagers changed and along with it their social role.

Like women, they were not recognised for their work in the household and their removal from the workplace to the classroom meant that they brought little or no income into the household. They came to be portrayed as a privileged age group, enjoying the relaxation of play and not appreciative of their academic education; an idle burdensome crew with time on their hands and the physical and mental capacity to cause mischief.

There was another aspect to this process. Put to work at seven, the youth had little time to forge an identity, even though as 'junior' workers they had a doubly exploited position in the family and society. Nor was the space afforded for large groups of youth to associate. Capitalism changed all that by bringing in widespread corporate education of adolescents. It created an identity and a means of collective empowerment.

Teenagers had been transformed from a productive asset to, in the short-term at least, an unproductive irksome burden. Their education and "free time" were intended to benefit the state not to challenge and threaten it. The state determined to mould them for its needs and to ensure they knew their place in the world, which in turn meant leaning on the children's parents to keep them under control. Divide, revile and rule came into play; a method of control that we shall see was practiced in relation to children in care and in orphanages especially. If the child was not to be trusted, so the adolescent had to be considered a morally debased threat to society.

Edward Long, an 18th century British plantation owner had written that they: *"seem almost incapable of making any progress in civility or science. They have no plan or system of morality among them... They have no moral sensations; no taste but for women; gormandizing, and drinking to excess; no wish but to be idle."* (The History of Jamaica, Edward Long, 1774).

Long was justifying his exploitation and brutal treatment of his Black slaves but the same comments would soon grace the pages of British journals regarding adolescents. The Edwardian drawing rooms passed seamlessly on from deploring the sulking, lazy Blacks to the moody, idle teenagers. In adolescence, capitalism had created a new identity, dressed it, characterised it and set to work creating a biological explanation for it.

The "Insanity of Adolescence"

From the 1880s, British psychiatrists increasingly began to refer to the "insanity of adolescence" and a noted work in this field was by Scottish psychiatrist, Sir Thomas Smith Clouston, who described his view of this new social phenomenon: *"At puberty and adolescence ... the affective faculties, the social instincts, the altruistic organic cravings, the delight in poetry and romance, the sense of duty, all arise in so different and definite a form as compared with their previous existence, that we must conclude that great tracts of brain substance, which had before lain dormant, have now awakened into activity."* (Developmental Insanities, T.S. Clouston, in Daniel Hack Tuke, ed. A Dictionary of Psychological Medicine, J. & A. Churchill, 1892).

In the same work Clouston referred to one 16-year-old patient as having been struck by the "Melancholia of Adolescence". Considered an eminent psychiatrist, Clouston was also said to be a fervent believer in "masturbational insanity" whereby masturbation was both a symptom and cause of insanity. He and other psychiatrists commented that most of the men they observed in the lunatic asylums masturbated. That the youngest were adolescents led the often very religious psychiatrists to conclude evidence of a causal relationship.

Adolescents would bear the scorn of Christian religious society. These young people were the epitome of the Biblical 'Original Sin', described by the 16th century French theologian, John Calvin as: *"... a hereditary, depravity and corruption of our nature, diffused through all the parts of the soul, rendering us obnoxious to the divine wrath... "*

One female care activist related to me how even in the 1960s the nuns in her orphanage would tie her and her young friends' hands to the bed at night if they were even suspected of masturbating.

Militarism and Adolescence

With increasing conflict between the imperialist powers, schools were also the convenient place for the preparing and disciplining of young men for the enlisted and conscripted armies. The more the military relied on adolescents, the more the screw was turned against them with official society turning into a barking sergeant major to prepare the recruiting pool for defence of the national interest on the battlefield.

Technical developments and the rise of the nation state, meant the nature of war combat was changing and younger men would be involved. The average age of troops killed in the American Civil War was 27 but the USA's soldiers that died in World War I were on average four years younger and one in five of those were teenagers. Despite official UK policy not permitting recruits to fight till they were 19, a quarter of enlistees were under 18 and up to 250,000 participated in World War I (Is it Counterproductive to Enlist Minors into the Army? Gee & Taylor, The RUSI Journal, Volume 161, 2016 - Issue 6).

Adolescents became at once the fodder of war and the butt of the establishment.

By 1932, the conservative American novelist, Corra Harris, was writing in the country's press declaring in an article entitled, We Made It Too Easy for Them: *"What could have happened 40 years ago that took the stamina out of the men and women who were to become the parents of these amorphous youths whose accent of conscious superiority indicates so clearly immature minds? We ourselves had lived as pioneers, abstemiously, obediently, with few pleasures, and under hardships that produced strength of character. The idea was to give our children more happiness and a better chance. We have made it so easy for them that too many of them have become unfilial and egotistical..."* (Parents and Children, Yesterday and Today, Harris, The Saturday Evening Post, May 28, 1932)

Twenty years later, the notorious FBI head, J. Edgar Hoover would publish a report, warning: *"...the nation can expect an appalling increase in the number of crimes that will be committed by teenagers in the years ahead,"* and by 1955 President Dwight Eisenhower was calling for the congress to: *"assist the states in dealing with this nationwide problem."* Western governments and their media have continued this barrage into the 21st century, making a regular pastime of launching attacks on the moral character of adolescents, all with the aim of pressurising the adult population to partake in the repression of their teenage children.

"Biologizing" Adolescence

Since Clouston and the early psychiatrists have long been largely discredited, government treasuries have funded universities to conscript armies of scientists to find new concepts and chemicals to justify the societal repression of adolescences all based on 'protecting' society by understanding the inner workings of the child that evolves into the marauding, irresponsible, pre-civilised adolescent (the delayed Original Sin).

However, as early as the 1920s, the anthropologist, Margaret Mead, visited Samoa and studied the female children in a tribal culture and concluded that Samoan children experienced none of the trauma as displayed in Western adolescents (The Social Organization of Manu'a, Mead, 1930). She concluded that American adolescent trauma was a societal issue rather than one innate to teenage humans.

As celebrated as Mead's research work was, on this point Western developmental psychologists, doffed their cap, ploughed on and moved past her. Educationalist, Professor Gowri Parameswaran, in 2019 observed how psychological analyses of childhood was torn of its socio-cultural text and driven deep inside the body of the young child and the adolescent: *"Since the beginning of the science of developmental psychology, which began more as a descriptive endeavor than a predictive one, biology has been selectively used to locate behaviors within one's body and not in the social context within which these behaviors arose ... By the end of the 1920s, there were hundreds of articles published exploring childhood and adolescence as psychological and biological phenomena, a significant rise from barely a handful a decade earlier."* (The social historical roots of the concept of emerging adulthood and its impact on early adults, Gowri Parameswaran, October 2019, Theory & Psychology)

Almost a century after Mead, psychologists, Epstein and Ong, argued that adolescent trauma is not primarily due to chemical changes in the young person's brain but is a product of modern society, pointing out that not only Margaret Mead but many other anthropologists since had studied scores of cultures around the world where teenagers did not suffer the trauma common to adolescence in the Western world: *"American-style teen turmoil is absent in more than 100 cultures around the world, suggesting that such mayhem is not biologically inevitable. Second, the brain itself changes in response to experiences, raising the question of whether adolescent brain characteristics are the cause of teen tumult or rather the result of lifestyle and experiences."* (Are the Brains of Reckless Teens More Mature Than Those of Their Prudent Peers? Epstein and Ong, Scientific American, August, 2009)

Neurological and psychological studies indicate that changes take place in the brains of modern day adolescents in Western societies, in particular significantly improving their ability to absorb and ponder abstract ideas. However, the idea that the brain of teenage humans predisposes them to generationally unique traits, such as increased angst and discontent, is contradicted by evidence from other cultures.

Neither is it supported by historical evidence of the brain's development in pre-capitalist Western societies. We have shown that adolescence as we know it today did not exist in pre-capitalist societies. As such, adolescence is a social construct. Biologization ignores the critical developmental social processes.

In this context, given scientists accept that the brain responds to and shapes to deal with circumstances and challenges, a more socially beneficial direction of neurological research would be to place the development of the brain during adolescence in the context of the social construct. Hitherto most research has been faced the other way, or upside down, seeking the source of the social construct in the biology, rather than a holistic approach, placing the biology within the entirety of its evolving environment.

The Brain, Social and Societal Stress

That a person's experience of their environment can change the brain has now been accepted by many neuroscientists. This research primarily focussed on foetuses, babies and infants, while little consideration was given to the plight of adolescents, as reflected in the observations of neuroscientists, Romeo and McEwen who in 2007 wrote:

95

"Although much is known about how exposure to stress and stress hormones during perinatal development and adulthood affect the structure and function of the brain, relatively little is known about how the pubertal brain responds to stress." (Stress and the Adolescent Brain, Romeo & McEwen, Annals of the New York Academy of Sciences, 2007)

By 2012 Eiland and Romeo in their 2012 paper, Stress and the Adolescent Brain, felt able to assert from research that experience of stress at a time when the brain was rapidly developing could impact heavily on its functioning: *"Numerous studies have identified a link between exposure to stress and the perturbation of many neurobehavioral processes."*

The authors concluded: *"... stress at prepubertal and early adolescent stages of development affect the morphological plasticity of limbic and cortical brain regions, as well as the enduring effects of adolescent stress exposure on these brain regions in adulthood. We suggest that, due to a number of converging factors during this period of maturation, the adolescent brain may be particularly sensitive to stress-induced neurobehavioral dysfunctions with important consequences on an individual's immediate and long-term health and well-being."* (Stress and the Developing Adolescent Brain, Eiland & Romeo, Neuroscience, Nov 2012)

What the work of these neuroscientists exposes is the fallacious simplistic biologization of adolescent behaviours based on the societal convenience of explaining away teenage trauma. Some of these scientists have begun to explore the impact of social stress on adolescents, which may open up to more specific understanding of the impact of societal stress.

Wadman et al in 2011 usefully defined social stress as *"... the feelings of discomfort or anxiety that individuals may experience in social situations, and the associated tendency to avoid potentially stressful social situations."* (Social Stress in Young People with Specific Language Impairment, Wadman, Durkin & Conti-Ramsden, Journal of Adolescence, 2011)

Social stress is used to refer to any social situations ranging from relations with one's family, to the first day at a new school, to a party, to being part of a community perceived as having low social status and facing the impact of discrimination on the grounds of colour, ethnicity, religion and gender.

Consideration of the impact of social stress is based on the observation that humans are social beings. Maintaining positive social relations is not only desirable but fundamental to our survival and prospering. No man or woman is an island. Scientists acknowledge that threats to these positive social relationships and one's confidence to develop further social relationships can cause deep anxiety and stress.

As adolescents prepare to step out into the world and develop their self-esteem and self-identity, their ability and confidence in building the social capital of positive social relationships becomes critical. This process, with its doubts, setbacks, uncertain results and advances, suggest neuroscientists, can become major sources of stress i.e. social stress, which then impacts on the adolescent brain.

Bingham et al, in their 2011 paper, Early Adolescence as a Critical Window During Which Social Stress Distinctly Alters Behavior and Brain Norepinephrine Activity, referenced this aspect. Quoting several sources, they wrote:

"...studies show that stress during adolescence determines future behavioral strategies used to respond to subsequent stressors or environmental challenges. Social stress has particular relevance to adolescents. Adolescence is characterized by an increase in child–parent conflict, search for autonomy, and a shift in social interaction from familial to peer relationships. With an increased importance of social signals and activity, there comes an increased potential for adverse social interactions to elicit a stress response." (Early Adolescence as a Critical Window During Which Social Stress Distinctly Alters Behavior and Brain Norepinephrine Activity, Bingham, McFadden, Zhang, Bhatnagar, Beck & Valentino, 2011 American College of Neuropsychopharmacology, 2011)

The impact specifically on the adolescent brain was clearly stated by Romeo in 2013:

"Stress happens. It is a fact of life. However, the type of stressors we experience and how we respond to them change throughout our life. Adolescence represents a stage in development when both of these aspects of stress are in flux. .... Specifically, adolescence is marked by significant shifts in hypothalamic-pituitary-adrenal (HPA) axis reactivity, resulting in heightened stress-induced hormonal responses. It is presently unclear what mediates these changes in stress reactivity and what impacts they may have on an adolescent individual. However, stress-sensitive limbic and cortical brain areas that continue to mature during adolescence may be particularly vulnerable to these shifts in responsiveness. Consequently, perturbations of the maturing adolescent brain may contribute to the increase in stress-related psychological dysfunctions, such as anxiety, depression, and drug abuse, often observed during this stage of development." (The Teenage Brain: The Stress Response and the Adolescent Brain, Romeo, Current Directions in Psychological Science, 2013)

So here we have some neuroscientists beginning to accept from their research that teenage trauma may not be a simple function of adolescents' biology but the pressure and stress which their social (including their domestic) environment places upon them at a time when, like the butterfly newly emergent from its chrysalis, they are particularly vulnerable.

The next step is for scientists to understand societally generated stress and some social scientists are beginning to understand the additional stresses experienced for example by ethnic minorities (e.g. Psychophysiology in African-American Samples: Howard University Studies, Harrell, American Psychological Association, 2013).

There is some way to go before society begins to fully understand and propose remedies to the impact of societal stress imposed on genres of people because of their age, gender, ethnicity, legitimate preferences, their class or caste. In relation to research regarding the impact of racism-induced social stress on the psychology and physiology of the Afro-American population, Harrel, an American professor of clinical psychology, wrote in 2013:

"We recognized that racism constituted an important source of stress in African American life... the work on the physiological impact of racist stressors is still in the early stages. Psychological and biological factors that contribute to individual differences in responses are still being identified. We suspect that available measures of facets of racial identity and subjective responses to racism are saturated with demand characteristics... Racism may impact physiological outcomes and health through a variety of psychophysiological pathways." (Psychophysiology in African-American Samples: Howard University Studies, Harrell, American Psychological Association, 2013).

The experience of racism as a societal form of social stress is acknowledged by Harrell and many other academics, so opening up the paths to further research. In contrast, it is notable that when academics refer to social stress in relation to adolescents, they commonly highlight social stress as a function of adolescents' relations with their family and peers but omit the wider societal aspect. For example, Van Roekel et al. in a nevertheless very instructive paper regarding early adolescence concluded:

"One of the most important developmental tasks during adolescence is to be able to develop satisfying relationships with peers and create more autonomy from parents. This substantial shift in social relationships during early adolescence could result in success or failure of this developmental task, which could explain the intense emotional states and increased emotional variability during this period." (Social Stress in Early Adolescents' Daily Lives, Van Roekel, Ha, Verhagen, Kuntsche, Scholte and Engels, Journal of Adolescence, Nov 2015)

It is only in the last century that academics have begun to consider the impact of the societal stress on women generated by sexism. The turn to research into the stress impact of racism on non-Whites is even more recent. Both were driven by academics from these oppressed sections of society. The experiences of their peers drove them to recognise sexism and racism respectively and to link societal prejudices with social stress.

There is as yet no army of adolescent academic researchers to drive forward understanding of the impact of childism, which probably explains why such research has barely begun. This will require academics to reacquaint themselves with their child-eye, to develop a genuinely child-centred approach and intensely interrogate the 'conventional wisdoms' with which we are surrounded and challenge, as had to be done in regard to sexism and racism, many of the prejudicial premises that have surrounded so much of social research.

For example, Epstein and Ong's paper, referred to above, challenged the "conventional wisdom" as they termed it that adolescents immature brains meant that teenagers were greater risk takers than adults. They discovered the opposite. One's child-eye wisdom might remind one that as a child one was far less likely to take risks when one was uncertain of one's environment. Many care-experienced people can tell stories of the setbacks of being moved to a new home with new rules and a new school and having to work out all over again how to survive and prosper in the new setting. After all, knowing the threats is one of the fundamentals of risk management.

When Epstein and Ong pointed to the absence of teenage trauma in so many non-Western cultures it should have flagged up to other researchers the importance of inquiring whether the levels of social and societal stress are the sources of the decisive difference in regard to modern industrial societies. Put very simply, if racism is a source of societal stress for ethnic minorities, then a non-racist, perhaps ethnically uniform society would not expect to see this type of social stress, similarly in regard to gender discrimination. So, one might ask whether a society which doesn't evince teenage trauma reflect a culture with less prejudice towards adolescents and vice versa.

A useful alternative approach framework may be provided by that of Liberation Psychologists such as Ignacio Martín-Baró and his particular narrative therapy approach. A Latin American social psychologist,

Martín-Baró concluded that the predominant narrative in societies is generated by and to meet the ideological needs of the ruling strata. However, in El Salvador where he practised, Martin-Baró observed that the members of the oppressed groups were pressed to accept and absorb this narrative, which dominated the media and social welfare systems.

The many impoverished rural and urban communities did not fit into the dominant narrative. As a result, their peoples often had low self-esteem, considered themselves as failures and with all that goes with these traits, reinforced the narrative. In his book about racism in the USA, John Howard Griffin alluded to the impact of the prevailing narrative when he wrote:

"Your blanks have been filled in far differently from those of a child grown up in the filth and poverty." (Black Like Me, Griffin, Houghton Mifflin, 1961)

Martin-Baró considered that the same could be applied to other countries and that the dominance of the ruling strata's narrative leaves those who don't thrive in society labelled as 'failed individuals' and that many absorb the narrative and so absorb low individual and collective self-esteem to the extent that they go on to serve the narrative, reinforcing their oppression.

Martin-Baró concluded that it is the role of those seeking to empower and improve the lot of the narrated-down to challenge the ruling narrative by fostering the repressed individuals' development of a strong alternative narrative. He aimed to lift up these communities by establishing, through them a new narrative for them, which was aimed at empowering their communities. In El Salvador, Martin-Baró's work was considered such a threat to the ruling strata that his printworks was blown up and he would later be executed by the US-backed regime's Death Squads.

The Martín-Baró narrative approach can apply as much to teenagers as it did to the villagers of El Salvador and as it does to women and to the Black communities. Historically we can see that Black is Beautiful, Black

Power, Sisterhood, Me Too, Black Lives Matter were all part of self-generated counter-narratives.

Society's predominant adolescent narrative of smouldering contrariness, insolence and violence brought on by a raging biological time-bomb leaves little room for teenage self-assertion and supports societal insistence on its authority to apply surveillance, stigmatisation and discrimination to the age cohort. Biologization and infantilisation of adolescents is part of the predominant narrative.

Liberation Psychology focussed on deconstructing the prevailing ideology and its predominant narratives that lead to negative identities, suppressing self-esteem and building a new narrative for the oppressed groups. Radical deconstruction and reconstruction based on the social group challenge the homilies and conventional wisdoms that are often taken for granted, like vigorously raking and dethatching the crusted matted earth, allowing oxygen to flow and plants to flourish anew. For social psychologists to take this route requires deconstructing psychology itself and understanding the social bases of its routes and how it supports or challenges the predominant narrative.

It is considered that once groups with low collective self-esteem become aware of how a prevailing narrative impacts on their self-esteem, they are released to establish their own narrative. In his 1968 work, Pedagogy of the Oppressed, Paulo Frere termed the process one of conscientization. Understanding the source of their oppression and low self-esteem they can begin to act and find new ways to improve their lives and empower themselves and, in this way assist society as a whole

In their paper published in 2009, Sonn and Lewis usefully explained the Liberation Psychology method:

"... from a liberation perspective there is a focus on deconstructing ideologies, narratives, and resources for identity that are negative and engaging in processes of reconstruction in order to promote liberation and opportunities to self-determine identities and futures. Deconstruction is central to the disruption of internalized oppression because it is concerned

with disrupting negative social and cultural scripts and taken-for-granted social and political understandings that inform identities. Through this process critical consciousness is raised, and what has been seen as natural and taken-for-granted is problematized." (Immigration and Identity: The Ongoing Struggles for Liberation, Sonn & Lewis, Springer, 2009)

Hence deconstructing societies' prevailing narratives regarding adolescents with their focus on biologization and infantilisation, and then rebuilding the narrative based on how these young people see their world would counter the impact of low self-esteem and offer communities a radically different view of adolescence.

In more current social work terms, it is basing one's work on the views of the service user or client – but cut loose from the deadweight of the dominant ideology.

Deconstruction and narrative therapy have been and are used as treatments for some adolescents but a much wider service could be provided by the creation of a new narrative for adolescents as a whole – a reframing. In this regard, the time for standard narrative therapy approaches to generate interaction and data collection for any one cohort is relatively much shorter than for other studies, especially given the transitioning in adolescence. Consequently, the research hurdle that immediately presents itself is that, compared to favella communities, ethnic minorities and women, the adolescent cohort is so much more in flux.

Liberation Psychology which is unashamedly eclectic in its choice of research methodologies, emphasises using any tool that works or "By Any Means Necessary" to lean on Malcolm X. So, the search may be on for sharpened tools. Nevertheless, all social research data represents only a snapshot in time, which serves to emphasise the societal need to provide the resources required to conduct this research. It also points to the need to assist the young people to successfully advocate for themselves.

Academics sourcing government or corporate funders sufficient to allow such societally challenging research campaigns to take on a head of steam may be a major hurdle in a world where the boundaries of academia are being trimmed to meet corporate demands.

However, reframing adolescence will be critical to taking our societies forward. In summation, neurological and psychological studies indicate that changes take place in the brains of modern day adolescents in Western societies, in particular significantly improving their ability to absorb and ponder abstract ideas. However, the idea that the brain of teenage humans predisposes them to generationally unique traits, such as increased angst and discontent, is contradicted by evidence from other cultures.

Neither is it supported by historical evidence of the brain's development in pre-capitalist Western societies. We have shown that adolescence as we know it today did not exist in pre-capitalist societies. As such, adolescence is a social construct. Biologization ignores the critical developmental social processes.

In this context, given scientists accept that the brain responds to and shapes to deal with circumstances and challenges, a more socially beneficial direction of neurological research would be to place the development of the brain during adolescence in the context of the social construct. Hitherto most research has been faced the other way, or upside down, seeking the source of the social construct in the biology, rather than a holistic approach, placing the biology within the entirety of its evolving environment.

As Johnson, Blum and Giedd concluded in their 2009 paper regarding modern research into the adolescent brain and health policies:

"...the focus on pathologic conditions, deficits, reduced capacity, and age-based risks overshadows the enormous opportunity for brain science to illuminate the unique strengths and potentialities of the adolescent brain." (Adolescent Maturity & the Brain: The Promise & Pitfalls of Neuroscience Research in Adolescent Health Policy, Johnson, Blum & Giedd, Journal of Adolescent Health, 2009)

The Societal Mess of Adolescence

The arguments of Parameswaran, Epstein et al that scientists and government have been in a process of infantilisation of teenagers and young adults, points to the scientists offering societal justification for 21st century governments intensifying oppression of young people by discriminatory acts such as raising the age for eligibility to receive the adult minimum wage.

Parameswaran wrote: *"The consequences of biologizing adolescence has been to eliminate this age group from the workforce while enforcing a strict regime of surveillance on youth."* (The social historical roots of the concept of emerging adulthood and its impact on early adults, Gowri Parameswaran, October 2019, Theory & Psychology)

The condition of the modern adolescent is to be a biological adult but at the same time a societal child beset by a muddled array of constraints driven by varying concepts of mental and physical capacity, responsibility, self- and societal-harm, benevolence and privilege, all mixed with concepts of the age of majority, the age of maturity and the age of adulthood with a dose of religious considerations for good measure; the sum of which emerges from the political cooking pot with strictures such as the age of sexual consent, the marriageable age, the school-leaving age, the purchasing alcohol age, the driving age, the entering into bars age, the contract signing age, the voting age, the political candidacy age, the full-time working age and the minimum wage age, the smoking age, the gambling age, the watching sexual films age, the watching violent films age and the possession of guns age; the ages for which will all vary from country to country and occasionally from region to region and town to town.

The teenager crosses a line in the sand and she can vote. She crosses another line and she can marry and party in the street. She crosses back at night and she can find herself in a police cell. For nine years or so, the adolescent must accept transiting through this half-adult half-child stage. Nor is where the nine years come from scientifically based. That in some countries the full set of 'adult' rights may be conveyed over 10 and 15 years once more underlines the political nature of adolescence.

Some authors have likened these various rights to a calibrated set of permissions. One is left with the image of a wizard who has experimented for years by pouring a variety of potions into a cooking pot, recording which ingredients and spells caused the pot to implode and which took the roof off his tower. He finally emerged from his tower with a book of recipes to produce an adult without breaking the pot or bringing down the tower. The wizard has no rationality for the recipe save for what he can get away with. The ages of rights and responsibility are similarly an ad hoc jumble representing reactions to events.

Adolescents and the Voting Age
The voting age, for instance, is widely taken as the sign of adulthood; when young people fully take their place in a democratic society. Democracy is said to be rule by all the people for all the people but what happened to the 2.2 billion people classified, because they are not yet 18 (or in some cases 16) as children in this equation? Or are people under the age of 18 or 16 not people?

By this definition a British teenager can travel from London where she is not a person to Scotland where she becomes a person, and daily repeat the same process to four other parts of the country, changing like Jekyll to Hyde from person to non-person at nightfall. Travelling around the globe would produce as many conundrums. In Brazil and Argentina, the voting age is 16, in Indonesia and Greece it is 17, in France it is 18, in Taiwan 20, Malaysia 21 and United Arab Emirates 25.

The Emirates' voting age of 25 appears to be an anachronism but it is commonly the age which many Western countries use to accord young people full adult benefits. Similarly, the age of criminal responsibility in Bangladesh, the Emirates and Kuwait is 7, in England and Syria it is 10, in Gambia, 12, in Russia and South Korea, 14, in Guinea Bissau, Cuba and Portugal, 16 and in Luxembourg it is 18.

Luxembourg aside, the nine-year range of minimum voting age across the world matches up to the nine-year range in the minimum age for criminal responsibility and the nine-year range (7 to16 years old) of child soldiers used in combat. This nine-year stretch reflects political adolescence. – the age gap between on the one hand being considered responsible for one's actions harming others and their property and on the other being given responsibility for the governance of society. The range of the gap varies from one country to another depending on cultural, political and social histories and once more emphasises the degree to which adolescence is only fruitfully viewed as a social construct.

The Biologization of Democracy

"Age-based policies are not exceptional; policies are frequently enacted in the face of contradictory or non-existent empirical support. Although neuroscience has been called upon to determine adulthood, there is little empirical evidence to support age 18, the current legal age of majority, as an accurate marker of adult capacities." (Adolescent Maturity & the Brain: The Promise & Pitfalls of Neuroscience Research in Adolescent Health Policy, Johnson, Blum & Giedd, Journal of Adolescent Health, 2009)

The Western concept of democracy was conceived as an instrument of social control by those who were empowered within those societies. It therefore excluded the oppressed – women, children and slaves. From the Greek city-states onwards there has been an evolution and at each stage the empowered believed that they had reached the 'most equable order of things'. Rights and responsibilities were shared out between the empowered. The disenfranchised were tossed a handful of nominal rights and bucket loads of duties.

The notion of equality for all sat uncomfortably particularly with those sections of the population who were consigned to being property and marginalised. We have illustrated how at each stage when democracy became exposed as oppressive to particular oppressed sections of the population the ruling elite sought rationalisation both in their religion and in pseudo-scientific justification of what were social constructs, namely the exclusions of the disempowered. Hence the pseudo-science of biologizing of slavery, ethnicity, gender and adolescence.

The Basis of Universal Suffrage

Democracy or majority rule (aptly described by De Tocqueville, John Stuart Mill and Marx as the tyranny of the majority over the minority) is a very crude rule for running any society. It does not guarantee tolerance for the minority, nor equal treatment. For example, today, less than a century after women first got the vote in many Western countries, women are still generally paid less in large parts of the workplace, suffer discrimination and terrible harassment. Many laws are still interpreted by the courts in a discriminatory fashion when applied to women. Nevertheless, having a voice in the democratic system remains a major lever for socially and economically oppressed and exploited sections of society.

With universal suffrage allowing voting for all adults, the notion of equality of all before the law and equal rights for all, is left sitting even more awkwardly in regard to children, particularly when it comes to voting.

Democracy is based on a vote for all citizens so that all decisions about organising society are agreed collectively. It is not based on electing the most knowledgeable or most competent. Certainly, in countries like the UK and Canada there is no assumption of mental capacity that excludes voters and no competency or mental health requirement for candidates. There is no illiteracy bar, no objection to people who have no knowledge of politics voting or a bar on people voting for a candidate because the family, the priest or the landlord has told them which way to vote. Nor is there an objection to people not voting because they are not interested – save for in countries where it is compulsory.

Yet, the arguments against a radical reduction in the voting age allowing adolescents (as children) to participate in democracy amount specifically to the above, namely:

- Adolescents do not have the reasoning power to make rational choices

- Adolescents have neither the experience or knowledge of life to make informed choices

- Adolescents will be told how to vote by their parents

- Electoral turnout is generally low amongst the under 30s so adolescents will not be interested

The arguments for denying adolescents' suffrage because of their age are flimsy in the least. The first issue of contention is that these grounds for disenfranchisement are not applied to those above voting age. The second is that the vast range of minimum ages used for exclusion in different countries around the world demonstrates that those ages have little or no basis in science. The third, if not final, contention is that if democracy is rule by all the people for all the people, then the exclusion of over 2 billion people means that democracy has still to be reached.

Another case for the defence of the current voting age is that parents will vote to protect their family and hence their children's interest. However, we have already seen that a parent and an adolescent's idea of their best interests (as in the past with husbands and their disenfranchised wives) may be very different. A child may want the best possible education but the parent may not wish to pay the taxes or fees deemed necessary to pay for that education and it is known, for example, that parents may decide to send their sons to fee paying schools and their daughters to state schools.

Electoral Bias Against Children and Young Families

Across, Europe, only a third of households have dependent children in them, leaving the electoral voice of families with dependent children in a small minority.

For example, according to the Office of National Statistics (2020) only 30% of UK adults live with dependent children and these 13 million adults are easily outnumbered by the 15.5 million people aged over 60. Hence, we should not be surprised that successive British governments have paid more attention to protecting the incomes of the retired whilst one third of all children are left to grow up in impoverished families (Department of Work and Pensions 2021). As a result, British children are almost twice as likely to live in poverty as the country's pensioners, 18% of whom AgeUK reported as impoversihed in 2021).

The above example demonstrates how defining majority rule as that of adult majority rule may currently be working against children and families with dependent children. Were children to have the vote that would go some way to evening up the electorate. In this regard, some have suggested that parents receive proxy votes for their children. Between 1893 and 1919, Belgium gave an additional vote to property-owning fathers and similar ideas have been raised in the French and German parliaments. However, these ideas, based as they were on childism, would only underline the oppressed position of young people.

Giving the vote to all adolescents under 18 via school- and college-based polling booths could be a start. If an American 12-year-old can have a licence to carry a loaded weapon, which can take away someone's life, why can't they have a vote to shape their own lives?

The question has to be asked as to whether, if adolescents had the vote, politicians would be so keen to introduce special laws to confine and impose curfews on teenagers, so keen to sanction the right to pay adolescents below the rate for the job, so keen to increase the costs of higher education and cut youth unemployment benefits? Young families generally represent half and more of society but the skewing of the electorate places them in a small minority tempting the politicians to rest on the votes of the aged rather than the broad spectrum of society.

An additional argument in defence of the voting age status quo is that children should be left to enjoy their childhood without the burden of adult issues. They paraphrase Rousseau's notion that children should be left to play. However, they miss the contradiction that adolescents are expected to spend more time working on their education than the 35-hour working week expected of government employees. What is supposed to be so enjoyable about sitting in a classroom all day with hardly an hour's break?

The only defence left is that the minimum voting age is a rough approximation of when a person will have sufficient faculties to make a reasoned informed decision. Yet the same case was made in defence of excluding women and ethnic minorities from the democratic processes.

The voting age delineation is a "rough approximation" created by the empowered to suit the needs of the state and capitalist society. Its only merit is that at present there is no storm of protesting young people demanding the right to vote.

The question may yet arise for politicians whether they prefer to give more adolescents the vote or have school students, students and apprentices marching out of classrooms and taking to the streets demanding climate change policies, anti-racist action, an end to police harassment a decent minimum wage etc. The voting age is an arbitrary line drawn up by empowered citizens to exclude the disempowered, and as with women's suffrage we see how historically it is edging towards recognising the rights of the oppressed but will need mighty shoves to move it forward. Yet the emergence of a 'youffragette' movement to push reluctant governments over the line could dwarf the last century's seminal movement for women's emancipation and go well beyond the simple concession of the vote.

History also shows us how on many occasions the struggles of the oppressed for emancipation were eventually rewarded with voting rights when it was deemed to be in the interests of one or other of the ruling elites within that society. Hence voting rights for America's blacks were first achieved as the country's protectionist northern industrial class was struggling to defeat the free trade policies of the agrarian south. Lincoln's declaration of freedom for the Black slaves was a decisive blow both undermining the Confederacy's economy and enrolling tens of thousands of Black slaves in the fight for freedom, and so leading to the crushing of the Confederate armies.

The woman's suffragette movement had reached a high level of intensity but was still being passionately resisted by the time of the First World War. Enrolling women into the war effort and post-war revival was intensified by the threat of Bolshevism and women first got the vote in the UK, Germany and the USA at the end of the war in the immediate aftermath of the Russian Revolution. Japanese women won the vote at the end of the Second World War and the Vietnam War saw the USA bring its voting age down to 18. In Japan the recent reduction of the voting age from 20 to 18 has been put down to the then ruling party's wish to push through constitutional reform.

Haunted by the spectre of the 1917 Russian Revolution and the uprisings in Germany, the British government did give votes to 19-year-olds in 1918 but only if they were men in the armed forces. They soon took that right away and almost 50 years would pass before Britain's 18-year-olds were all given the vote courtesy of Harold Wilson's Labour government who reduced the age from 21 to 18.

The 1960s began more than a decade of upheaval amongst Europe and North America's youth with mass student movements, anti-war, anti-nuclear, anti-racism and anti-repression protests. The threat of communism and revolt continued to loom large and while the conservative sections of the establishment resisted extending the franchise to 18-year-olds, the more far-sighted elements sought to give youth a sense of a greater stake in official society.

The prevailing arguments in Britain's Labour government were summarised in the Cabinet papers: *"It is arguable that to give young people of 18 the vote will channel their political energies into regular forms of political activity and away from the kind of violent demonstration in which students have recently been indulging (or at least that the more stable among them will be less tempted to violent and dramatic forms of demonstration if attempts to exercise political influence by orthodox means are not frustrated by the lack of a vote)."* ('The last milestone' on the journey to full adult suffrage? Adrian Bingham, June 2019, historyandpolicy.org)

Pressured by the anti-Vietnam War revolts, the USA reduced the voting age to 18 in 1971. The pressure of the French and German student and youth movements forced their governments to follow suit in 1974 and 1975 respectively.

There is a great deal of evidence to show that for today's mainstream political parties, lowering the voting age is an issue more based on political calculation than religion, science or morality. Young people are considered more likely to vote against the parties openly supporting the establishment whilst being more supportive of radical or left-wing parties.

In a 2009 general election, an under 18 voting project in Germany saw 127,000 young people casting their vote at polling booths. Whilst almost half (48%) of all adults voted for the Christian Democrat/Christian Social Union, Free Democrats establishment parties, only one quarter (27%) of under 18s did so. (The German U18 Project Experience, Sylvain and Marisa dos Reis, 2009)

It is not surprising that Germany's Social Democratic Party and the Left (Linke) Party support votes at 16 but the conservative establishment parties are against. This is currently mirrored in the UK where the ruling Conservative Party is the only mainstream party opposed to extending the franchise.

In 2020, on the basis of a Green Party initiative, the Belgian government agreed to lower the voting age to 16 for the European Union elections but held back re-elections to its own parliament where a two thirds majority is required. Otherwise only Austria and Malta currently allow EU votes at 16.

The issue of the voting age highlights the global political, social and governmental confusion over adolescence. The contradictions between human rights, children's lack of rights, the infantilising and biologizing of adolescence and the needs of a modern economy are reaching a crisis as the world moves into a new era. The old methods of education, child-rearing and exploitation of young people are inadequate and the more governments turn the screw to intensify those methods, the more they fail not only the family but also the future of society.

In her 2016 article, The End of Adolescence, University of California Professor Paula Fass goes laments that the prevailing government and social scientists' concepts of adolescence have crumbled as a rational framework for understanding and providing for American teenagers:

"Although we still use the term 'adolescence', its cultural signals are mostly irrelevant. It no longer describes the period of training required to function

as an adult in the 21st century, nor does it distinguish the boundary between the knowledge of children from those who have reached puberty. For parents, adolescence is an untrustworthy way to understand how their teenage children mature: they cannot clearly connect the sexual practices of their young progeny to stable mating in marriage, nor can parents see how schooling during adolescence will lead their offspring to satisfactory adult work. The idea of a tentative moratorium that gets resolved once teenagers create stable identities seems far-fetched, since the identities of even those in their 20s and sometimes their 30s are still in flux. Some have blamed helicopter parenting for the long delay in maturity, but regardless of its specific role, the path to adulthood has become much more tangled and uncertain." (The end of adolescence, Fass, 2016 https://aeon.co/essays/adolescence-is-no-longer-a-bridge-between-childhood-and-adult-life)

And the world wonders why the teenager questions adult authority. When Sir Walter Scott wrote his immortal stanza: "*Oh what a tangled web we weave when first we practice to deceive,*" (Marmion: A Tale of Flodden Field, Sir Walter Scott, 1808), he may as well have been referring to the position that two centuries on Western society has got itself into regarding its seed, its source of fresh energy and progress, its promise of a better future - the reviled and oppressed teenager.

Today's teenagers are yesteryear's adults, denied the modern political rights and labours of adulthood but tied to the state compulsion of education. It is not at issue whether adolescents of today have a materially more comfortable existence than their counterparts of the same age 300 years ago. Simply that they are historically no freer than their counterparts of 300 years ago and that the gap between their "freedoms" and those of their elders has widened. As much as adolescents' physical comforts may have improved their psychological security appears to have deteriorated yet they are expected to become the future soul of humanity. As the Christian Bible warns: "*What does it benefit a person to gain the whole world, and forfeit his soul?*" (Mark 8:36, The Bible - St James Version)

Whether Western society willingly ignores how adolescents perceive these contradictions is uncertain. Even young children often show they have the capacity to perceive social injustices i.e. situations contrasting with their received notions of social fairness. Most have the capacity to determine whether they or their peers have been treated unfairly; for example, being punished for what they have not done.

This capacity can be multiplied several times over in adolescents. So, it should not be hard to understand why many adolescents become either angry or cynical whenever they contrast all that they are being taught about equality and rights of adults (and occasionally children) with the reality of their condition where they own nothing, can labour for nothing, can be physically chastised at will but must accept the 'will' of their parents, people who society and corporate education declare are not their owners and who must respect and care for them.

Origins of the Mystery Wall

Content

This chapter looks at the processes rooted in property relations that lead to the erection of the Mystery Wall. It argues that the Wall has its origins in property relations and arises from the state's division of spheres of responsibility between parents and corporate educational institutions. It contends that the corporate education process further commodifies and collectivises young people's transit through adolescence. We consider the impact on the adolescent of the parented/home world and the school world being respectively and contrastingly domains of private and corporate property.

Family and Corporate Education: Two Worlds Propping Each Other Up

Children are still essentially the private property of their parents and this attitude is pervasive in the corporate world of academia and government. The contradictions remain between the reality of the atomised nuclear family and the collective corporate world of education. Adolescents are left to bear the brunt of this.

State school education played a key role in this process by establishing the parented world as having no merit to a place in the curriculum.

Children were the private property of the parents and the state in the 20th century formed a crushing pact with those parents that they could do as they wished with their offspring so long as the children were delivered to school in reasonable condition (in modern terms: to not ring any safeguarding bells) to undergo their academic education and conditioning to prepare them to participate in adult society. Meanwhile, the parents were left free to contribute to society by raising more children or earning an income. It was an uneasy and far from child-centred compromise.

With the growing power of the state, women's battles against domestic abuse, for equal rights and property ownership, government has felt confident to make further inroads into the castle. Since the 1970s, there has been a growth in schools being used as the state's launch point for family interventionism in the form of support services and social work visits but these inroads are still mainly only applied to families considered to be failing to deliver their children to school in a fit state to learn. For the most part the state still sees a benefit in maintaining the wall between children's academic education and their parented lives.

Erecting the Wall
The parented world was the domain of private but personal property and the incomprehensible decision-making handed down by adult autarchy in the form of demands on the children.

For the duration of the school day, parents ceded a portion of their property rights over their children to the educational establishments.

In school we became corporate property. Our school world was the domain of private but corporate property and regulated decision making handed down by adult autarchy in the form of demands on us pupils.

The Mystery Wall separated our parented home world from our corporate school world.

Teachers in England whom I questioned recently as to their level of interest in their students' domestic situation, commented that they only considered such matters if the young person was incapable of being educated or was performing erratically. This wasn't surprising as academic teachers, in the UK at least, are not adequately trained to play a pastoral role.

It is easy to think of several reasons for students' silence but these also need to be placed in the context that pre-adolescent children often freely and innocently talk about their home lives and adults not uncommonly discuss their domestic situations with colleagues in the workplace, are socially encouraged to discuss their domestic issues with friends reflected in popular idioms such as "a problem shared is a problem halved". This total and mutual silence is unique to adolescence.

I wanted to see what were the features that created this Mystery Wall that led to the domestic lives of adolescents being so shielded from the outside world and to consider its impact.

I considered the development from the child to the adolescent stage where young people feel increasingly empowered by physical and intellectual development, a growing sense of self-efficacy and spheres of mastery. This in particular, as the psychologist Piaget pointed out, is powered by their increasing capacity for abstract thought. Adolescence is also a key pre-adult stage where the young person is consciously or unconsciously having to prepare for adult life when they will be expected to contribute to a collaborative collective society. They must prepare to be of value to others outside their parental world. For them at least, assessing and developing their sense of self and self-worth becomes a key driver.

Adolescents have three primary learning spheres: domestic, academic/corporate and peer-based. The academic and peer-based learning environments are mainly outside the home and overwhelmingly for much of the year find a base in school settings. In this sense these settings are distinct from the domestic setting. There are major differences between these learning environments and especially when compared to the domestic setting. All can comprise a proportion of academic learning as opposed to non-academic learning (such as life skills, hobbies, sports etc) but the proportion of formal academic learning is overwhelmingly via the school and generally least in the domestic setting.

The domestic learning environment is often inconsistent, unstable, and contradictory and may pay little attention to rationality. It is dominated by autarchic parents in a setting where the young person is disempowered. The young person has little control over that environment. Learning in peer-empowered settings may also be inconsistent, unstable, random and contradictory but the adolescent has an element of control, can walk away and is free to develop their own sense of rationality regarding their peers' behaviours.

In comparison to the above, the academic learning environment is often rigid, stable, relatively consistent and focuses on the rational. The nominal structure of the school gives students little power and in practice they are commodified. However, the very commodification of the students gives them a collectivity, which in turn gives them an important lever to power. At the most elementary level, adolescent school students en-masse can generally physically and emotionally overwhelm a school teacher or alternatively lift them to a higher status. In this setting the adolescent students experience collective empowerment such as rarely occurs in parented settings.

Tanti et al in their instructive 2008 paper on the development of self concepts during adolescence referenced other authors' previous research regarding the environmental changes impacting on young people passing through this critical stage into a collectively peer empowered setting, when stating:

"...the social world of pre-adolescent children is comparatively stable and narrow, as it primarily involves quite familiar and intimate social contexts of family and primary school (Simmons & Zhou, 1994).

"In contrast, early adolescents experience an abrupt and considerable change in their social world (Benedict, 1954; Eccles & Midgley, 1989) with the significant transition from primary to secondary school where the social world becomes markedly wider and more complex (Gecas & Mortimer, 1987; Lewin, 1939). Coinciding with this marked transition in social context, early adolescents become very concerned with a sense of belonging and affiliation with social groups (2000; Newman & Newman, 1976).

"In this context, early adolescents also show changes in their social relationships as they begin to move away from parents and toward their peers, reflecting the adolescent separation/individuation process (Blos, 1979; Collins & Repinski, 1994)." (Tripartite Self-concept Change: Shifts in the Individual, Relational, and Collective Self in Adolescence, Tanti et al, 2008)

Commodification, Collectivism and Alienation

That the setting for this collective peer-based engagement is the school environment has its own bearing on the adolescent. Property relations come into play. The young person is expected to attend school to be educated into becoming a functioning member of society and most importantly to contribute as a component of the workforce.

In the Western world, the family is expected to send their adolescents to school and, so long as the young person attends school in a reasonable state to be educated, teaching staff ask no more questions about the adolescent's home life. The home life is not generally expected to be part of the academic establishment's concern. Their pupils are commodified to the extent that the adolescents are judged almost entirely on their academic attainments and the schools are primarily judged on academic and value-added performance.

This process of commodification lays the basis for collectivisation of the students who are, in the name of standardisation, for the large part stripped of their individuality and rigidly treated as near homogenous groups. They are being topped and tailed to suit the production line, rather than the other way around, a routine very sharply reflected in

Pink Floyd's globally popular award-winning teenage anthem, "*Another Brick in the Wall*".

This rigidity is strongly backed up by disciplinary regimes, intimidating adolescents into compliance. Having collectivised the students, the academic regime has also given them great potential power as the adolescents when operating collectively can easily take control out of their teachers' hands, as shown most dramatically when school students take mass strike action.

The students are commodified and so collectivised to achieve economies of scale. In the strictly academic sphere, they are introduced to seeing themselves valued not for themselves or their value to others but for their role in the productive process. The teaching regime is so focused on developing adolescents as academic commodities that they lose sight of their pupils as individuals with other valuable qualities.

A popular refrain amongst many young UK adults is: "*After years of being told I wasn't going anywhere because I was rubbish at Maths and English, I gave up at school.*" Giving up on academic education may not necessarily be a bad thing, but this is often accompanied by withdrawal and isolation from wider peer collectives and extreme alienation where the adolescent becomes consumed with the notion that they have no value to others. The self-harm which ensues from these stations may also include violence to others and other anti-social behaviour but only displays the tip of the iceberg regarding teenage trauma generated by the social system under which the West lives.

In turn, adolescents commodify the teaching staff and give little concern to teachers' home life or wellbeing unless it interrupts the educational process. This is reflected in the classroom more regularly in pupils 'ganging up' and using their collective power to make an unpopular teacher's life 'hell'. These collective demonstrations often represent adolescents' first real experiences of exercising their new found power in relation to adults. The pupils often see their actions as fun but for teachers they can be a traumatic or chastening experience of impotency, putting in brutal focus the unhealthy nature of the commodification process for adolescents and teaching staff alike.

The Parental Castle

The Mystery Wall, separating the parented and academic world into deep siloes, operates for academia as it enables their teaching staff to maximise their focus on developing their students as academic commodities. Neither are they instructed in pastoral care. Their students' lives and wellbeing outside of school are considered the sole responsibility and consideration of the young person's parents or carers.

This division of care however, arose from the basis of property relations rather than care. Centuries ago, as British capitalism began to burst the country out of the grip of feudalism, laws were established which gave men jurisdiction over life in their home or dwelling. As cited above, British law ruled that "an Englishman's Home is his castle." Effectively the state came to a pact whereby property-owning men were allowed control of their own affairs within the household (including beating their wives senseless) so long as they were compliant to the rest of the laws laid down by the country's rulers. This was the extent of the freedom conceded by capitalism to give the population a sense of ownership in the system.

Later under pressure the state conceded property rights for women, one man one vote, then universal suffrage. Throughout this time the state has made only nominal inroads into the home with laws on rights for women and children. Notably even the application of the latter to domestic life are largely kept in abeyance unless called into action by social outrage.

The freedom to act as one wishes on one's own property is one of the last freedom's left to advanced capitalist society's yet is also limited by various laws governing behaviour to neighbours while at the same time being extremely constricting since the rest of the land is owned by others and the state. In this tiny space the adolescent is the subject of the parental autarchy.

As a result, parents shelter their domestic life and that of their family behind the Wall, beyond the gaze of most of society, including the teaching staff. So long as the legal status quo is not breached, the teaching staff have little option but to accept this constraint. In turn, the parents as directed by the state, hand over their children to the corporate world for their academic education. They accept this aspect of the loss of control over the young person's development on the basis that they have the right to an element of reporting back and consultation with the teaching staff.

Nevertheless, they only have restricted access to information on the development of the child because the teaching staff only have a limited view, which is comprised of the pupil's academic development and overt school behaviours but very little of the young person's peer-to-peer learning. Meanwhile the teaching staff have an even less restricted and subjectively permissioned view of the young person's learning, academic or otherwise, in the home environment.

The Adolescent Transition: When Two World's Collide

The evolution of their child to adolescence on the way to adulthood poses major issues of change for parents. The old autarchic methods of nurturing, control and protection are no longer so effective. Both parents and adolescents attempt to renegotiate the relationship. This process does not take place in abstraction; life with the family remains a learning environment for the adolescent (and for the parents), even if it is not an academic one.

The domestic learning environment is in contrast to that of school. The adolescent's learning environment is atomised rather than collectivised and in conditions of disempowerment as opposed to the peer empowerment offered by the classroom. In contrast, learning within the family environment tends to be a chaotic, unstable process with inconsistent boundaries, rule application and discipline. In the nuclear family, the adolescent is subject to the control of their parents with whom they often share a long history and complex emotional relationships, which continue to evolve and impact on verbal and non-verbal communications. On the other hand, at school, adolescents generally have had a very brief history with their teachers and with barely any serious emotive content.

The predominant Western societal view is that the two learning environments work in tandem but in reality, especially for the adolescents striving to discover their identity and assessing their self-worth, the two worlds often work in contradiction; the one tearing down the work of the other. And while adolescents may find peace in the relatively stable and peer-empowered academic setting, they cannot take this empowerment home.

The impact of the emotional challenges of the parented world may be much more difficult to manage resulting in a gnawing away at whatever additional sense of self-esteem the young person has gained from their academic and peer-empowered environments. Little wonder that they return to their cage as the surly individual. As they trudge back home at the end of their school day, they often never know quite whether on arrival they will need their slippers or goloshes, their umbrella or sunglasses.

THE MYSTERY WALL

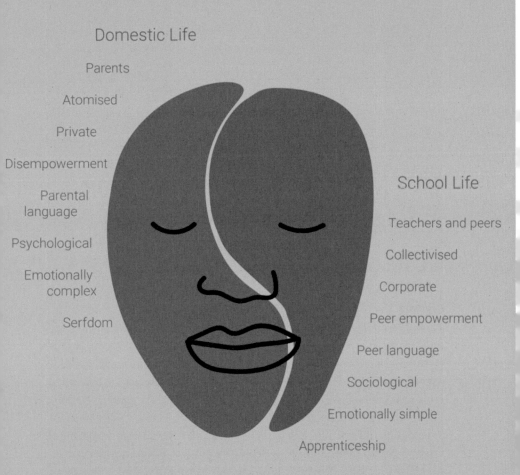

Domestic Life

Parents

Atomised

Private

Disempowerment

Parental language

Psychological

Emotionally complex

Serfdom

School Life

Teachers and peers

Collectivised

Corporate

Peer empowerment

Peer language

Sociological

Emotionally simple

Apprenticeship

Adolescents and the Mystery Wall

The Mystery Wall Separating Adolescents' Atomised and Collective Worlds

Content

This chapter considers the functions and mechanisms of the adolescent's Mystery Wall, protecting the seeds of self-esteem and self-identity as they germinate in the fields of peer group collective empowerment. It argues that adolescents' rapidly developing self-efficacy is expanded within their collectively empowered peer groups; this in contrast to their disempowered atomised condition in the parental home. This sense of developing self-efficacy brings about a qualitative change in parental relationships necessitating a complex often dramatic period of negotiations which challenge both the self-esteem of the adolescent and the nurturing skills of the parent.

The Wall acts to protect the adolescent's self-esteem by siloing the parental world. Adolescents bring in additional cement for the Wall by consciously and subconsciously developing communication barriers with specific functions for parents, teachers and peers. Parents nurturing aspirations are frustrated as they find themselves blocked off from large parts of their adolescents' peer empowered world.

The Separation of Adolescents' Atomised and Collective Worlds

Whilst the classroom is not the only place where adolescents can experience collective empowerment, in the school setting, they often form friendships involving more than one other peer. The peer group setting gives them an autonomous collective of friends and associates. That collectivity allows them to experience collective empowerment (ability to achieve goals that they could often not expect to achieve through individual activity). Moreover, they generally enter the group as an autonomous act, not one dictated to by their parents or other adults.

Finding a peer group, no matter how loosely connected, to settle into can be difficult for some adolescents when attending a new school. If the situation continues it can be disconcerting as they watch others settle in and take advantage of the benefits of collective empowerment. The difficulty and vulnerability of social isolation can be experienced very quickly. Adolescents can take time to find a suitable group, depending on commonality of tastes, experiences, culture, levels of intensity of group commitment. This fluidity of changes in associates also reflects the rapid manner in which each member of a group is absorbing new experiences, new information and new insights.

This is a critical stage when the young person is beginning to explore their self-worth. Once settled, the collective self-esteem added by the group improves their sense of self-worth.

When analysing academic outcomes amongst 2,800 Australian students, AJ Martin et al. sought to use social identity theory to explore this role of the collective in developing self-esteem.

"Social identity theory is also relevant. Individuals' self-concepts are based on their membership to their social group (Tajfel, 1978; Tajfel and Turner, 1986). Social identities are most influential when the individual has strong emotional connections to a group and when membership in a particular group is considered by the individual to be central to their self-concept. The individual garners self-esteem through affiliation with the group, typically through influential processes such as within-group assimilation (pressure to conform to the group's norms) and intergroup bias (favorably appraising one's own group relative to other groups). These processes are particularly powerful in peer groups (Leaper, 2011)." (Boarding and Day School Students: A Large-Scale Multilevel Investigation of Academic Outcomes Among Students and Classrooms, Martin, Burns, Kennett, Pearson and Munro-Smith, Frontiers in Psychology, January 2021)

Crucially, on the other hand, rejection by the group or inability to locate in a group impacts negatively on their sense of self-worth. Peer-belonging (to be or feel popular) becomes a measure of value. In a brief 2011 paper for Current Directions in Psychological Science, DeWall and Bushman outlined the stakes for humans in general:

"Being motivated to have positive and lasting relationships conferred a tremendous advantage among our evolutionary ancestors. With no fangs, fur, or claws, and with long, vulnerable childhoods, humans are ill-suited to fulfil their survival and reproductive needs living in isolation. Given these vulnerabilities, early humans survived harsh environments by depending on small groups of other individuals to meet many of their survival and reproductive needs. The benefits of acceptance and group living extend beyond protection from predators and providing mates to spread one's genes to future generations. Cooperative group living enabled early humans to share and receive resources from each other, thereby making it unnecessary for individuals to carry the entire burden of their well-being on their own shoulders. Therefore, social rejection is experienced as "bitter" in order to motivate individuals to avoid a negative state in which they do not receive the benefits of inclusion, which ultimately decreases their survival rate. Because our ancestors evolved in small groups, social rejection likely signified a death sentence." (The Sweet and the Bitter, DeWall & Bushman, Current Directions in Psychological Science, 2011)

Just how painful the neurological process can be for adolescents and people as a whole as they search to accommodate themselves in groups of their peers was highlighted by DeWall:

"When people experience social rejection, their hearts literally slow down and they experience motivationally tuned changes in progesterone, a hormone associated with social-affiliative motivation. Social rejection and other forms of social-evaluative threat, defined as a context in which a person can be judged negatively by others, increases the release of the stress hormone cortisol and stimulates production of proinflammatory cytokines. In terms of neural correlates, social rejection increases activation in brain regions (e.g. dorsal anterior cingulate cortex, anterior insula) that are associated with the affective component of physical pain (i.e. the 'unpleasantness' aspect of pain, as opposed to the sensory component on knowing that one is experiencing pain)." (The Sweet and the Bitter, DeWall & Bushman, Current Directions in Psychological Science, 2011)

Indeed, DeWall and his associates tested their hypothesis that the pain of social rejection was felt in the same way as physical pain, and found their theory borne out. They hypothesised:

"Because there is some shared overlap in neural regions associated with physical pain and social rejection, numbing people to physical pain may also diminish the pain of social rejection."

DeWall et al reported that their tests demonstrated that the impact on the brain of social rejection could be dealt with in the same way as when treating a physical pain and that:

"a daily dose of acetaminophen.... an over-the-counter analgesic commonly used to treat physical pain was effective in reducing emotional responses and neural correlates of social rejection."

Collective empowerment becomes a key building block in the adolescent search for self-worth – as witnessed on the flip-side by the reaction when experiencing rejection by the group.

The collective world of academia and peer collectives gives adolescents the space to marshal their own resources. The peer collective is the key. No amount of praise and encouragement by parents or teaching staff can protect adolescents' sense of self-worth if they are rejected by their peer groups. In their research into the development of self-concepts Tanti et al. concluded that the peer groups become so important to adolescents that they begin to use those groups as part of their self-concept:

"Through the subphases of adolescence people showed increasing use of collective terms, reflecting the incorporation of social group memberships into the self-concept. Further, although mid-adolescents unexpectedly showed slightly increased use of the individual self, the content of the individual self became markedly more reflective of socially embedded attributes.

"Finally, while the use of specific relationship terms decreased in adolescence, the relational self shifted focus from the parents to the wider social network of peers. Thus, the findings show that as people move through adolescence, they develop a stronger sense of their social identity." (Tripartite Self-concept Change: Shifts in the Individual, Relational, and Collective Self in Adolescence, Tanti et al, 2008)

Whilst, the adolescent's peer-based world is expanding and exploring ever new areas, their domestic/parented world appears to be either standing still or deteriorating.

In their domestic world, the parents are trying to adjust to their increasingly empowered child, now an adolescent. Having towered over their child due to their superior physique, knowledge and emotional skills the parents were used to the relatively simple tasks of nurturing and protecting their child. They readily employed lies, obfuscations and silences in their belief that they were in the best interests of their child. Now that past world is challenged. The developing intellect of the adolescent equips them to challenge the adults.

Tanti et al. referenced others' research to illustrate the shifting allegiances of adolescence away from their parents and towards their peer groups:

"Many theorists describe early-adolescence as a time of beginning to disengage from the internalized standards of the parents (Blos, 1979; Levine, Green, & Millon, 1986), in order to move toward more autonomous functioning. In fact, Csikszentmihalyi and Larson (1984) showed that time spent with family decreases during adolescence, from 25% for early adolescents to only 15% for late adolescents.

"Further, Steinberg (1988, 1989) provided evidence of increased psychological distance between children (aged 10 – 15 years) and their parents, with the adolescent's advancing maturation. Not surprisingly, peer groups appear to replace the parents by providing a supportive and understanding self-reference point (Marcia, 1983), and research shows adolescents spend one third of their waking time with peers though only 8% talking with adults (Csikszentmihalyi, Larson, & Prescott, 1977)." (Tripartite Self-concept Change: Shifts in the Individual, Relational, and Collective Self in Adolescence, Tanti et al, 2008)

The adolescent increasingly finds support and succour in peer groups. For the adolescent a new and empowered world is opening up but it is a world which the parents can barely touch, and furthermore a world increasingly foreign to the adult with its own language, codes, and cultural preferences. Many parents now face the prospect of trying to nurture and protect their child but in conditions where their autarchy no longer stretches over all spheres of their adolescent's behaviour. Part of parental nurturing is to ensure that their child will not be drawn into activities that will threaten the young person's development, whether academically or otherwise.

The concerned parents often draw lines in the sand for their adolescent but the teenager often sees this as an extension of the autarchic control that they faced as the young child whom they have left behind. The adolescent reasonably demands parole but the parent wants to apply tags and behaviour orders. Negotiation can be a stressful even violent time for parents and adolescents. Nevertheless, given the way in which society is currently constructed, the complete abandonment of the negotiation process presents perils for both sides.

Much of this arises unintentionally due to the rapidly evolving relationship between the adolescents and their parents generating periodic rounds of negotiation and renegotiation of adolescent "freedoms" and duties, negotiations which involve complex psychological issues with history on both sides and which may not necessarily be bilateral but involve both parents and even considerations regarding siblings. Adolescents do not find themselves in a strong position. The law and property relations are on the parents' side, reducing the young person to a serf pleading for freedom from the master. Although for some adults this can feel like it is the opposite with the parent begging for some family time to keep the family together.

Even the adolescent with the most affectionate view of their parents may feel frustrated that their parents are displaying a lack of confidence in their ability to comprehend, for example, the threats posed by membership of their peer groups. The adolescents, sensing that the parents have little knowledge of the goings-on in their peer groups, bristle at the lack of confidence shown in them and their choice of associates.

In all this negotiation, which at times may be an intense daily event, the parents' case is often undermined by their having to deal with the many other aspects of their lives, including other close relationships and hence parental behaviour can appear inconsistent, arbitrary, irrational and unstable.

The parents bring into play their own view of what constitutes their child's identity and self-worth, which itself can be construed by the adolescent as a full-frontal attack, aimed at destroying the young person's emerging sense of identity and self-worth.

For teenagers, who generally still retain a sense of respect for, and complex emotional ties with their parents seeing them in this light for the first time can of itself be traumatising. The first time that the adolescent dares to stand up against their parents... is the first time. Rather like lovers who enter unexpectedly into their first major row, adolescents generally enter their first negotiations with their parents without any concept that they will be negotiating, and that they, like Napoleon, will require more than a few campaigns to reach their goal.

Having lived under the yoke of their parents for many years, adolescents have often tolerated far more of their parents' irrational statements, lies, obfuscations, false promises and mood-swings than their parents wish to remember. They have an arsenal of information to throw back at their parents. Where the parents don't recognise this both sides can be in for some heavy fighting. "Why? Because I say so!" is no longer the crushing coup de grâce.

Adolescents, new to negotiations for their freedoms, make mistakes, blurt out unreasonable demands and accusations, but then have to live with the consequences.

For the adolescent, the Mystery Wall acts as a protection of their collectively empowering peer-based world from being infected by the barely comprehensible, seemingly irrational, emotionally confusing developments in their parented world. The Wall protects adolescents' crucial search for self-worth amongst their peer group or collectives. Nevertheless, by siloing these worlds and drawing a curtain across their parented world, adolescents create a dangerous dichotomy because the two worlds are both busy shaping their identity and sense of self-worth but are left to generate often contradictory messages. The result is to complicate and undermine adolescents' search for identity and their sense of self-worth.

The Mystery Wall of Adolescence

Adolescent's Domestic Life	THE MYSTERY WALL	Adolescent's School Life
Parents		**Teaching Staff & Peers**
Atomised		Collectivised
Private		Corporate
Disempowerment		Peer Empowerment
Semi- structured		Structured
Unstable Environment		Stable Environment
Unstructured Learning Experience		Structured Learning Experience
Parental Language		Peer language
Psychological		Sociological
Emotionally Complex		Emotionally Simple
Inconsistent Reward System		Consistent Reward System
Unstable Punishment System		Stable Punishment System
Serfdom		Apprenticeship
Secret Society		Public Society
No Trespassing		Qualified Entry

The Wall as a Barrier to Others

Furthermore, the Wall strengthens as it leaps from its passive cognitive use into active service as a means of cocooning both worlds to protect them from invasion by others. As much as parents are denied access into adolescents' peer collective-worlds, so peers are prevented access into their friends' parented worlds.

Barring Parents

Regarding adolescents' protection of their peer-collective world from parental scrutiny, this reaction is brought about as a primitive step on the road to adulthood. The young person's search for identity and self-worth is one which only they can go through. Adult assertion and support can play only the crudest part as the young person tries to make sense of their increasingly complex world.

This appears to the young person as a solitary journey which only they can go through, particularly because adults stand outside the complex interactions within the peer group/collective. In reality the journey is along a road that is far from solitary as neither parental interactions nor peer interactions can be extricated from the process.

Adolescents, carefully stepping their way through those peer interactions fear that adult intervention or their following of adult advice will shift the complex balance of those peer interactions against them. This is not surprising because neither the adult nor the adolescent has all the words to convey the myriad of those interactions and the emotional angles linked to each one.

On this stormy ocean, the adolescent rarely finds peace in self-reflection. The process may heighten senses of difference in identity with the parents. This is often construed as adolescents rebelling specifically against their parents. However, teenagers, in beginning to define their identity will also do so by identifying their differences with those around them, whether it be siblings, subgroups of their peers or their parents.

(Indeed, this process of differentiation begins much earlier. As a Mixed-Race child, I was still four years old when I learned from others that I was a Black child, which meant I was not a White child. I became Black in

135

England where people were White. I was not in my country but I did not know my country. I had no country. Like many children, I learned much of what I was from being told what I was not.)

Often a more appealing route out of the complexities of domestic conflict is one which directs towards safe havens, distractions absorbing the self in peer-interactions and other activities such as sport, music or academic studies. Even these pathways may not suffice and the young person may seek solace in substance abuse and other potentially harmful practises.

Parents habituated to their role of nurturing and protecting their child to the best of their ability now suddenly find their adolescent reaching into spheres outside the parental reach. Their initial reaction to feeling frustrated is often clumsy.

The teenager reacts by cementing the Wall using silence, obfuscation or outright lies. The parent reacts by demanding the truth; the information that they feel they require to take back control of their child. They are disappointed at their child not being forthcoming and using forms of deception, yet these forms of deception are exactly the same as they themselves have used to control and nurture their child. They have not only trained the child in deception (through play at least), in academic education they have also given them the weapons. Deception through silence, lies and obfuscation are critical elements of both the adult's and the adolescent's armoury.

Parents' insistence on knowing all the information about the adolescent's peer-collective world signals a lack of confidence in the young person. The young person often lacks the words to describe their newly complex world and may justifiably fear that by miscommunicating they will threaten their engagement in their new collectively empowered world. They may not want to lie because they do not want to signal that they do not wish to be disrespectful for their parents and lose their affection. Hence the safest route will often be to draw a veil, but if the parent presses, produce a lie.

Teenagers, Truth and Empowerment

A key-word Internet search for English-language material on adolescents and truth brings up an ocean of material focussed not on truth but how to deal with the lying adolescent; and all this around the premise that lying is a societal sin. The authors and researchers seem oblivious to the fact that most adolescents have experienced a childhood peppered with parental lies, white lies and obfuscations of the truth. Learning when and when not to lie is part of growing up, of self-empowerment.

There are so many of us who, as children, were beaten for our truths, which adults construed as lies. They told themselves that punishment would teach us to "tell the truth", whilst all the while they were busy dressing up their own deceptions as "white lies". What did they expect we would conclude when we learned that they had no more claim to sit at the table of truth than we had? How would the world benefit when we realised that we were deceived? That we were not beaten for truth but to force compliance to their will.

For the most part, the physical mismatch between adults and children does not result in a climate of domestic violence. Instead, parents and adults empowered with greater knowledge try to use this advantage over young children to nurture, control and steer children's thought processes. Yet, in doing so, parents commonly use lies, white lies and obfuscation. Would society benefit from teaching children what it preaches to adults; that lying has its place?

Western society, Hinduism and the Abrahamic religions of Christianity, Islam and Judaism sanctify white lies i.e. lies told for the greater good. Yet this is only in the subtext. Most religious institutions' loudest refrain, shouted from the hilltops is that lying is a terrible sin and in civic society perjury, lying in the law courts, is often dealt with as a bigger crime than the crime itself.

Conversely, Western constitutional practice has many governments asserting their right to suppress uncomfortable information and awkward truths for decades and to tell "white lies" and Plato's "noble lies" to others, for what they argue is the "greater good", whilst jailing others for lying or even just staying silent.

Yet white lies, no matter how benevolent the intention, are nevertheless lies and distortions of the truth. Consider, for example, Father Christmas and all the fabulous stories told by the world's major religions, which later the inquisitive child, adolescent or young adult will be told are not strictly true but are interpretations, 'pious lies' or fables. Literate adolescents can easily learn that vital elements of 'facts' they have been told are either fantasy or that they conflict with the scientific knowledge being passed onto them in their academic classes and studies.

To protect their fledgling empowered world, adolescents often bring into play what they have been learning throughout childhood about the use of untruths, fantasies and the silence of secrets.

We encourage our children to engage in fantasy and use their imagination for their amusement. They learn to play with truth and untruths. In their peer groups they learn about secrets with their secret hiding places, dens and secrets to surprise. They learn that fantasies, untruths and silence are tools, first of play; then of protection. Not a few will soon enough hear: "Don't tell your father."

They learn like adults that lies, obfuscations and silence have their uses. For the adolescent these become part of the cement of the Mystery Wall. This cement is also being employed by parents and teaching staff and for the same purpose.

However, when adults feel the need to intervene to nurture, protect of control the adolescent they feel disempowered if they cannot squeeze out the information, which they believe they need from the young person. They demand that the young person tells them the truth (which may not of course always be the facts of the matter). They often insist on being made to feel that their child has taken them seriously, which takes the form of, for example, insisting that the young person looks them in the eye, does not smirk or pull faces at them.

Both parents and teachers demand honesty and respect from children. They hope the child's honest replies enable them to protect and control the children in their care. They feel disempowered over their children if they perceive or discover that the children have miscommunicated with them.

Adolescents gather more knowledge and communication skills and their lives becomes more complex as they spend more time away from their parents. The balance of power between them and the adults in their sphere begins to change. The adolescent finds that not only is possession of truth empowering, so too can be the denial of access to the truth via lies, obfuscations or silence.

The adolescent learns that denying others access to their truths gives them new found power, in particular to protect their own space and activities from parental and others' scrutiny. A charity researching street children in Kerala, India referred to how they had to respect and accommodate the young people's approach to truth:

"Street involved children are smart talkers and have cultivated the art of relating to people and the technique of smart talking or giving standard replies to safeguard their identities. Instances of fake responses were also observed as a way of avoiding certain issues regarding street life and the staff, although aware of this, had to accept their responses at face value." (Don Bosco Veedu study, Trivandrum, India 2014)

Deliberate miscommunication is a sign of a young person trying to empower themselves by denying the parent or carer that information which the young person feels may be detrimental to their own (or their collectives') wellbeing. However, the parent is thrown into a quandary and sometimes a frenzy. How can they protect their child if they don't know what is going on in the child's life? The balance of power has changed and no amount of threats and pleading will bring that balance back.

It is also an indication to the parents that they are having to move into another phase in their own lives, one that might also be perilous, meaning that it is not an entirely comfortable place for them either. Dark thoughts and forebodings may rush through the minds of the parents. It is a short stretch from "my adolescent is out of my control" to "adolescents are out of control."

In denouncing the adolescent for lying, the parent can at best add guilt to their teenager's trauma. The adolescent still wants to respect and be respected (or 'loved') by their parents but now that prospect is endangered if they refuse to hand power back to their parents. On the other hand, if they hand power to their parents then this may destroy the complex edifice of relationships which they have built up with the collective or their peers and friends. The bond between parent and adolescent can face rupture, especially because the adult's demands may appear hypocritical, appearing to demand a higher moral stance from the young person than they, the parents, have displayed.

Mutual trust is replaced with distrust or wariness, a cagey cat and mouse game of testing one another out, testing not only the new boundaries and tolerances, but also one another's capacities to support each other's worlds. The more communication the better.

For adolescents, deliberate miscommunication and silence are part of the cement that binds the Mystery Wall; and the same can be said of academic teachers and parents. Somehow mutual understanding and trust must be forged to weaken that cement, find possible passages through the Wall and keep doors of communication open.

Unfortunately, the process of communication with adolescents is not helped by the instruments of adult society. Governments and mass media often pander to parental and adult fears. The mass of youth must be controlled and shaped into productive employees for society, fitting in with the societal status quo. But in their teenage years they are bursting with conscious and unconscious insights into the irrationality and contradictions of society irrationalities, which many adults have either incorporated into their thoughts or resolved to acquiesce to.

The "adolescent rebellion" that French psychologist Maurice Debesse identified in his 1936 work, "La crise d'originalité juvenile", has its roots not in puberty but the teenage application of rational abstractions to the

Bad Faith and seemingly irrational contradictions that surround them, defying both Aristotelian formal logic and Platonic dialectics.

The maddening irony for parents is that, with the knowledge foundation based mainly on what their parents and formal education has taught them, they often have other ideas about what society and/or their future should be. For this sin they are barely trusted as individuals and frequently feared when they combine into their collectives.

Adolescents and Teaching Staff

Adolescent apprehensions re-adult intervention are not helped by a) parental apprehension at losing control over their children's behaviour, b) schools almost exclusive focus on academic attainment and c) societal prejudices expressed against teenagers and their collectives.

Parents' and the teaching staff's main focus is often on the adolescent's academic achievements and parents, especially, tend to justify this on the basis that other matters can be resolved later once their young person has laid the basis for their employability. The emphasis on academic results as the sole means by which teaching staff and their schools are assessed has been intensified in the neo-liberal world. Parents may have other concerns such as fears of their children facing discrimination, cultural isolation and bullying. Schools may address these but, for example, the English government's school comparison charts feature nothing of the pupils' perceptions of their experience either academically or otherwise.

The teaching staff can glow with 30 'nerds' or 'swots' and the parents might be filled with pride and expectation but how do these adolescents feel that they have been set up for life amongst their wider peer group is not measured yet is so crucial. Governments hand that role to the parents but the process is not in the parents' control, it is often in the peer groups that operate based around the adolescent's school life.

The overwhelmingly academic results-based approach may be suitable for developing automatons and humans who are just adjuncts to or replacements of machines but flies in the face of developing socially engaged individuals. In many areas, the young person is told to think but mainly to the extent of absorbing knowledge rather than applying it to life. They are told to think of others but not to fully engage with their peers because their real value is to the employer and the workplace. To parents the adolescent's peers may have little value but to the adolescent they are critical to assessing their ability to make their way in the world beyond the workplace.

Few adolescents dream of spending eight hours a day in the workplace then spending the rest of their day alone. Indeed, Western culture sees the ultimately atomised individual as a danger to society rather than a paragon (a situation sadly borne out by the profile of many mass, random killers).

Society demands socialised individuals ready to interact collectively but gives a negative value to this in the education of the adolescent. Most teenagers, faced with the peer groups and collectives before them, instinctively grasp that this purely academic approach does not contain all the answers to their parallel search for self-worth.

For adolescents, the journey is complex as they begin to understand, in the peer group setting, that their self-worth is not defined solely by academic or other personal individual achievements but primarily their interrelationships with their peer groups/collectives. At the same time, they have to find means of coping with the conflicting focus, if not demands, of their parents and teaching staff.

Parents and adults' behaviour often leaves the adolescent more isolated and left feeling unsupported in handling their participation in peer collectives. A consequence may be poorer judgements re-seeking a balance in regard to personal academic development and acceptance in the peer group/collective and also in regard to participation in "anti-social" peer activities. In the former case, we have the example of adolescents concluding that their academic or other individual achievements may be a barrier to building their relationships with the peer group and so neglecting their studies, which may be a wrong or right step for them.

Risks of Crossing the Wall: Adolescents

The trigger to this discourse was the observation that as adolescents we unconsciously applied this Mystery Wall to keeping out our peers. This is perhaps the most instructive of aspects. In discussing this observation there are those who initially identified the cause for this behaviour was teenage fear that the disclosure of "private" family information to their peers could open them up to ridicule and abuse, also implying that they could not trust their friends. This could well be the case in some instances but is more likely due to uncertainties brought about by the changing nature of social relationships during adolescence.

However, this also assumes that the teenager can make sense of or even frame the fast-evolving changes in relationships at home and so be confident enough to convey this picture to their peers. Whilst on a sociological level most adolescents would assume that their peers experience similar parented lives, at a psychological level, the interactions between individuals in the family are so complex and dynamic that only by expressing what they considered to be happening could the adolescent have any confidence that their peers were having similar experiences. The latter requires being able to frame and articulate those processes.

Meanwhile there are other more mundane domestic events which could be discussed in relative safety but these are also subject to the blanket embargo. The risk is not so much of bullying but of not being understood or of revealing information that might risk or undermine their status in the peer group.

That the Mystery Wall is similarly erected to face the teaching staff tells us more. Teenagers considering revealing aspects of their home life to teaching staff must weigh up the consequences should their parents be informed of those disclosures. The power imbalance in the home is such that the disempowered adolescent risks reprisals from the parents not only for the nature of the information relayed but also for the very act of revealing information about their parented world without the permission of the autarchic parental power.

Students face the threat that their parents might react by throwing them into the family 'dungeons', removing some or all of the little freedoms left to them. If the Englishman's home is his castle, then his children residing therein have a status little better than that of a serf. The adolescent is not empowered to reveal private information about the parents' castle. Only when they reach adulthood do they commonly feel empowered to do so.

Risks of Crossing the Wall: Teachers

Crossing the Wall also poses risks to the teaching staff and parents. For the academic teaching staff, largely untrained in pastoral care, they risk professional and parental censure should they intervene in any way regarding the student's parented world.

The staff also risk placing the child in further difficulty because they have no say in the home and no guarantees of how those parents will react in the domestic or in the public sphere. Teachers are trained to teach in a formal setting rather than to approach a child's education in a holistic manner. Failed intervention could result in sanctions. They also face the danger of parental disengagement with the school. Unless the din is unbearable or the teacher is imbued with an overwhelming sense of pastoral duty, the staff are expected to turn a deaf ear and keep the portcullis firmly closed.

Risks of Crossing the Wall: Parents

On the other hand, the parents' intervention in the adolescent's peer-empowered world risks at best the adolescent resenting the invasion of the parental autarchy into their empowered arena and feeling their status in the peer-group to have been undermined, but also risks the young person being thrown out of their peer collectives and left isolated with their quest for self-worth back at the starting point.

Parental uninvited intervention in the affairs of their adolescent's academic world (aside from as an adjunct to the teaching staff ensuring that teenagers have space to do their homework) risks undermining their status as parents and generating amongst teaching staff prejudicial attitudes towards their children and communications with those parents.

Should they consider disclosing to the teaching staff their parenting difficulties they fear the consequences of the social stigma and humiliation attached to their apparent inability; a stigma which may stretch beyond the school staff to their social circles and conjure up the horrific spectre of social service intervention. Even if parents approach the school to protect their child, they face major risks. An example of the risks of parental intervention is when parents request the school to protect their children from reported incidents of bullying. The school intervention can at best often only protect their pupil within the school grounds. At worst it exposes the child to more intensified bullying unless more peers rally in the child's defence.

Siloing the Two Worlds

All the above risks encourage adolescents, teaching staff and parents alike to further reinforce the Wall between the adolescent's parented and academic worlds. For the teaching staff and parents this appears relatively simple with rules set out for behaviour, responsibilities and territories. For the adolescent seeking to establish their own territory in these spheres of ownership, the situation is far more complex.

All parties to some degree use lies, obfuscation and silence as tools to protect their territories. For adults, this is largely seen as normal and tolerable behaviour unless it generates aggressive conflict between the parties. For the teenager, using these methods is more complex. This deliberate miscommunication may be part of an adolescent's self-empowerment process but at the same time it challenges the parental autarchy, creating conflict. The teenagers are nevertheless busy cementing the Wall to protect the parts of their world where they feel empowered, and which also contain the kernel of their journey to assess their self-worth.

The differing property relations and division of labour between parents and teaching staff allow for the siloing of the parented and academic worlds. For the adolescents this appears to have some advantages but it also cuts off applying the collective empowerment of their peer collectives to their domestic situation and challenging the parental autarchy. This is of particular importance when it comes to issues of child abuse, whether physical, sexual or psychological. Generally, only in extreme circumstances will adolescents proactively disclose to other adults in such situations because they are already losing blind faith in the adults entrusted with their care, namely their parents. The risks of contacting other adults are great especially because, post disclosure, they have ceded control of the situation to the adult autarchy.

Family and Corporate Education: Two Sources of Alienated Existence

Recent studies of the impacts of the contradictory demands of the privately parented world and the school world on adolescents appear rare. From their research some sociologists, such as Eccles et al. point out that: *"Adolescence is a time for renegotiating the power and authority relationships within the family."* (Schools, families, and early adolescents: what are we doing wrong and what can we do instead? Eccles, Flanagan, Lord, Midgley, Roeser and Yee, 1996)

They postulated that life at school with its: *"broadened exposure may lead the early adolescents to question the legitimacy of their parents' rules."* They also identified a countervailing pressure on parents whose concern regarding their children's growing sexuality drove them to taking repressive measures, intensifying teenagers' sense of grievance.

Yet the parental autarchy is often reluctant to cede all but nominal ground. Eccles's research found a mismatch in the dialogue between parents and their teenage school children: *"The parents reported that they included their children more in family decision-making than the children perceived to be true."*

The study also noted how those adolescents who became increasingly disillusioned with their ability to impact on family decision-making fared worse at school.

It is common for modern sociologists to approach alienation as a malfunction of capitalist society rather than a logical condition for humans living under capitalism. In contrast, Karl Marx considered that alienation was a direct consequence of class society and identified its source in humans being objectified as commodities able through work to deliver added value. He argued: *"A direct consequence of the alienation of man from the product of his labour, from his life activity and from his species-life, is that man is alienated from other men. ... man is alienated from his species-life means that each man is alienated from others, and that each of the others is likewise alienated from human life."* (Political Science for Civil Services Main Examination, p. 11, Karl Marx)

In their teenage years, adolescents emerge into a society dominated by this alienation with all the malfunctions that it manifests such as Bad Faith, lack of sense of fulfilment in work, undermined self-worth and commodification of family and friends. The corporate world of academia insists that it is teaching adolescents to be rational. However, the huge contradictions between society's mores, actions and outcomes encourage any moderately perceptive teenager to conclude that they are witnessing insane irrationality.

Somehow academia must try to place a shroud over the chaos of contradictions and stitch up any gaping holes with a needle, threading a patchwork of words such as complexity, compromise, intricate, innate, tradition, acceptable, love, black holes and God, 'grow up' and 'when you're older'. Should teenagers place their thoughts on the collective experience of their privately parented world into this mix, then the whole shroud could fall down, exposing the absence of any humane rationality. Hence, the Mystery Wall and the Englishman's home remaining as the parental castle.

As Harter points out, adolescence, with its transitional social and learning settings, is a distinct period of dynamic and dramatic changes in regard to self-esteem and studies show that in early adolescence, self-esteem can take a nosedive for up to 50% of the teenagers. (Self-perception profile for adolescents: Harter, S. 2012 University of Denver, Department of Psychology and Causes and Consequences of Low Self-Esteem in Children and Adolescents, 1990)

Since adolescents, in preparation for their futures, must learn to survive in the world of their peers rather than their parents' it is logical that they focus on developing their self-identity within the spheres of their peer group empowered collectives. Given their primary attention is on their peer groups, their reaction is only rebellion in the sense that parents are denied their prior status as the adolescent breaks out of the protection of the parental cocoon and looks to settle down in the new semi-independent world of their emerging self-identity's new cocoon provided protection by the Mystery Wall.

Consequently, where adolescents are expected to spend the majority of their daylight hours with their peers, peer acceptance is crucial to a sense of self-worth. The lowering of self-esteem in early adolescence is entirely understandable as the young people begin the not always comfortable journey to seek and test out peers with whom they can feel relaxed and accepted.

No amount of praise from teachers and parents can protect a youth from the devastation reeked by peer rejection. Conversely peer acceptance brings qualitatively increased empowerment, protection by the group, sources of resilience and the self-esteem of being valued by the group.

The very chasm between the relative rationality of the school world and the irrationality of their parented world leads to the two worlds being siloed. Parents peering through a secret window into the school cannot recognise their child. Teachers peering into the parental home cannot recognise their pupils. The pupils peering into their own homes can so not make sense of its chaos that they can barely even recognise themselves.

If books are read through the filter of one's own knowledge and experience so too are other educational and information inputs. The young person has to absorb these inputs through the contradictory experiences of their home and school worlds. Little wonder that they are often tempted to drown out the resulting din by putting on the headphones and blasting their brains with heavy metal music.

Ultimately the Mystery Wall protects adolescents' crucial search for self-worth amongst their peer groups/collectives. This is a journey which only they can go through, particularly because adults stand outside the complex interactions within the peer group/collective. Adolescents, carefully stepping their way through those interactions, fear that adult intervention or following adult advice will shift the balance of those interactions against them.

What British adolescent has not used the response: "Fine," to repel a parent's inquiries as to how their day went at school or at the sleepover? What parent hasn't had their questions as to what happened at the birthday party met by a teenage: "Nothing"? The Wall was erected, sometimes politely, yet firmly like a hand-off of a would-be tackler by the rugby player carrying the ball, but at other times with a grump, and a grump that would become still grumpier should the parental quizzing to grab the ball persist. The matter was closed and the teenager's world of collective engagement protected.

Societal Oppression of Adolescents

Content

This chapter deals with government and media portrayals of adolescents and the impact they have on society. It then goes on to consider how this propaganda is perceived by adolescents and looks at how this might negatively impact on not only the collective self-esteem of adolescents but also their attitudes to other adolescents. It considers the levels of trauma faced by adolescents in today's Western societies and whether, by poisoning the well of collectivity and collective empowerment from which teenagers draw their self-esteem and self-identity, governments and their media are the primary cause for the rising tide of adolescent mental ill-health.

The Enemy Within – The Propaganda of Adolescent Oppression

For adolescents, deliberate miscommunication and silence are part of the cement that binds the Mystery Wall; and the same can be said of academic teachers and parents. For a society to advance, somehow mutual understanding and trust must be forged to not necessarily weaken that cement but to find possible passages through the Wall and keep doors of communication open for meaningful engagement.

Instead, the process of communication with adolescents is to a large part obstructed by the instruments of adult society. Each generation of parents that raises children has to face a challenge to their nurturing capacity when their adolescents reach out for adulthood. This fear that they are losing control is replicated from one generation to the next but is part of the 'letting go' process which all people who care deeply for others feel.

Rather than sooth and work through these fears, governments opportunistically seize upon them and ministers and mass media often hype up the propaganda and pander to the prejudice of childism. The interests of the controlling exploitative state requires that the mass of youth must be controlled and shaped into productive employees for society, fitting in with the societal status quo. But in their teenage years young people are bursting with conscious and unconscious insights into the irrationality and contradictions of society. They have other ideas about what their future should be. They are barely trusted as individuals and almost feared when they combine into their collectives.

Consider why so many adults become apprehensive when they see a group of young people as opposed to other adults on the streets? Only if there is an adult presence in the group, will their fears be eased; equally, if those youth are in spaces designated for their recreation such as a football pitch.

Youth are the oppressed "enemy" like the "natives" were in the African and Indian colonies, never respecting the Imperial assertion that they were incarcerated for their own benefit. Reminiscent of the days of Empire, it is common to hear mention of "*groups of youths hanging around street corners*" as a euphemism for a threatening environment and accompanied by demands for the authorities to disperse the rabble. Yet these are young humans acting out their crucial development into social beings. Perhaps we, the broken-in adults, when seeing the collectively empowered teenagers, recoil at the mirror image of our collectively empowered selves which we have been taught to loathe and fear? How should young people react to a society that simultaneously ignores, despises and represses them and rules them out as stakeholders?

Adolescents being out of control and youth criminality have been recurring governmental and mass media themes in British society for decades. From the 19th century social reformers taking orphaned children off the streets and placing them in workhouses or orphanages, the establishment moved on to mass education as a means of preparing the unruly youth for work or military service.

In a 2021 article for International Modern Perspectives on Academia and Community Today, which looks back over a decade of media coverage of youth crime, Angela Rogan points out that: *"Historically, youth crime has been depicted as an exponential social problem increasing In severity and occurrences. The extent of the United Kingdom (UK) political and media focus on youth crime within contemporary society demonstrates this phenomenon continues unabated. Sensationalist media headlines from right-wing mainstream media and harsh policing policies by the conservative government continued to fuel these debates aimed at tackling the supposed increasing surgence of youth crimes in the UK."* (Rogan, The Demonisation of Delinquency Media 2021 https://impactjournal .qub.ac.uk)

Half a century beforehand, during the 1960s, the British media were obsessed with gang crime and the massed youth gangs styled as Mods, Rockers, Teddy Boys or Greasers and apoplectically outraged by the open challenge to the prevailing social mores of armies of young Hippies and Yippies. Fast forward just one generation and that societal outrage was seemingly conveniently swallowed up by nostalgia. The societal trauma which was induced had gone the way of many traumas and been driven into the deeper recesses of societal memory.

Evidence contradicting assertions that young people were increasingly out of control were conveniently brushed aside. For example, in 2001, the National Association for the Care and Resettlement of Offenders analysis of UK crime statistics had revealed that youth crime had fallen between 1993 and 2001 to leave Britain as the country in Europe with the lowest crime rates for young people.

Yet, the new millennium continued with media and government expressions of outrage concerning teenage "unruliness". The British Crime Survey 2002/3 revealed that 33% of people regarded "*teenagers hanging around on the streets*" as a problem and in 2003, the English government introduced the Anti-Social Behaviour Act with Dispersal Orders giving police the power to disperse groups of two or more persons.

Moving on a few more years, one might reasonably have concluded that Britain's once polite well-mannered youth were fast becoming feral when seeing the Daily Telegraph headline on April 7th in 2008, which declared: "*Youth crime 'up by two thirds in 10 years'*".

However, four months later, the opposite was revealed to be the case when The People, a British tabloid, on August 10th, 2008 published extensive research on youth crime, declaring:

"VIOLENT BRITAIN? IT WAS WORSE IN THE 60s - THE PEOPLE SURVEY FINDS 'LOVE' KIDS PUT TODAY'S TEEN YOBS IN SHADE."

The report conveyed a positive picture of life for modern youth compared to that of the prevailing rosy nostalgic view of Britain's Swinging Sixties?

"Teenage violence is one of the biggest fears for people in Britain today - but the problem was actually far WORSE in the Swinging Sixties. Youngsters of the so-called Love Generation were almost TWICE as likely to prowl our streets armed with a knife. The number of girls carrying a deadly blade in 1968 was DOUBLE the level of today. And despite 30 teens being stabbed to death in the UK already this year, the study gives the lie

to claims the country is in the grip of an unprecedented epidemic of youth violence.

"But among the class of 68 - brought up in the shadow of violent running battles between Mods and Rockers - that figure was nearly 200. And while 48 of today's kids said they WOULD use a blade if they got caught up in a street fight, 86 of the older generation admitted they HAD. The gender breakdown between the two generations is just as alarming in the year Georgie Fame topped the charts with The Ballad of Bonnie and Clyde, more than a quarter of boys and a shocking one in eight (12.5% - Editor) girls confessed they had carried a knife. In 2008, the figures are 17 per cent of boys and just 7 per cent of girls. The number of teenage VICTIMS of crime has also plunged since the heady days of flower power.

"Back then, nearly half the youngsters who had been targeted by crooks were assaulted - and a third had suffered sex attacks. For the 2008 group, just over a third have been assaulted and 14 per cent have been preyed on by perverts. Even the number of kids getting into trouble with the police has dropped dramatically. One in five of the 1968 generation admitted falling fall of the law. But only 13 per cent of today's youngsters say they have ever clashed with cops." (The People, August 10, 2008)

Nevertheless, the rest of media ignored these dramatic and positive findings and continued to cherry pick statistics to alarm and bludgeon the British public. An IPSOs/MORI study in 2006 found that 71% of media stories about young people were negative and a third of articles concerned the issue of crime (Insos MORI, Attitudes Towards Teenagers and Crime. London: 2006).

The impact of mass media's barrages of ephebiphobic, anti-adolescent propaganda is palpable. The Institute for Public Policy Research (IPPR) in 2011 claimed that more than 1.5 million Britons had considered moving home because of young people "hanging around" their neighbourhood.

The IPPR also reported that British adults were twice as likely as German adults to cross the road when they encountered teenagers committing anti-social behaviour. (The Independent 22nd September 2011)

Eight years later, in 2019, The Guardian newspaper carried a headline: *"Rising Youth Crime Reflects Wider Social Problems"* and included letters from a Member of Parliament and representatives of organisations working with young people. However, the UK Ministry of Justice youth crime report for the year ending March 2019 demonstrated that youth crime was massively decreasing:

"There were just over 60,200 arrests of children (aged 10-17) by the police in England and Wales...This has decreased by 77% over the last ten years, with a decrease of 5% in the last year....

"Around 8,600 youth cautions were given to children in England and Wales. This is a decrease of 91% compared with the year ending March 2009, with a decrease of 23% in the last year."
(https://assets.publishing.service.gov.uk/government/uploads/system /uploads/attachment_data/file/862078/youth-justice-statistics-bulletin-march-2019.pdf)

The British government's Youth Justice Board highlighted the huge drop in recorded youth offences over the decade 2010-2019.

- The number of children who received a caution or sentence had fallen by 82% over the last ten years.
- The number of arrests was 74% lower than the year ending March 2010.
- The number of first-time entrants had fallen by 84% since the year ending December 2009.
- In the year ending March 2020, there were just under 49,100 proven offences committed by children which resulted in a caution or sentence in court. This was a fall of 75% from the year ending March 2010.
- There were around 24,600 children proceeded against at court in the year ending March 2020, a fall of 76% compared to ten years ago.
- There were just under 16,900 occasions where children were sentenced in all courts in the latest year, which was 78% lower than ten years previously.

In the year ending March 2020, there was an average of just over 780 children in custody at any one time. This was a reduction of 68% from ten years ago.

Ministry of Justice-Youth Justice Board, Youth Justice Statistics 2019/20)

Of course, there are those who try to dismiss such statistics, claiming that much crime is not reported, that figures may reflect a decline in police numbers or a massive rise in ability or willingness to report crimes but that only proves the point of the disingenuity of the media and government in their attempts to shape public attitudes using trumped up "facts" and may also tell the story of a major disconnect between the public and the law enforcement agencies.

Critically, despite British media and government's nationwide and decade long clamour about the 'epidemic' of teenage knife crime, young deaths from knife crime, tragic as they are, still stand at less than half the levels reached in the 'Swinging Sixties' over 50 years ago... when many in the government, the media owners and judiciary were in their teens.

Rogan's 2021 review of media coverage as against government statistics on youth crime concluded: *"...contemporary media and political representations of youth crime in England and Wales, were highly unbalanced, unsubstantiated, and unjustified particularly between 2008 to 2018 when contrasted with figures on youth crime reported by the UK MOJ & YJB (2019) showing a decline."* (Rogan, The Demonisation of Delinquency Media 2021 https://impactjournal.qub.ac.uk)

This prevailing media and government narrative of unruly adolescents was notably contradicted during the 2020 UK pandemic, a year characterised by youth led protests especially about their treatment. The main anti-racist Black Lives Matters marches were triggered and led by teenage Black youth. The school students marched over their school grades, the students protested about their incarceration in university halls of residence and went on rent strike over their fees.

All this was at a time when much of adult society was locked down at home. The big cities were empty save for the essential workers and the youth. For months on end, the youth all but had the deserted city centres to themselves. There was no looting, no scene of mass violence. Indeed, when the youth took to the deserted city streets in their tens of thousands during the illegal Black Lives Matters marches not a pain of glass was broken, and this despite cases of heavy-handed policing as directed by the government. If a few statues were damaged it represented a highly political act against provocative symbols implying White supremacy and glorifying those who profited from the cruel and barbaric slave trade.

South Africa

A bloodier more violent tale of youth in protest occurred in the young people's battles with South Africa's White racist brutal apartheid regime in the latter part of the 20th century. History records the hugely important role that school-age children played in combatting apartheid and eventually overthrowing the regime. In action, on the streets and in the schools and colleges, the youth heroically asserted their 'citizenship'; the right to a say in their lives.

If those who actively forge the creation of a new state are considered to be legitimate members of its citizenry then South Arica's young people and the youth of the post war colonial revolutions have a clear-cut case for inclusion. The heroic long-running role of the youth in the South African political revolution deserves particular attention. During the many years that Mandela was in prison, hundreds of thousands of school-aged children took to the streets in battles against the apartheid regime when the state's sheer brutality deterred others from raising their voices. Tens of thousands of these youth were incarcerated and tortured and several thousand met their deaths at the hands of the security forces.

In 2011, Bray and Moses, in Children and Participation in South Africa: Exploring the Landscape, offered a brief summary of the role of the "children" in the struggle against apartheid:

"The prominent position of children in South African history owes much to their leadership of resistance during the peak of apartheid's repressive regime. Guided by struggle politics, on June 16 1976 school children in Soweto marched in protest against government's insistence that all lessons be taught in Afrikaans (neither the first or second language of these nor the vast majority of South Africa's children). The South African Minister of Bantu Education and Development, MC Botha, issued a decree in 1974 that made the use of Afrikaans as a medium of instruction in black schools compulsory from Standard 5 onwards [from the last year of primary school to the last year of high school]. ([http://africanhistory.about.com/od/ apartheid/a/AfrikaansMediumDecree.htm](http://africanhistory.about.com/od/apartheid/a/AfrikaansMediumDecree.htm)).

"The African Teachers Association launched a campaign against the policy, but the authorities implemented it anyway. The government responded with bullets, injuring 220 children and killing 23. Outraged, children and adults across the country took to the streets and over 500 children were killed in clashes that year (Truth and Reconciliation Commission, 1998).

"Children's involvement in active resistance to apartheid continued into the 1990s, gaining momentum after 1984. They confronted illegitimate government structures in their immediate environment by rejecting Bantu education and instituting boycotts of school, rent for municipal housing, and consumer goods purchased in white-owned stores. They also attacked municipal beer halls in protest against their fathers spending money on alcohol, money that swelled government coffers.

"The government and its allies responded with uncompromising brutality According to the Truth and Reconciliation Commission Report (1998):

All the available figures indicate that the largest number of children and youth was detained between 1985 and 1989, during the two states of emergency. Of 80,000 detentions, 48,000 were detainees under the age of twenty-five.

"In the popular imagination during the struggle, youth came to be regarded in polar opposite terms as at once 'heroes' (of the liberation struggle) and 'villains' (violent, threatening and uncontrolled). The heroic

image of South Africa's urban youth was founded on their prominent role in leading resistance to apartheid. ....

"In the years since the advent of formal democracy in South Africa, anecdotal evidence and media reports suggest that public protest has persisted sporadically as a mechanism for children's participation in matters of public concern. Over the last few years, there have been several reports of learners protesting publicly over school governance issues. The response by schools has generally been heavy handed, and the reactions of teachers and parents suggest that in democratic South Africa this form of engagement by children is becoming increasingly delegitimized, especially where the concerns of children are not shared by (powerful) adults." (Children and Participation in South Africa: Exploring the Landscape, Bray & Moses, - in Education for Participatory Democracy: a Grade R Perspective: Perspectives in Education, Volume 29, 2011)

The youth were lauded as the revolution's heroes and heroines. Yet, with apartheid abolished and Mandela freed, the youth were re-infantilised and denied the dignity of the citizenship and 'freedom' that their role in the creation of the new society clearly merited.

In the same anthology, Henderson, Pendlebury and Tisdall's *Theorising Children's Participation: Trans-disciplinary Perspectives from South Africa* pointedly highlights this historic contradiction:

"In South Africa, for example, the first democratically elected state established in 1994 emerged out of the highly politicised 1980s in which children and young people played a seminal public role in resisting the apartheid state. With a sense of urgency in creating a 'normal' society there emerged in public discourse a capitulation to the normative. Generations and genders were called upon to resume their so-called 'proper places'. This was a process that infantilised children. Their vulnerabilities were emphasised and calls for increasing protection were linked to a desire for moral regeneration within the society. Ironically, the latter processes marked movement towards a place of conservatism. The visibility of children and young people in public spaces decreased. There was shrinkage of space of children's informal participation in political

space and the emergence of uneven and sparse arenas for their formal participation in processes of governance and policy formation."

(Theorising Children's Participation: Trans-Disciplinary Perspectives from South Africa, Henderson, Pendlebury and Tisdall, in Education for Participatory Democracy: a Grade R Perspective: Perspectives in Education, Volume 29, 2011)

Hence as the new South African state modelled itself on the prevailing capitalist democracies, the youth were remarginalized and effectively disenfranchised. From being hounded off the streets because of the colour of their skin, they now find themselves dispersed because of their adolescence. From being denied a say because of their colour they are now denied a say on account of their age.

Those looking for a more modern analogy to societal attitudes to young people, should also consider the media and government treatment of immigrants. Needed by employers as a ready pool of cheap labour, governments and much of the mass media nevertheless portray immigrants as a threat to the rest of the population and denigrate them to the extent that the rest of the workforce becomes oblivious to the miserable wages and working and housing conditions migrants are forced to accept.

Where teenagers are concerned, official society acts like truth and respect are dispensable and secondary to the need for suppression. The parallel with colonial rule and immigration is complete.

Similarly, regarding the colonial people and foreign migrant families, there is no indication that any government ministers or mass media moguls give any consideration to the impact on adolescents' mental health of the ephebiphobic attacks raining down on them. Sharma and Agarwala writing on collective self-esteem (where the individuals broaden their view of self to their being part of a group e.g. ethnic minority, team, gang etc) point to evidence by Trung Lam and others that show: *"positive mental health such as life satisfaction and well-being of an individual is strongly predicted by collective self-esteem."*

(Self-Esteem and Collective Self-Esteem Among Adolescents, Sharma, & Agarwala 2015, Dayalbagh University, India)

Adolescents' Collective Grievance Expressed

Adolescents' sense of collective grievance and oppression found a willing outlet through the popular music industry which thrived off a profitable market, pushing out music tracks highlighting the teenage condition. Much of this grievance came through in the songs' lyrics and have repeatedly returned to the same emphatic themes for decades.

In her 1961 song, "Don't Treat Me Like a Child", Helen Shapiro captured the basics of adolescent angst:

"Well just because I'm in my teens and I still go to school

Don't think that I dream childish dreams. I'm nobody's fool

Don't mother me that makes me wild. And please don't treat me like a child

It's often said that youngsters should be seen and not be heard

But I want you to realise that is quite absurd

Don't wanna be so meek and mild so please don't treat me like a child

Gonna be my own adviser 'cause my minds my own

Then I will be much the wiser. My own point of view has got to be known."

Here are just a few of the most overt track titles with the musicians that made them popular over the last six decades and more.

I'm Not a Teenage Delinquent, Frankie Lymon (1956)

Don't Treat Me Like a Child, Helen Shapiro (1961)

My Generation, The Who (1965)

To Be Young, Gifted and Black, Bob & Marcia (1970)

Talking the Teenage Language, The Lost Generation (1971)

Teenage Revolution, HELLO (1974)

Teenage Lobotomy, The Ramones (1977)

Bored Teenagers, The Adverts (1978)

Teenage Kicks, The Undertones (1978)

Germ-Free Adolescents, X-Ray Spex (1978)

Smells Like Teen Spirit, Nirvana (1991)

Young Offender, Pet Shop Boys (1993)

Teenage Dirtbag, Girls Aloud (2006)

Here's to Never Growing Up April Lavigne (2013)

Seventeen Forever, Metro Station (2008)

Angry Young Men, All Good Things (2016)

How many teenagers who lapped up these tracks in their rooms, on dance floors and in concert halls found solace in them is uncertain but the tracks reflected a sense of fighting off self-loathing uniquely imposed on their generation by society. There is no other generation in the West at least that can identify its unique collective pain.

The Teenage Pressure Cooker

One thing is certain is that society will pay a bigger price than ever if it continues to suppress its offspring, its youth. The pressure cooker that is being applied to adolescents and the delay to their expectations may explode. The post war period was marked by the huge social and political rebellions that broke out across the globe on the 1960s and 1970s. Most people of the era recall the swinging sixties, the Hippies, the Yippies and mass marches against war and racism. However, there were also vast national armed uprisings of young people determined to get the yoke of colonialism off their backs. Young workers, peasants, young soldiers and young students sacrificed their lives fighting for a better world.

Earlier, a group of young teenagers in the residential care of Standon Farm, an English approved school and driven to despair by their treatment, rebelled taking up arms which resulted in the shooting dead of one of the staff. It was a warning that largely went unnoticed but it is no accident that the 1968 film, "If", portraying a group of boarding school adolescents staging a savage insurrection and killing their staff and governors though banned by state television at the time is seen by buffs as one of the top ten British films of all time. (The 100 best British films, Time Out, October 2017)

Youth Rights or Age Discrimination?
Notably in the last 50 years since the Western world's youth rebellions of the 1960s and 1970s, whilst Western governments have donned the badge of the UN Declaration of Rights of the Child, adolescents have increasingly had their rights taken away. That women are giving birth later in life is a reflection of the declining situation facing young people with lower salaries and employment uncertainty leading to delays in leaving the parental home and in finding a suitable home to begin a family. According to the European Union, in 2017, 39% of young adults were still living in the parental home when they reached the age of 30 (European Union Statistics on Income and Living Conditions, http://appsso.eurostat.ec.europa.eu). In the UK today, 20% more 15 to 34-year-olds are living with their parents than was the case in 1995 according to statista.com. The Guardian (18th October 2020) reported that one third of single adults in the UK in their thirties were still living with their parents.

In England, teenagers have lost the right to leave school, the right to equal pay for equal work, the right to housing and equal unemployment benefit, are not considered adult until they are 18 and yet at ten years of age are considered to be of sound enough minds to face conviction for major crimes if they have been found to be involved.

In 2021, the British government set the English national minimum wage for 16- to 17-year-olds at half (52%) and for 18- to 20-year-olds at threequarters (75%) of the "adult" rate which they would have to wait another 3 years for (www.gov.uk). The excuse that employers will not take on young people unless they are cheap labour is based on the notion and prejudice that young labour is less competent, less able to deliver. There are many examples of why this is inbuilding age discrimination. A young person, for example, can have two years more experience when applying for a job in a certain field than a 30-year-old. If it is a job involving manual labour, the young person may be so much the stronger. If it is a job involving in-depth interviewing young people about their lifestyle preferences the young person may be so much more attuned. It also begs the question as to whether people who are 'over experienced' or 'over qualified' should be paid less because they might be disinterested in the job and not deliver.

The British government's Low Pay Commission, commented in its 2019 Review of the Youth Rates of the National Minimum Wage: *"21 to 24-year-old workers generally do the same work as older workers, with minimal differences in experience and productivity, particularly in low-paying sectors."* (A Review of the Youth Rates of the National Minimum Wage, 2019, Low Pay Commission). With the government setting the tone for underpaying the under 25s, the commission reported, even at the age of 21, a young person in work could only expect to earn 60% of that earned by a 30- to 50-year-old. In 2021, eleven years on from the Equality Act barring age discrimination in England, young people reaching adulthood at 18 still have to wait another five years before they have full entitlement to the government's recently introduced National Living Wage.

The excuse that employers will not tolerate higher wages is exposed by the fact that the government is itself a major employer. In the UK, the nationally and locally government funded public sector employed 5.6 million people in 2020 (Office of National Statistics, December 2020), almost one in six of people in paid work. If governments wish to be true to their statements about the living wage and human rights then the minimum wage should be a right not an age privilege, and be the absolute minimum paid to government, government contractors' and government-subsidised companies' employees whatever their age. Private sector companies would be pressured to follow suit or lose out on the recruitment of vibrant young workers.

Many governments also operate cash benefits' top up schemes for workers with families. The UK government tops up the wages of workers with families out of recognition that the employers are not paying them sufficient to live on. Governments could equally apply the same to the national living wage with a non-means-tested cash benefit payments to all young people and covering the shortfall in the wage paid by the employer. Why do they think that a young couple at 16 need to eat less than at 30?

According to the Commission, Britain was not unique on the international scene in regard to exploiting young workers. In Europe most governments set lower minimum wages for young people. Britain came out as the worst in Western Europe. Belgium, Germany and Ireland at least offered the full adult minimum wage to young people at 18. New Zealand offers the full minimum wage at 16 whilst across the water a 16-year-old on the legal minimum wage in Australia can only expect to receive 36.8% of the adult rate. Nevertheless, there is a huge caveat to this and that is that many governments stipulating such minimum rates for young people also add a rider that they do not apply to jobs classified as apprenticeships, training, work experience or internships where rates are often much lower or allow for unpaid labour.

The same wealthy countries that have signed up to the UN rights of the child declarations against exploitation legislate regularly for the exploitation of young people in the work place. A band of psychologists and neurologists are now claiming that their research indicates that in today's world the psychology of adolescence continues to the age of 25. Nobody should be surprised, given the way Western governments have undermined the rights of young people and stripped them of the means by which to secure a reasonable independent living and be able to create a secure family home.

In effect, young people in England are legally not considered adult until they are 21 and over, a retreat from 50 years ago when the age of suffrage was reduced to 18.

Adolescents are not considered able to make decisions about who should represent them on their town council or in parliament until they are 18, but the same minors are able to sign up for the British armed forces at 15 years and seven months, whereupon they must serve for another six years. These young people will not be allowed to sign most other legal contracts or buy the most violent films or video games, purchase fireworks or get a tattoo until they are 18. The decision they made as a minor is considered reasoned enough to leave them just over two years later dying, being crippled for life or in some cases leaving behind their children. Foreign fields are littered with the blood of British teenage combatants. Yet at 16 they were not considered wise enough to place a cross on a ballot paper.

Britain's Youth Charter 2019 Legacy Manifesto

Mission:

- *Sport, culture, art and digital technology - social and human development for life*

Vision:

- *Youth and communities engaged, equipped and empowered to contribute to a 21st Century Global Society for All.*

Opportunity:

- *To invest in the potential of our 21st Century Global Citizens.*

Objectives:

- *Engage, equip and empower young people and communities to maximise their social and cultural integration and active participation.*

Values:

- *Positive happiness and fulfilment through active human and social engagement*

- *Positive mental and physical fitness for all*

- *Commitment to excellence and collaboration for all young people and communities*

- *Dignity, honesty, integrity and respect of self in all that we do*

(YC 2019 Legacy Manifesto, www.youthcharter.org)

Many governments have attempted to display a concern for young people. Aside from signing up to the UN Declaration, many have youth charters and youth commissions making lofty declarations about young people, how they should have a right to a decent future and how they should be treated. But when the European Union lists the World Scout Movement, which is run by adult scoutmasters and commissioners amongst its six most recognised European youth movements, then young people must watch out (European Youth Portal, https://europa.eu/youth/get-involved/).

Inspect the British government's Youth Charter and you will find that they are woefully short on specifics to end youth exploitation. It talks of empowerment but ignores the built-in disempowerment. The African Youth Charter and the Iberoamerican Youth Charters have lofty statements but like the British charter offer no short-term targets for specifics that will end exploitation. None of them sign up to equal pay for equal work, which is fundamental to the emancipation of young people.

The world is already beginning to witness what happens when governments and those in power refuse to take action or try to fob young people off with platitudes, dead-end consultations and enquiries. All the youth charters and commissions have stood for years declaring against racism but it took millions of youths taking to the streets and scores dying to secure any serious action by governments and businesses.

Reviewing the Black Lives Matters demonstrations in Britain and Europe, most were called by adolescents, declared illegal by many governments and boycotted by most politicians. They were not initiated by political, trade union or NGO leaders, by priests or cardinals; they were called by the voiceless. The structures of democracy of Western society failed the youth and the ethnic minorities and were bypassed as millions of young people marched, occupied buildings and tore down symbols of racial oppression.

What was equally noticeable was that the 2020 world anti-racist revolt occurred less than a year on from the global explosion of youth-led school and student strikes inspired by the teenager, Greta Thunberg and demanding climate change. In 2019 an estimated six million people in in 150 countries took strike action over climate change. Notably in the UK, the climate change strikes were condemned by many education chiefs and the Black Lives Matter marches were condemned by police and the leaders of the mainstream political parties.

Even the 1960s youth rebelllons against war and apartheid did not witness such a global take up of teenage led initiatives on this scale.

Faced with their issues and concerns the new generation are heading in a different direction, as forewarned in Britain's EU referendum when the young generations voted for internationalism and the elderly for separation.

It is as if the world's established political parties and governments have treated the youth with contempt, focussing instead on the fears and prejudices of the over 30s, stoking nationalism and other concerns instead of answering the real crises facing young people or dealing with the world's problems.

Millions of young people have demonstrated their preparedness to take action for a better society. Adolescence should be an exciting time of understanding the wonders of the world and applying oneself not only to enjoying those wonders but also participating in making the world a better place.

We recognise the abused who turn to self-harming, yet we have a whole society, a corporate body slashing at its adolescent offspring, lacerating, wrenching and bruising its own seed - the teenager, the painful reminder of abandoned aspirations to live in a harmoniously beautiful world and the residue of society's self-loathing. The pain is past on because it knows no other way and, as is common with self-harming, it won't get to a solution until it admits that there is a problem.

Meanwhile, society excuses itself and blames the adolescent's hormones and poor parenting rather than investigating and acknowledging the root causes within its own paranoid contradictory approach to education and child/youth development

Impact of Attacks on Self Esteem and Self Worth

"Our children are our greatest treasure. They are our future. Those who abuse them tear at the fabric of our society and weaken our nation."
Nelson Mandela, 22 November 1997.

It is striking that while the recorded Incidents of youth crime in the UK have gone down dramatically over the last two decades, that according to the Mental Health Foundation, the figures regarding young people's sense of mental wellbeing have been going in the opposite direction (Mental Health Foundation, www.mentalhealth.org.uk). Has society so crushed the spirit of adolescence that significant layers of young people have turned to self-loathing?

Beyond the overt media and government attempts to besmirch adolescents as feral would-be criminal threats to the rest of society, is the even more insidious covert portrayals of the young people as threats to each other.

The mindset is such that thousands of child psychologists, psychiatrists, medics and social workers are so focussed on the extremes or the most easily observable extremes of children's experiences that they avoid questioning the status quo. Some would justify this approach on the grounds that they must focus on "what they can change, not what they can't". This is fundamentally the same approach as the Climate-Change deniers, the economic Trickle-Down theorists and the proponents of capital punishment. It is also unfortunately the approach that is infesting the world of social science, based so heavily as the academic world is on national government and commercial funding.

The question has to be raised as to whether, in the West, governmental focus on short term political advantage and the commercial funders' focus on profits is strangling at birth any searches for societal truths that in any way challenge the commercial status quo.

In the world of parenting adolescents, the result of the social sciences' deliberations on adolescents' problems is to turn the adolescents and parents against themselves. For example, Dr Marc Bush, Chief Policy Adviser at YoungMinds, referring to the causes of depression for 14-year-old girls is quoted on the organisation's website, stating:

"We know that teenage girls face a huge range of pressures, including stress at school, body image issues, bullying, and the pressure created by social media. Difficult experiences in childhood – including bereavement, domestic violence or neglect – can also have a serious impact, often several years down the line." (https://youngminds.org.uk/blog/1-in-4-girls-are-depressed-at-age-14-new-study-reveals, 2021)

His emphasis on the negative impact of the teenager's peers (via body image, bullying and social media threats) and the extremes of domestic abuse downplays the role of nuclear family and the handling of adolescents' transition within it. The nuclear family remains sacrosanct. Instead, the youth mental health charity's chief policy advisor highlighted the negative impact of adolescents' peers in the form of body-shaming, bullying and social media... i.e. the major threat to adolescents was other adolescents.

Increasingly the media, government and child development professionals point to issues such as peer-bullying, body-shaming, social media and even youth fashion trends as the primary causes of teenage trauma. Such issues clearly have a big impact but they are very far from the whole story. The world of the peer collective has threats but it also has major benefits, which is why adolescents head there. Association time, which for young people we might usefully call socialisation time allows for collective empowerment, building self-esteem and delivering mutual support, socialisation time also builds mutual knowledge eroding prejudice and combatting bullying whilst inclusion can combat the anxieties that generate trauma.

Nevertheless, we have seen above how in schools the sphere of a young person's education described as play, playtime and school breaks continues to be undervalued. As a result, the peer collective world of young children and adolescents has been under attack for half a century as valueless time that can be replaced by time that governments consider has 'real' market value – adult-directed quantifiable learning. Experts have warned that, in cutting school breaks and playtime to a minimum, educationalists are attacking children's socialisation time, their collective world, and so potentially driving down their time for developing emotional intelligence and driving up trauma. Like the pupils wishes for longer school breaks those experts who do tell uncomfortable truths are ignored.

The long-term drive to marketise education, with the efficiency and value-added of teaching staff based on children's ability to complete examination papers, by commoditising young people, also atomises them. They must be shaped and regimented to fit the needs of the teaching establishment, so school breaks are a luxury, unregimented interaction with other children is a distraction and an administrative luxury. Marketised education of young people demands that they are atomised precisely at the time when adolescents' healthy transition to adulthood demands collective engagement and empowerment with their peers.

The dire impact on pupils' mental health of the pandemic wholesale closure of schools and subsequent isolation of young people from their friends has been much stated and globally used as the main reason for early reopening of the schools. Association and collective empowerment are fundamental to adolescent development. As previously stated, if adolescents cannot engage and find themselves valued amongst their peers, how on earth are they expected to feel sufficient self-worth and have sufficient social engagement skills to survive in the adult world?

Many scholars, consciously or otherwise, also overlook the fact that youth already often have and are benefitting from their "community" i.e. their peer collective, and one where they are over time increasingly empowered by independence from adult controls. The research of Tanti et al. in 2008 led them to conclude that there exists a significant lack of academic research of the role of peer group collective identity, self-esteem and empowerment and that this constitutes a serious weakness in understanding adolescent development.

"...our research shows that the collective aspect of a person's self, or his or her social identity, becomes increasingly important during adolescence. More specifically, the findings suggest that a person's social identity may shift from a relational focus on the family during pre-adolescence to a focus on the wider peer network during early-adolescence, with an increased incorporation of social group memberships into the collective self during late adolescence.

"Such findings suggest that the almost exclusive study of the personal identity in the adolescent developmental literature is limited."

(Tripartite Self-concept Change: Shifts in the Individual, Relational, and Collective Self in Adolescence, Tanti et al, 2008)

However, there is little indication that academic funds and research have been redirected to this area over the last decade. Indeed, given adolescence is the only generation which is the focus of such negative attention one would expect that governments and social scientists would be clamouring to organise the collection of clear auditable transparent data concerning adolescents. Yet, on an all-Britain level, at least, this is far from the case. Whether it be on crime, mental health, housing, there is no visible attempt to systematise data collection for analysis across the range of issues and assertions said to be of concern to governments and social scientists. It is ironic that 20th century UK governments probably had better data informing them about the state of the colonies than their counterparts have of adolescents in Britain today.

Meanwhile lawmakers' actions are informed without the support of a studied evidence-based analytical approach to understanding the underlying causes and the tracking of trends in behaviour, trauma etc. It leaves the question open as to whether governments consider propaganda wars against teenagers to be preferable to seeking genuine solutions to the social problems generated by their trauma.

Meanwhile Maslow's hierarchy of needs for the atomised individual continues to reign supreme. Crucially, having failed to take into account the role of adolescents' peer groups, the scholars also ignore the impact of the wholesale attacks on these peer-based communities made by governments and the mass media. There is no consideration given to the impact of denigrating and undermining these peer groups, which play a crucial role in adolescent development. Governments give free reign to the process of driving adolescents to fear and despise the very community of which they are a part. Divide and rule and propaganda designed to encourage self-loathing are tactics for dealing with one's enemies but Western ruling elites employ this approach towards their societies' children and refuse to take responsibility for their fundamental role in the process.

Acceptance as part of the collective and especially voluntary acceptance as part of a group/collective lends them a sense of value and self-worth, of being valued by their peers. It also opens the door to increased empowerment of the young person. The collective, the 'gang', the group offers the adolescent respite from the disempowered 'childish' existence of their home lives.

Nevertheless, the impact of this imbalanced corporate social messaging focussing on teenage collectives as a threat to the young people themselves, whilst benefiting those with an interest in suppressing adolescents or profiting from adolescent trauma, is to create further problems for parents and adolescents alike.

The adolescent needs to engage with peer-collectives for their development of self-worth but the parent is pressed to fear the very thing that is so vital to their personal growth. This clash often only increases the antagonisms in the adolescent's home due to parental reticence to "permit" their young person to become involved in the peer-collectives.

With the imbalanced messaging also featuring on youth media channels and in online magazines, the more pernicious impact on adolescents is the undermining of their confidence in engaging with their peer-collectives. Those peer collectives may contain threats but they are life and without engaging the young person cannot be expected to learn how to personally deal with and manage those risks. Attacking the collective self-esteem of adolescents may leave them further atomised but this goes counter to the interests of creating a harmonious society.

The horror created by the teenage mass random shooters in North America's schools and colleges is the tragic blunt end of this process. Adolescents growing up to hate themselves and hate their peers. Almost twenty years ago the study of Leary et al of mass shootings in the USA should have warned governments of the systemic damage generated by atomising teenagers. In 2003 Leary and colleagues analysed 15 cases of school shooters, and found all but two suffered from social rejection:

"Case studies were conducted of 15 school shootings between 1995 and 2001 to examine the possible role of social rejection in school violence. Acute or chronic rejection—in the form of ostracism, bullying, and/or romantic rejection—was present in all but two of the incidents. In addition, the shooters tended to be characterized by one or more of three other risk factors—an interest in firearms or bombs, a fascination with death or Satanism, or psychological problems involving depression, impulse control, or sadistic tendencies" (Teasing, Rejection, and Violence: Case Studies of the School Shootings, Leary, Kowalski, Smith & Phillips, Aggressive Behaviour, 2003)

An alternative approach would be to encourage the empowerment of peer collectives which would give them the confidence to tackle the causes of their trauma rather than hide from them. But this, of course, would have potentially longer-term unsettling consequences for those controlling the current social order.

This teenage-peer-threat propaganda completes an oppressive circle; teenagers are not only a threat to adults but also to themselves. Again, the approach is very reminiscent to that with which the British Empire ruled its African and Asian colonies. The only other time we hear this language applied to social groups is when talk is made of the criminal fraternity.

Teenage is Trauma

In a society reporting huge drops in adolescent crime rates, one would be excused for considering that this reflected an increased sense of wellbeing amongst Britain's young people. However, the statistics indicate that for a significant layer at least, the opposite appears to be the case with the stresses and strain leading to increased self-harming, hospital admissions and suicides.

In 2018 the Mental Health Foundation reported a steady rise in the proportion of young people reported to be suffering from "mental health disorders", especially anxiety and depression and with a higher propensity regarding those in late adolescence:

"The last survey, conducted in 2004, found that 1 in 10 children aged 5-15 had a mental health disorder (either emotional, behavioural, hyperactive, or other). In the newly released 2017 figures, this has risen to 1 in 9... When we include older children and look across all children and young people aged 5-19, we find that 1 in 8 (12.8%) have at least one mental disorder.... This change was largely driven by an increase in emotional disorders (including anxiety and depression), which for 5-15-year-olds rose from 3.9% in 2004 to 5.8% in 2017." (How Many Children Have Mental Health Problems? Mental Health Foundation 2018)

The Guardian in 2021 reported that the number of children aged nine to 12 admitted to hospital having hurt themselves intentionally rose from 221 in 2013-14 to 508 in 2019-20. The same article also reported that the rate of self harm amongst young people doubled in the six years to 2020. (Sarah Marsh, 16 Feb 2021, The Guardian, UK)

Meanwhile Public Health England (Public Health England, Children and Young People's Mental Health and Wellbeing, March 2020) reported that between 2012/13 and 2018/19, the self harm admissions' rate for females aged 10 to 24 rose from 508 per 100,000 population to 690 per 100,000 population – an increase of 36% though the rate for males remained roughly constant at around 200 admissions per 100,000 population.

Suicides in England and Wales of 10–14-year-olds in 2019 reached an historic high, whilst the number of 15 to 19-year-olds committing suicide almost doubled between 2010 and 2019 to get back to their late 20th century levels. (Young People's Wellbeing: Research Report, October 2019, Department for Education)

This picture is grim but only a reflection of the level of the problem. Nonetheless they highlight the intense pressures, social and societal stress that society as a whole is placing on adolescents. Some professionals in the psychological field promote the notion that traumatic stress only relates to the witnessing of, or exposure to extreme or potentially life-threatening events (e.g. American Psychological Association, https://www.apa.org/topics/trauma).

This concept can be extremely misleading and may reflect only those professional services that are on offer rather than the experience of those suffering from trauma. However, if we take extreme events to mean abuse in its many hideous forms and take the Blackfoot tribe's hierarchical needs, then we can begin to focus on society's macro failings to provide safe spaces for young people and primarily the impact of government-led stigmatisation and discrimination with its clinging on to childism and notions of the family that have outlived their usefulness.

As Britain's foremost mental health charity, Mind, stresses: "*What's traumatic is personal,*" in other words only the individual can know how they feel about their experiences and which they found to be traumatic. The generic trauma experienced by adolescence is an interpersonal trauma, which may be placed on top of having experienced or witnessed extreme events, psychological, sexual or physical abuse. However, in understandably focussing on the latter aspects, the professional can lose sight of the much more societally uncomfortable issues which challenge the beatification of the nuclear family.

Mind makes the point that trauma can be induced in several scenarios including:

- *"Living in a traumatic atmosphere*

- *Being affected by trauma in a family or community*

- *If you've been harassed, bullied or discriminated against."*

(https://www.mind.org.uk/information-support/types-of-mental-health-problems/trauma/about-trauma)

All these factors can describe aspects of the adolescent experience within the family and societal setting. Notably, the experience of being harassed, bullied, discriminated against or having one's identity challenged are also very pertinent expressions of how adult society treats teenagers as a whole. The intense government and media propaganda aimed at encouraging support for the adult surveillance, patrolling and discipling of adolescence, by focussing on adolescents as a threat not only to society but to other teenagers, poisons the very well of collective empowerment from which they draw their self-esteem and shape their identity. By raising the bogey of their teenage peers, government and media devalue adolescents in other adolescents' eyes and set the tone for self-doubt, self-loathing and peer-loathing.

Research shows how in early adolescence, young people's attendance at their new school triggers social stress. They are challenged as to how they will cope with their new peer groups. By raising the threat of other teenagers, adult society only increases the prospects of social stress for these young adolescents, adding a liberal dose of unwarranted societal stress.

The youth are driven to develop a split identity, burying each to suit the changing needs of coping with his/her environment. Adolescents are driven to alienation by that inability to identify their true self - a self continually battered by the contrasting pressures brought about by the siloing of their private and public life by walls as forbidding as those of the ancient ghettoes. Forced into this compartmentalisation, they live double lives becoming doubly alienated both from their home self and their school self. They duck and dive to cope with the different realities and the differing expectations of those that rule their alternate worlds.

In this context, it is hardly surprising that the USA's National Institute for Mental Health, list of early warning signs of psychosis, reflects the portrayal of many adolescents:

- *"Worrisome drop in grades or job performance*

- *New trouble thinking clearly or concentrating*

- *Suspiciousness, paranoid ideas or uneasiness with others*

- *Withdrawing socially, spending a lot more time alone than usual*

- *Unusual, overly intense new ideas, strange feelings or having no feelings at all*

- *Decline in self-care or personal hygiene*

- *Difficulty telling reality from fantasy*

- *Confused speech or trouble communicating."*

(https://www.nimh.nih.gov/health/topics/schizophrenia/raise/fact-sheet-early-warning-signs-of-psychosis.shtml)

The above reflects how close to the edge society finds its adolescents. Adolescence is years of what some term as interpersonal trauma. It is no random accident that so many combust at 15, opting out of attempting further meaningful dialogue with parents and teachers alike about their personal situation. Many others learn to live in a dual world, hiding truths from their incomprehensible parents or acting like prisoners, only leaving their cells to be fed or take exercise.

So, society uses othering and labelling to explain away the symptoms of this trauma, describing the young person as *"just being a teenager"* until, that is, the crisis breaks the boundaries. Thereupon the young person becomes a 'yob', the defendant or a patient.

Sadly, in the UK this process is borne out by those statistics at hand.

Mental Health First Aid (MHFA) England claimed that in the UK

- Half of mental ill health starts by age 15 and 75% develops by age 18

- About 10% of young people aged 8-15 experience a low sense of wellbeing with rates much higher amongst the teenage years

- Up to 25% of teenagers have experienced physical violence in their intimate partner relationships

The MHFA painted a saddening picture of the average English classroom where the children will be experiencing all the strains of adolescent life and on top of that:

- 10 children will have witnessed their parents separate,

- 8 will have experienced severe physical violence, sexual abuse or neglect,

- 1 will have experienced the death of a parent

- 7 will have been bullied

(Mental Health Statistics 15/10/2020 https://mhfaengland.org/mhfa-centre/research-and-evaluation/mental-health-statistics/)

In its 2020 report of its longitudinal study of those born in the UK during the year 2000, University College London painted a stark picture of the mindset of modern youth with almost a quarter (24%) of 17-year-olds reporting self-harming and one in 14 (7%) attempting suicide, reflecting the tip of the iceberg of adolescent trauma.

The authors of the report placed their findings in the context of reported widespread increases in adolescents experiencing mental health problems and find that these appear to increase for those in their mid-teens:

"24% of young people report self-harming and 7% report self-harming with suicidal intent by age 17.... Increasing rates of mental health difficulties in this generation have been reported consistently, with very high prevalences of common mental health difficulties reported in large school-based and population-based studies to date. This report highlights that these increasing prevalences are also present for more severe indicators of mental illness, including self-harm, and self-harm with suicidal intent. At age 14, around 16% of cohort members reported self-harming ever, and now at age 17 the 12-month prevalence of self-harm is almost 26%, highlighting large increases in the short span of three years in mid-adolescence." (Mental Ill-Health at 17, University College London, 2020)

Adolescents in Corporate Residential Settings

Content

In previous chapters it has been argued that capitalism's development and capitalist property relations' growing contradictions with the needs of the modern nuclear family are a major contribution to adolescent trauma. This chapter considers how taking young people out of the nuclear family settings impacts on their transition through adolescence. It looks at the peer collective empowerment in Boarding School and Orphanage/Children's Home environments and how this impacts on management practices. We discuss the removal of the many negotiation stages involved in the adolescent transition.

The Corporate Orphan World, Empowerment and Disempowerment

We have discussed how capitalism's development and capitalist property relations' growing contradictions with the needs of the modern nuclear family are a major contribution to adolescent trauma. We consider how taking young people out of the nuclear family settings impacts on their transition through adolescence.

Initial reactions to discussions concerning the difficulties and stresses imposed on the family and parenting by capitalistic social relations, are often that it is the family and parents that are the problem rather than the contradiction between capitalism and the family, between capitalism and parenting. This is an understandable defensive mechanism whereby parents in particular reach out to consider what else they could have done to become better parents. The answer may be very little. Given all the pressures of modern life, most parents try their hardest to raise their children to take their place as adults in the world. This chapter considers whether parenting in corporate settings offers any clues as to the previously highlighted issues regarding family parenting of adolescents.

Part of my fortune of being "corporately parented" (as care was labelled in the 1990s) was to experience its collectivity – of being treated as part of a collective and acting collectively.

My mother had handed me over at birth to the Barnardo's children's charity. In doing so she had to sign a standard form giving her agreement to the charity bringing me up as it saw fit. When she transferred her property rights to Barnardo's Homes, I became corporate property and part of a notional collectivity of thousands of children, and later a part of the collectivity of children in each orphanage I passed through.

In The Golly, I referred to the collective aspects of our life in the Southport orphanages. Whilst we had by no means suffered the deprivations and horror of Anna Freud's orphaned Bulldog Bank's children (reference An Experiment in Group Upbringing, Anna Freud & Sophie Dann, 1951), some of the behavioural similarities were striking, we:

- had little knowledge of our parents

- had been moved around a lot

182

- had few opportunities to form attachments with ever-changing temporary caregivers

- endured basic living conditions

- often showed each other great warmth and care and nurtured our younger ad hoc siblings

- Only turned to adults for permissions and to request items that were unavailable to us.

We often stole together, played together, journeyed together, attacked together, defended together, suffered together. For many years, we were an ever-replenished gang and experienced its empowerment. I wrote that, as an eleven-year-old, one of my advantages over the other newbies when arriving at my large grammar school was that: "*I was already institutionalised, already used to fitting my individualism into the needs of an authoritarian system.*"

I hoped readers would see that I had qualified what I meant by institutionalisation, as being used to spending time as part of a large institution rather than the looser use of the term when applied to individuals. The online Cambridge Dictionary explains institutionalisation in the following pejorative manner: "*If someone becomes institutionalized, they gradually become less able to think and act independently, because of having lived for a long time under the rules of an institution.*" (Cambridge Dictionary, https://dictionary.cambridge.org)

It is not hard to show the sloppy, unscientific and prejudicial nature of this statement. How did this work traditionally for Oxbridge university undergraduates a a majority of whom would have spent most of their childhood living in boarding schools?

We will discuss below how the British state, which has closed down so many English orphanages, still funds places for children in care at boarding schools because of the lack of residential children's homes and foster placements.

When any organisation uses drugs, acute sensory deprivation, brainwashing and abuse it can erode the ability to think and act independently. Tied down to a bed for years, the leg muscles will lose strength and forget the ability to walk. As Goffman pointed out in Asylums, his celebrated 1961 essays on institutionalisation in psychiatric hospitals, the inmates' mortification of self and consequential loss of identity was not brought about simply by incarceration. The key driver was the accompanying physical and social abuse. (Asylums: Essays on the Condition of the Social Situation of Mental Patients and Other Inmates, 1961 Erving Goffman)

The greatly misused term "institutionalisation" was and remains an excuse for bad management. Living in an institution with large groups of people does not of itself reduce their capacity to act or think, isolating them in single cells twenty-four seven and plying them with Ritalin might.

On the contrary it could be argued that when children are herded together and treated as corporate property rather than being left as atomised private property in the nuclear family, the very collective and more stable behavioural boundaries involved in the corporate and collective experience increases empowerment of the young person enabling them to think more clearly and more boldly. They may be more able to think independently and rationally because of the relative freedom and rationality offered by the collective.

Significant aspects of the above and below observations regarding orphanages also apply to the boarding (public) schools that were used to educate the children of the rich and the upper middle class. Adolescents in both these care settings enjoyed a much lower degree of regime change compared to their parented peers who attended day schools.

The advantage, which I had when entering secondary school in being accustomed to an institutionalised setting, was not only being used to the setting but also a greater experience of operating in a group or collective and an understanding of the benefits and accommodating within the collective setting. I enjoyed time spent with children of my own age but

I had also learned, at close quarters, to live, benefit and learn from much older adolescents and got used to nurturing children younger than I, all in a mixed sex environment and with young people from a variety of backgrounds. Added to which, I was burdened with no sense of academic expectation imposed by my carers and no sense of responsibility to them.

The lack of academic expectation in the orphanages accompanied the freedom from close complex emotional bonds between the staff and the young people. The corporate approach left little to be renegotiated with our carers during adolescence. We each day left for our new secondary schools leaving behind our carers who displayed no more anxieties regarding how we would fare in our changing world than before. We simply switched one corporate world for another.

As I wrote in The Golly: *"I experienced the adult world around me like a place on Earth experiences the Sun, which sets the rules, tolerates no objectors and is arbitrary in its temper. The Sun holds both the power to provide and to pleasure, and the strength to destroy and punish. Like primitive man with the Sun, I knew something of the adult world around me, and its effect, but understood little of its laws. If primitives worshipped the Sun, so I grudgingly bowed down to the wolves and other adults in my life in order to secure my passage."*

The disadvantage of my institutionalised upbringing was not a product of the institution but its management. As a teenager, I used to consider that I had an 'inferiority complex'. I didn't quite understand the roots but we were conditioned to feel inferior and unwanted. We understood that we lived as a courtesy of others' charitable donations and should be grateful. We were chided for our ingratitude and on more than one occasion informed that we were the worst behaved children of all the country's orphanages. We weren't told that Barnardo's were paid by the government to look after us or that there were homes where there were full scale riots. To compound this, I was Black and my father deemed a 'savage' in a very, very White sleepy seaside resort in racist post war Britain.

In my care files (but notably not in my school reports), I was referred to as having a chip on my shoulder regarding being in care i.e. I resented being in care. Having a 'chip on one's shoulder' was a term used then to refer to someone with a deep rooted angry and potentially violent resentment regarding their situation. It was a term commonly used in reference to Black people and sometimes twinned with 'inferiority complex'.

White professionals would refer to a Black person as 'having a chip on their shoulder' about being Black and, as such, inferior. In reality that chip was about being treated as inferior, disrespected and disempowered for the colour of one's skin. In my teenage years, my chip focussed on my experience as a Black person. I had internalised, and so could not get a clear view of the more pervasive constant demeaning treatment that we were suffering at the hands of those managing our care.

That sense of inferiority was the general experience of teenagers in orphanages. Bad management sought to devalue us and the value of our words. This allowed them, at best, excuses for poor management and, at its most heinous, cover for their exploitative and abusive behaviour. Our stigmatisation was needed by the abusers to use as a counterweight against our collective will and testimonies.

The orphanage charities commodified us children. We were the capital they traded on for an income from the government and the philanthropic middle classes. They were happy for us to sing Christmas carols to the governors but desperate to denigrate the truth in our young voices. We were plagued with Original Sin. They had saved us from the gutter but swore the gutter remained within us and expected that we would return there. At best we were worthy of going on to become domestic servants, labourers, factory hands or military fodder. Minimised expectations allowed for minimal investment in our upbringing. They perpetuated and needed our inferiority complexes.

The apparent economic and managerial benefits of treating us children, the corporate property, as a collective, laid the basis of our collectivity.

Within the maze of corporate property, we found the crannies where we could hide away and enjoy our freedoms – in the dormitories, in the leafy grounds, in the parks, on the beach and on the streets. This collectivity gave us a level of empowerment. If we couldn't deal with the various forms of abuse in the orphanage, together on the streets we could harass and chase down the flasher who exposed himself to our young girls, we could defend each other and look out for each other. We had one another to play with and to protect.

We were a gang and as such empowered. Much modern literature treats youth gangs as threats. Yet many of these gangs offer precisely the types of experience of operating in collectives that adult society has to offer. The threat is that such collectives of youth may involve greater adherence to their rules as opposed to those of the gesellschafts. Not by any means all of these impacts are centred on criminal intent. Nevertheless, even those that may be described as criminal, as collectives, offer a gateway to some of the routes to self-esteem to which adolescents aspire.

Maclure and Sotelo's 2004 conclusions of their research into Nicaraguan youth involvement in gangs underscore the role not only of gangs but also of adolescent peer group collectives. The reader is invited here to replace the words "gang membership" with those of "peer group" to see how important such collectives are for young people.

"As all our youth respondents indicated, gang membership allows them to 'fit' in with a community of peers. It provides them with feelings of stability and confidence that they are unable to attain in other ways. Excluded from mainstream social institutions, and having no obvious prospects for personal fulfilment as defined by a dominant middle-class discourse in Nicaragua, they have opted for gang membership as a way to attain a positive social identity and a semblance of control over their lives. The gang provides them with a social framework through which they can construct who it is they are in relation to their peers and to the larger social system. By facilitating their participation in collective activities oriented towards the specific ends of status and power, gangs help to augment

youth self-esteem. At the same time, however, these young people are aware that there is a price to be paid for gang membership.

"In making the decision to join gangs, most youth recognize that they have placed themselves in overt opposition to dominant social institutions. Yet in the absence of resources and other choices, it is gang membership that offers them the social bonding and support that they ardently desire." (Youth Gangs in Nicaragua: Gang Membership as Structured Individualization- Richard Maclure, Melvin Sotelo, Journal of Youth Studies Vol. 7, No. 4, 2004)

Brotherton and Barrios in their 2004 study of gang life in the USA were even more explicit, emphasising the empowerment aspect. They defined a gang as:

"A group formed by young people and adults belonging to marginalized social classes, which provides its members the construction of an identity of resistance, an opportunity for individual and social empowerment, a voice of challenge to the dominant culture, a refuge from the tensions and pressures of daily life of the neighborhood or ghetto, as well as a spiritual enclave where sacred rituals can be generated and exercised." (The Almighty Latin King and Queen Nation, Brotherton & Barrios, 2004: 23)"

They highlight the young people's very real sense of empowerment especially contrasting with their disorienting domestic experience of being doubly disempowered; being disempowered within a disempowered family unit (A Decade of Gang Research: Findings of the National Institute of Justice Gang Portfolio, Scott H. Decker University of Missouri–St. Louis 2002).

Numerous revelations from many survivors and staff who passed through the post-war orphanages illustrated how the fear of the power that we young people could exert as a collective was a major factor in management using physical, psychological and sexual abuse as a counterweight. This was notably a tactic more common to war zones, humiliating and disempowering communities in occupied territories.

In society as a whole, it was common for the media to refer to young people in care as "yobs" and so justifying repressive measures. Even the supposedly polite language of referring to us young people as "troubled children" carried a huge stigmatisation permissioning repression.

When they feared the power of the young people, they sought to terrorise and atomise us. Hence the establishment's response to the widespread revelations of abuse in the orphanages was to close them. If they couldn't manage collectives of youth by repression, they turned to atomising the children by sending them into the relative secrecy and isolation of foster care, and very much out of the public eye.

The common recurring trait to condemn youth gangs per se reflects parallel continuing societal attempts to disempower, whip into line and chain down young people as mentioned earlier in the chapter on the societal oppression of adolescents. The chapter referred to 2003 when, the British Labour government introduced anti-social behaviour legislation giving the courts and police special discriminatory powers to control young people to the background of media claims of rising youth and gang crime. In 2004, Hallsworth and Young pointed out the fallacy. Violent crime was declining and that there was no evidence of rising gang crime. Instead, they argued, the conflation of collectives of youth on the street and violent crime gangs was disingenuous on the part of the media and state. They wrote:

"...before we see in the gang menace a 'cause' of contemporary crime, it pays to put the problem into perspective. A key problem in attempting to do so is that the notion of a 'gang' is terribly permissive. It can be evoked in so many ways that delineating what is and what is not one remains problematic. When is a group of young men not a gang? Does it apply only when they are poor? If so, are the 'gang-like' qualities observed conferred or self ascribed? And just how many crimes do not involve group activity of some kind? Are the groups also gangs and if not why not? And if we want to firm matters up by arguing that, by gang, we mean an organised group pursuing a collectively agreed criminal goal, why apply the label to young people...

"More importantly we also need to be very careful about accepting the idea that when youths congregate collectively, crime and anti-social behaviour somehow emerge as a consequence. Many of the problems posed by groups of youths arise not because they enter into a collective that becomes immediately pathological, but derive instead from the ecology of the world in which they live." (Getting Real About Gangs, Hallsworth and Young, Centre for Crime and Justice Studies, Spring 2004)

Hallsworth and Young once again highlight how the collectivism which young people need for their development is demonised by official society. The closure of the large children's homes had more to do with fear of young people than fear of the child abusers who continued to be left free to roam society stalking other children. The British government's Home Office was busy funding the Paedophile Information Exchange while homes were being closed down and the notorious paedophiles Sir Jimmy Savile and Sir Cyril Smith to name just two were being protected from prosecution by senior government officials.

Adolescent Development at Boarding Schools

Given the Mystery Wall highlights how the adolescent is on a daily basis confronted with the contrasting and in many ways contradictory rather than complimentary learning settings of the atomised nuclear family and corporate collective schooling, it is reasonable to ask whether those residing away from their parents in residential or boarding schools benefit from a more consistent learning environment.

Background to Boarding Schools

Boarding schools are common across large swathes of the world and particularly for children's high school years. Focussing mainly on the boarding schools of Britain, Australia and the USA, Australia has around 170 boarding schools and the USA over 300.

The UK currently has around 500 boarding schools taking in some 70,000 pupils or 1% of the country's school age children. Around 10% of those are state run, accounting for 5,000 pupils. The rest are independent or private schools owned by a mixture of trusts, charities etc. Pre-pandemic, the private boarding schools were facing something of an identity crisis with foreign pupils accounting for over 40% of all boarders. Reporting average annual fees now at £35,000 per pupil and public apprehension over private boarding schools, the Financial Times, mouth of the British financial world, commented: "...*many of the pupils that made up their bread and butter - the middle- or upper-middle-class children of doctors, lawyers or other professionals, can no longer afford to board full-time.*" (Financial Times 25th October, 2019)

At the same time, the high percentage of foreign, and especially Chinese pupils, was claimed to be cutting into middle class perceptions of the schools offering a traditionally "British" boarding school education, added the Financial Times (ibid.). The paper quoted the case of a German family quizzing their child as to why his command of English had barely improved after a year of boarding in the UK. The boy's answer was said to be that he shared a room with three Chinese boys.

Meanwhile, the popularity of state-run boarding schools has increased with state schools offering paid boarding places for £10000 to £16000 a year whilst the educational aspect of their school stay is paid for by the state. The rise of such establishments catering for the adolescent age range is said to be for practical reasons such as "difficult family situations" but is also soaking up much of the middle-class defection from the high-cost private boarding schools, hence state boarding schools are largely the preserve of the country's middle classes. As with the private boarding schools, many high earning families with both parents working opt for the assistance of collective residential care rather than the nuclear family in order to take their adolescents through their school years.

This continuing trend notably runs counter to the prejudices and stigma attached to orphanages/residential homes for young people in care. The contradiction was graphically demonstrated in 2008 when Barry Sheerman MP, as Chair of the UK Parliament's Select Committee for Children, Schools and Families launched an investigation into boarding schools claiming that residential care was damaging for young people. Sheerman at least was being consistent as this same assertion had been used by successive parliamentary committees to defend the widespread programme of closing down orphanages.

Sheerman declared: *"There is quite a body of knowledge out there that suggests taking a child away at the age of eight or 11 to a boarding school is psychologically not the wisest thing to do for their development.... Lots of people argue, and there is plenty of psychological evidence, that the best place for a child to grow up is with a supportive family - whether it is one parent or two - for their social and emotional development. I do not mean just the Tory concept of 2.4 children, but a family with people who nurture you."* (The Guardian Newspaper, May 11th 2008)

It was an argument that might work when taking away the homes of voiceless orphans but it cut little ice with the sector or the rest of the vast number of boarding school-educated Members of Parliament.

In the same Guardian article, representatives of the private school sector, however countered Sheerman arguing that he was pitching himself at a past image of boarding schools.

"Vicky Tuck, principal of Cheltenham Ladies' College and president of the Girls' Schools Association, said: 'It is important to realise we are on a journey with boarding schools and the type of schools that led to that group are gone. The sorts of damage that people experienced in the past was as a result of a very harsh regime. It is not like that today.'

"Tuck said there were some schools in the past where matrons were strict, the food unpleasant, and children were cold, hungry or abused. But she argued that Criminal Record Bureau checks and the schools' inspections regime meant that no longer happened. 'We are living in a different world,' she said, 'At Cheltenham,' Tuck said, 'girls were in daily contact with their parents by email, phone and internet links - often chatting as much as if they lived at home.'" (The Guardian Newspaper, May 11th 2008)

Sheerman's investigations were bypassed by Parliament and the boarding sector was not only left to grow but by 2018 private schools as a whole were, according to The Guardian (5th February, 2019), receiving

£200 million in direct subsidies, over £100 million in fees and £2.5 billion in tax breaks from the state.

Ironically, by 2020. there were almost as many young people staying in government funded middle class state boarding schools as there were adolescents living in 'looked after' children's residential care homes.

The offer at English boarding schools has certainly changed significantly. Amongst other significant changes, traditionally the boarding schools were single sex institutions but today a sizeable number (over 100) offer mixed gender (co-ed) education. Now long-established public schools such as Harrow are to be found selling online academic courses at around £5,000 each.

Boarding & The Mystery Wall

From what has been considered to date regarding the Mystery Wall, education and the adolescent, one might expect the residential system of schooling to offer for teenage development certain advantages to that of the day school.

Day Student Adolescent's Domestic Life	THE MYSTERY WALL	Day Student Adolescent's School Life
Parents		**Teaching Staff**
Atomised		Collectivised
Private		Corporate
Disempowerment		Peer Empowerment
Semi- structured		Structured
Unstable Environment		Stable Environment
Unstructured Learning Experience		Structured Learning Experience
Parental Language		Peer language
Psychological		Sociological
Emotionally Complex		Emotionally Simple
Inconsistent Reward System		Consistent Reward System
Unstable Punishment System		Stable Punishment System
Serfdom		Apprenticeship

In contrast, the next table, shows that in term time there is little difference between the features of a boarder's academic and residential life. Even should parents be in touch online or visiting at weekends, in terms of learning settings, the parental input is severely reduced, permitting the young person to focus on developing themselves within the context of their boarding school lives. The adolescent's opportunity and need for constant negotiation and renegotiation of permissions and status with adults are both severely reduced.

The Mystery Wall separating Boarders' Worlds

Boarding Adolescent's Parental Life	THE MYSTERY WALL	Boarding Adolescent's Boarding Life	Boarding Adolescent's Academic Life
Parents		Teaching/Care Staff	**Teaching Staff**
Atomised		Collectivised	Collectivised
Private		Corporate	Corporate
Disempowerment		Peer Empowered	Peer Empowerment
Semi- structured		Structured	Structured
Unstable Environment		Semi-structured Learning Experience	Stable Environment
Unstructured Learning Experience		Peer language	Structured Learning Experience
Parental Language		Sociological	Peer language
Psychological		Emotionally Simple	Sociological
Emotionally Complex		Stable	Emotionally Simple
Inconsistent Reward System		Consistent Reward System	Consistent Reward System
Unstable Punishment System		Stable Punishment System	Stable Punishment System
Serfdom		Apprenticeship	Apprenticeship

From this perspective there are several aspects, which may be beneficial to adolescent development.

- Primarily, adolescents in residential schools are offered the opportunity to benefit from a collectivity of their peers on a 24-hour basis. The more intense focus on peer support, empowerment and nurture, allows their self-identity and self-esteem to develop uninterruptedly as they build up peer engagement skills. They are with their peers, speaking the same language (for their age) because they are at similar levels of development and enjoying similar amusements for their age.

- Secondly, residential schooling, by taking the child out of the parental home potentially creates a more stable foundation for development by eliminating the pressure and complications facing adolescents since they no longer have to handle the daily duality of learning settings.

- The boarding of rapidly developing adolescents potentially reduces the amount of time and potential angst involved in negotiating and renegotiating permissions with parents. Instead, in the modern boarding school staff take on the pastoral "in loco parentis" but only in a professional and corporate capacity and backed by corporate behavioural rules. The psychological background noise in any negotiation of permissions is severely reduced. Additionally, the less complex psychological relationship between pastoral carers and the adolescents should allow boarders to feel they can approach staff more as counsellors than gatekeepers when discussing personal and relationship issues.

- With residential schooling, the weekly and longer periods parents and boarders spend apart offer each party more time to contemplate personal development and other issues and, by taking away the chaotic background of daily stresses, invites parents in particular to focus on enjoying productive "quality time" with their children. This should lead to better rather than worse relationships between parents and their boarded children than exist between parents and day students.

Boarding School Detractors

The detractors of residential schooling such as the above quoted Barry Sheerman MP, commonly revert to attachment theories and claim psychological damage is done to the child by taking them away from their nurturing parents. They suggest that children deprived of parental love will find themselves incapable of loving. Many also associate all residential schools with criminal toleration of child abuse.

The detractors of private boarding schools go further, arguing that such schools are elitist, filling their pupils with notions that they deserve a better position in life than the rest of their generation. British boarding schools are commonly perceived as having strong cultures of child abuse, the perpetrators being not only teaching staff but also older pupils. The result, claims psychoanalyst, Professor Joy Schaverien, is Boarding School Syndrome characterised by depression, problems with relationships and long term emotional or behavioural difficulties (Boarding School Syndrome: The Psychological Trauma of the 'Privileged" Child, Joy Schaverien, 2015).

Schaverien particularly focuses on the practice of sending young, pre-adolescent children to boarding schools. However, many of her causal factors of Boarding School Syndrome can be put down to poor management rather than the lack of presence of the young people's parents. Nevertheless, British boarding schools have over many years been the source of very serious allegations of physical, psychological and sexual child abusive practices, which blur comparative studies between boarders and day students regarding their academic and non-academic outcomes.

Boarding School Proponents

The proponents of boarding schools in the UK, such as the above quoted Principal of Cheltenham Ladies College, counter that Schaverien and the Boarding School Survivors organisation are tilting at past windmills because, they claim, the schools have changed dramatically in the last 25 years and now have much improved focus on mental health outcomes, pastoral care and safeguarding practices.

For example, in my research, I received the following practitioner's piece from a former teacher at a well-established English boarding school:

Boarding, Adolescents and Pastoral Care: Kate Wright
"I have recently come across the arguments of Phil Frampton regarding the alienation that can be felt by adolescents. Frampton argues that many adolescents create a psychological Wall between their private home life in the nuclear family, where 'irrational parenting' can be the rule of life and their corporate school life where one has one's peers and the relatively straightforward structure of the school's routine. This creates a more 'peaceful' setting for the adolescent. Never the two worlds shall mix, which is aided by the fear the parents may have of the school making unwelcome inroads into their private sphere and vice versa.

"I am aware that Frampton wrote his childhood memoir: 'The Golly in the Cupboard' in part to show the advantages that the care system can bring to an adolescent's stability. The advantages of already having been in an institution and used to peer support and encouragement as opposed to those from the nuclear family background.

"Here I consider these issues from the perspective of life in a boarding School.

"I have taught and worked in a medium-sized boarding school in the north of England for sixteen years, twelve of those as a tutor to sixth formers and a teacher. Two of those years I was a resident tutor and felt much more 'in loco parentis' than I may ever have felt had I been in a state or day school.

"Regarding the idea of 'corporate parenting' which Frampton refers to as a phrase used in the 1990s regarding children in care. This is very much the experience of the average child in boarding school. 'Mum and Dad' are replaced with 'Housemaster/mistress, their spouse, the academic tutor, the resident tutors and the matron.' A special 'in loco parentis' relationship may also be struck up with the adult in charge of a favourite sport or extra-curricular activity.

"As a tutor, I have guided many 16- to 18-year-olds through mental ill health, relationship dilemmas, friendship problems, issues from home that as a day or state teacher I may have remained blissfully unaware of. As a resident tutor I have helped kids with cooking skills, tidying skills, known all about their boyfriends or girlfriends, have offered some sex education; have even been called on when there's a rat in the kitchen (what am I going to do?!) and had many a happy cocoa and 'Take Me Out' night round at my flat for international students who didn't want to go to the main school social events. I have had pupils cry on me many times and confide all sorts of home life dilemmas to me. The lines get blurred as a resident between 'Maths teacher' and 'Mrs W' who was always up for a chat and a cup of tea if needed. I knew full well that they had also chatted with Matron that night and would chat to the Housemistress or master the next day (I have tutored boys and girls). This I always saw as a massive privilege and a huge joy of the boarding environment and one I could see was helping the teens make sense of their world.

"The next idea is the importance of the peer group. As with Phil's gang of friends, this cannot be underestimated at boarding schools. Living with one's peers gives a sisterhood or brotherhood like no other. And in later years, who do you see when you see their photos of weddings, kid's baptisms etc? It is the year group with whom they shared a House or a dorm – all there in a faithful fraternity. In House they will always have each other's backs, especially within year groups. Across year groups too the bonds can be strong and the older ones will often look out for the younger ones.

"The last concept Frampton talks about is the potential dysfunction of the nuclear family compared with the more rational school experience. Our kids, although rich, may be returning to alcoholic mothers, anorexic sisters, tyrannical fathers, parents who simply work so much that they leave their offspring as latch key kids once the school breaks for holidays.

"A word of caution to end, however... if school is a hard place and they don't enjoy it for example through bullying, then home can be the oasis of calm and School the termly dread. One girl I knew spoke of how she was 'social top dog' at home with her home friends and 'bullied misfit' at school which left her with something bordering on a personality crisis.

200

"That said, by and large, when boarding works it works incredibly well indeed. I can see how life in care set Frampton up for life at school, just as life in boarding school can set kids up for life at university or college or the army. The importance of camaraderie and the bonds created shine through on each and every wedding photo and it is a joy to witness.

Kate Wright 20/11/2020."

The supporters of private boarding school education, aside from asserting that such schools offer a better quality of education, generally list three notable structural points appertaining to the issues surrounding the Mystery Wall. They highlight:

- A consistent and holistic learning setting

- Independence from parents

- Living and learning to grow in a community of peers

For example, the website ourkids.com included in its list of benefits

"The immersion in school life offered by boarding allows a holistic approach to learning that extends well beyond classroom walls."

"... independence from parents fosters self-reliance among boarding school boys and girls"

"Boarding school fosters a supportive "all in this together" community where kids have opportunities to learn collaboration"
(ourkids.com, 30th May, 2021)

Boardingschoolreview.com emphasises:

"You will get to live away from home."

"You will learn how to cope with life and all its many high and low points within a community of your peers who are going through the same things you are."

"You will learn to be responsible for yourself. You have to learn to get along with others because it is a community."
(boardingschoolreview.com, 30th May, 2021)

Boarding School Elitism
The history of the private boarding schools involves their use by the ruling elite to prepare their children, and sons in particular, to take their place as rulers of the country and empire. This was particularly made clear in the 1864 report of the government's Clarendon Commission. Simon reports in his historical work, "The Politics of Educational Reform":

"Finally, in order to complete the transformation of the public schools into purely upper-class preserves, it was necessary to get rid of the places which their founders had specified should be made available for 'foundationers' - poor and deserving local scholars who received free board and education. Winchester and Eton had 70 such pupils, Westminster 40, Charterhouse 44.... The presence of these local boys 'lowered the social tone of a school aspiring to attract the upper classes' and various attempts had already been made to reduce their numbers.

"The Commission ignored the protests of local residents - even denying them the opportunity of appearing as witnesses - and instead, set out how local privileges could be abolished... In this way, the upper-middle class 'divested itself of all likelihood of social contamination' and the public schools, originally intended for 'all classes above that of the Elizabethan pauper', became the monopoly of one." (The Politics of Educational Reform 1920-1940 B. Simon, 1974)

These schools had to prepare the children of the wealthy and heirs of the warlords for the brutal world of class exploitation, military domination and colonial rule. As such the process itself was often brutal. The boys had to be prepared for ruthless military realities, develop a taste for power and a callous disregard for the weak. In the school, privileges were reserved for the eldest pupils and generally those who proved themselves to be the strongest and most dominant in the pack.

The tone of the private boarding schools was set and, while many boarding schools have attempted to move on, from time-to-time public scandals and revelations at the more traditional establishments illustrate that much of that culture remains. As a result of this and historic revelations of widespread staff abuse of children in orphanages, the value of British residential schooling is marred in the minds of many, a perception reflected in the above quoted 2008 statements of the Chair of the UK Parliament's Children, Schools and Families Select Committee.

Nor do the antics of the public-school educated members of British governments help to convince society that public schools have their place in a meritocratic Britain.

Nevertheless, it could be contended that the latter issues and most of those raised by the boarding school detractors (as with those decrying residential social care) are more the products of ideological or bad management than the provision of residential schooling in itself.

Research
Relevant independent research and surveys regarding boarders' experiences at these schools is sparse and comparative studies with their day attendee counterparts even sparser. Nevertheless, there are studies which appear to bear out the claims of boarding school proponents. For example, in 2003/4, England's Commission for Social Care Inspection, surveyed the views of the country's boarders and their parents and considered that the young people generally conveyed a positive view of care.

Roger Morgan, the Commission's Children's Rights Director, making reference to the low public opinion of boarding schools, observed: *"The public caricature of boarding is of a negative environment of high physical bullying, poor care and extreme homesickness. These do not come through as major issues for today's boarders or their parents – and boarders themselves register fewer concerns about separation from family and homesickness than their parents."*

Furthermore, he quoted the self-completion survey results suggesting the boarders (aged 8 to 21) had reasonably high levels of satisfaction with their treatment in their schools:

"Three quarters of boarders (74%) said that their boarding school was looking after them very or quite well. Over a third (37%) commended boarding schools as having looked after them very well. Only 4% of boarders thought their schools had looked after them anything less than 'well enough'."

Other observations were instructive:

"The best things boarders listed were:

• *living with your friends (28%);*

• *making new friends (9%);*

• *out of class activities (6%);*

• *having independence (6%)."*

"Boarders' comments showed that friendships do not just happen because you are a boarder – you have to work on them if you live in the same place, but gain in doing so: 'It makes you a much stronger person if you are capable of keeping friendships even though you have to spend all your time together.'

"Very young boarders commented positively on always having friends around at school: 'There is always someone to play with.'" (Being a Boarder: A Survey of Boarders' and Parents' Views on Boarding Schools, Dr Roger Morgan, Commission for Social Care Inspection, UK 2004)

Just before the onset of the 2008 financial crisis, Charles Clarke, Education Secretary in the UK's Labour government, was considering offering more places in boarding schools to children in care or liable to enter care (Boarding School Plans for Children in Care, Guardian, UK June 13th 2003). The aim was to assist those children but also to reduce spiralling costs involved in the privatised care system. Some charities, such as the Royal Wanstead Children's Foundation were already part funding such activity. In 2007, the charity, lobbying for more government action, published a telling report on the most recent outcomes for the young people they had supported through boarding schools:

"Of the 97 children in the sample, 59 (61%) had been exposed to abnormal, threatening or abusive conditions in the family or home environment. A total of 93 (96%) faced serious problems and risk to their normal development. The study shows that many of the most vulnerable children in Assisted Boarding make quite dramatic early progress. Forty per cent of these children achieved or exceeded their peer group 'average' (on social, emotional and academic criteria) within two years, and 85% did so within 3 years. Thirty-nine per cent (39%) of those who had been boarders for at least three years became above average pupils during that time."
(Breaking Through, Royal Wanstead Children's Foundation, 2007)

The Foundation identified a clear benefit for a layer of young people who were withdrawn from the parental setting and placed with their peers in a more professional setting where care was pastoral.

In a far larger and more detailed comparative study comprising of 5,276 high school students (28% boarding students; 72% day students) matched by socio-economic status from 12 high schools in the United States, Martin, Papworth, Ginns and Liem analysed the experience and outcomes of both boarders and day students. (See Boarding School, Academic Motivation and Engagement, and Psychological Well-Being: A Large-Scale Investigation, Martin, Papworth, Ginns, & Liem, 2014, American Educational Research Journal)

As background to their own research the authors, drawing on the research of others e.g. Bronfenbrenner identified the differing socialisation contexts for boarders and day students not only in relation to their peers but also the staff.

"First, the residential environment of boarding schools provides a particular ecological context in the socialization process different to those of day students which allows boarding students to engage in a different set

of activities and interactions with peers and staff, thus providing differing opportunities for growth and development..."

(Boarding School, Academic Motivation and Engagement, and Psychological Well-Being: A Large-Scale Investigation, Martin, Papworth, Ginns, & Liem, 2014, American Educational Research Journal)

The authors also drew on many other studies which highlighted the pre-set boarding regime facing residential students:

"Second, to a greater extent than day students, boarding school life involves an elaborate system of regulation and tight scheduling of students' daily routines, dictating when they have to wake or sleep, eat meals, participate in recreational activities, prescribing how, when, and where they need to complete their homework, the standards for keeping their accommodation neat and tidy, as well as access to telephones and computers, to name a few... "

They argued that the differing settings impacted on students and in particular that boarding for some students could provide a less "toxic" home environment than the family for some students:

"Third, this results in differences in salient caregiver interactions. While boarding school may put some children further away from important relational assets such as the home, for others the boarding environment may provide a more stable environment than their own home or community, providing safety, security and less 'toxic' home environments and neighbourhoods..."

In their paper, the authors quoted similar research conducted in the USA for a 2013 study which was commissioned by that country's Association of Boarding Schools looking into differing outcomes for 720 boarding, private and public day students all matched by socio-economic status (see The Truth About Boarding School. Asheville, NC: The Association of Boarding Schools, 2013).

From the results of questionnaires completed by the sample, the authors concluded that many United States boarders had more positive perceptions of their schooling and development. Boarders (68%) were much more likely than day students (52% more likely than private day students and 60% more likely than state day students) to state that boarding school had helped them to develop in regard to non-academic outcomes such as self-discipline, maturity, independence, cooperative learning and critical thinking:

"Of those surveyed, 68% of boarding students, 52% of private day students, and 42% of public day students indicated that attending boarding school helped them develop on a range of non-academic outcomes (e.g. self-discipline, maturity, independence, cooperative learning, critical thinking).

The authors also found that boarders were more likely than day students to report that their schooling developed them both academically and for life at college, concluding: *"Based on these findings, it appears there are positive perceptions of the modern boarding experience."*

Their identification of the increased time boarders could spend with staff which could boost opportunities for mentoring is particularly relevant in the pastoral care role as reflected upon above by Kate Wright:

"Fourth, boarders typically spend a greater amount of time with teachers, coaches, and other school staff (e.g. boarding staff) and have greater opportunity to develop mentoring or personal relationships with them than day students (The Association of Boarding Schools [TABS], 2013)."

Martin, Papworth, Ginns and Liem's hypothesis (leaning on Bronfenbrenner) was that the differing learning settings would lead to differing outcomes in regard to both the academic and the non-academic aspects of the student's lives:

"Given the nature of students typically attending boarding school, and the structures and processes of boarding school, it seems reasonable to postulate that boarding school is an environment in which distinct proximal processes are influential. Thus, boarding may impact academic and non-academic outcomes differentially to day students (Bronfenbrenner, 1994, 2000). This, however, is an open empirical question; one the present study is designed to answer."

In their own study of Australian schools, the authors found few significant differences in the academic outcomes. However, it is notable that in the non-academic fields they identified several important differences. This led the authors to highlight major variances in the non-academic lives of boarders as compared to the non-academic lives of day students:

"Although there was mostly parity between boarding and day students, there were some significant differences. It is interesting to note that a greater proportion were on psychological well-being measures. Perhaps this is because boarders' academic lives are more similar to that of day students and that it is non-academic life where boarding and day students' lives are more dissimilar."

In psychological aspects such as adaptive motivation, growth goal setting, sense of meaning and purpose, life satisfaction and parent–child relationships, boarders scored much more positively than day students. The authors, again reflecting points raised in discussing the Mystery Wall, point to the fact that parents are not trained either to educate or nurture their adolescent children:

"In terms of psychological well-being, the positive findings for boarders' sense of meaning and purpose and life satisfaction were interesting. Again, it may be that boarders' access to trained educators on a more ongoing basis enables opportunities for pastoral development that are within the remit of such professionals (see Hawkes, 2010). For example, school staff receive professional development on the social-emotional needs of students (Becker & Luthar, 2002; Martin & Dowson, 2009), when as parents are not trained educators and are relative novices at each stage of their child's social-emotional development. In this light, it is also very interesting to note the positive findings for boarders and parent-child relations."

Of particular relevance were the authors' findingss in relation to parental attachments. Their analyses revealed that boarders' relationships with their parents were more positive than those of day students:

"In terms of attachment theory, it is very interesting to note that boarders' relationship with their parents was more positive than day students'

relationship with parents. This is somewhat consistent with Cree (2000) who found that boarding school did not diminish boarders' relationships with their parents."

In a study back in 2001, Dr Umar Lydia at Ahmadu Bello University in Nigeria had also found, when researching 15 to 17-year-old students across 12 schools in Kaduna State, that: *"Boarding school adolescent children tended to have fewer conflicts with their parents than adolescent students in day schools."* (An Investigation into Conflicts Between Parents and their Adolescent Children in Kaduna State: Implications for Social Studies Education, by Dr Umar Lydia, Ahmadu Bello University, 2001)

The Australian research team expressed uncertainty as to why boarders could emerge with better parental relations, which perhaps went against their understandings as per attachment theories. They speculated that it was to do with issues relating to day students having to do homework in their domestic setting. They also considered that better relationships between boarders and their parents may be due to the more positive interactions that parents may have with their boarding children during holidays as opposed to the daily interactions of parents with their day student children:

"The precise reason for this is unclear. Perhaps absence makes the heart grow fonder. Perhaps for boarders, the daily struggle with homework and study (Horsley & Walker, 2013) is shifted onto the school and away from parents, whereas day students and their parents continue with this struggle, leading to a decline in the parent-child relationship. Along similar lines, perhaps boarding parents can focus on more positive interactions that tend to occur during holiday periods and in 'good times'."

However, whether this means that the boarders miss out on richer and deeper relationships *"in all their dreadful complexity,"* with their parents, to quote Ian Craib, was not investigated, leaving work to be done. (The Importance of Disappointment, Craib,1994)

Modern IT allowing for ease of parental contact was also suggested to be a possible factor:

"It is also worth noting that modern boarding school is characterized by modern communications and so boarders are more frequently and extensively in touch with their parents and school-leave arrangements are less restrictive than in years gone by... In any case, boarding school did not seem to negatively affect boarders' perceptions of their parents and this has some relevance to attachment perspectives and boarding school."

Their speculation regarding what seemed to be their unexpected outcomes regarding adolescent-parental relationships backs up the points made about the limitation of parents in supporting adolescents in their development but clearly calls for more research. There appears to be a hint of an understanding that relations between parents and adolescents in the home may be strained but placing the differing tensions facing boarders and day students down to holidays and homework may reflect an idealised view of adolescent life. Follow up research would probably be more fruitful to investigate the impact of the author's casual observations that: *"parents are not trained educators and are relative novices at each stage of their child's social-emotional development."*

Writing later in The Psychologist, one of the co-authors of the study, A J Martin, commented on the breadth of differences in outcomes for the boarding and day students:

"We found significant differences between boarding and day students on eight out of 18 academic and personal wellbeing outcomes, after controlling for background characteristics such as socio-demographic, ability, personality, and school factors. Boarding students were significantly higher on adaptive motivation, academic buoyancy, growth goal setting, sense of meaning and purpose, life satisfaction, parent–child relationships, and extracurricular activity." (AJ Martin, https://thepsychologist.bps.org.uk/volume-29/june-2016/effects-boarding-school)

Conclusions Regarding Boarding Adolescents
Whilst the quoted boarding school findings go some way to support the suggestion that residential schooling gives room for adolescents to

develop with their peers and away from the psychological pressures of parental relationships, like much social research the strength of the objectivity is partly clouded by possible conflicts of interest and also the veracity of information contained in self-completion questionnaires. For example, there is always a degree of self-selection involved in the respondent sample for self-completion questionnaires.

Martin, Papworth, Ginns and Liem's study was also part-funded by the Australian Boarding Schools Association which is an organisation that *"exists to promote the interests of boarding schools in Australia by enhancing the well-being of boarders, facilitating the professional development of staff and advancing excellent practice among schools,"* (www.boarding.org.au) leaving those findings that might appear to be sympathetic to the marketing of Australian boarding schools open to question.

In their 2014 study, the authors also pointed to the historic dearth of significant quantitative studies of outcomes at boarding schools:

"Boarding school has been a feature of education systems for centuries. Minimal large-scale quantitative data have been collected to examine its association with important educational and other outcomes."

Their research conclusion, that when socio-economic status was taken into account the fact that there was little difference in outcomes between boarders and day students, may have had something to do with the reasons why there has been a lack of independent, boarding school or government interest in this area. Having schools, which the 1864 Clarendon Report intended to focus on developing an elite and which educated significant numbers of those appointed to oversee the mechanisms of government, subject to public scrutiny may not have been seen as beneficial to those in power, especially research that demonstrates that for all the fees paid the difference in academic outcomes is negligible.

However, if the wellbeing and overall education of adolescents is to be improved then comparisons of boarder and day student non-academic outcomes and views regarding their ongoing relations with parents may be a fruitful area of study. The findings of the above research generally support the notion that future research could be usefully centred on considering whether residential schools offer a less traumatic path towards adulthood for adolescents due to the following factors (as above):

- Adolescents in residential schools may benefit from a collectivity of their peers on a 24-hour basis, assisting them to develop their sense of self-identity and self-esteem and peer engagement skills.

- Residential schooling, by taking the child out of the parental home potentially creates a more stable foundation for development by eliminating the duality of learning settings.

- Boarding adolescents potentially reduces the amount of time and angst involved in negotiating and renegotiating permissions with parents

- With residential schooling both parents and boarders, weekly and longer separations may lead to better adolescent relationships with their parents than those of day students.

This is not to suggest that residential schools are necessarily the answer to smoothing the pathway for adolescence, rather the comparison may offer additional important clues as to how the level of trauma that characterises adolescence may be severely reduced. The comparison between non academic outcomes for boarders as opposed to day students may have helped to identify the cause of rather than the solution to teenage trauma.

Researching Adolescent Development at Orphanages

It has been argued that the Mystery Wall is generated by property relations dictating the differences in learning settings between the adolescent's parented and academic worlds. For adolescents, whether parented or fostered, the experience of the two worlds is sharply contrasting. However, the contrasts are much less so for those in residential or boarding care.

Parented/Fostered Day Student Adolescent's Domestic Life	THE MYSTERY WALL	Parented/Fostered Day Student Adolescent's School Life
Parents		Teaching Staff
Atomised		Collectivised
Private		Corporate
Disempowerment		Peer Empowerment
Semi- structured		Structured
Unstable Environment		Stable Environment
Unstructured Learning Experience		Structured Learning Experience
Parental Language		Peer language
Psychological		Sociological
Emotionally Complex		Emotionally Simple
Inconsistent Reward System		Consistent Reward System
Unstable Punishment System		Stable Punishment System
Serfdom		Apprenticeship

Similarly structured to adolescents' life at Boarding Schools, the table below shows that there is little difference between the features of an adolescent's academic and orphanage life. The individual's opportunity and need for constant negotiation and renegotiation of permissions and status with carers are severely reduced.

The Mystery Wall Separating Orphanage Day Students' Worlds

Orphanage Day Student Adolescent's Domestic Life	THE MYSTERY WALL	Parented Day Student Adolescent's School Life
Carers		Teaching Staff
Collectivised		Collectivised
Corporate		Corporate
Peer Empowerment		Peer Empowerment
Structured		Structured
Stable Environment		Stable Environment
Unstructured Learning Experience		Structured Learning Experience
Peer Language		Peer language
Sociological		Sociological
Emotionally Simple		Emotionally simple
Consistent Reward System		Consistent Reward System
Stable Punishment System		Stable Punishment System
Apprenticeship		Apprenticeship

As with boarding schools, the issue arises as to the impact of having a collectivised residential care domestic experience as opposed to one in the atomised nuclear family. Orphanage life brings substantial experience both of being commodified but also of collective peer empowerment. The regimes were very similar. In the modern world, despite armies of boarding school educated establishment figures still sending their children to become boarders, it is considered extremely counter intuitive to suggest that corporate residential care can offer adolescents a better all-round experience than can many families. That however is not the argument here. The issue is what can we learn from any research.

For similar reasons as may apply to Boarding School research, there is little reliable relevant research regarding adolescent development in orphanages or residential care settings. Much of the research is dogged by "careism" (as we defined in the first chapter) and national governments' social agendas regarding the assertion of the sacredness of the nuclear family as the only valid form of raising children. The base point of careism is the lauding of the nuclear family as the holy grail, the only child-centred vessel for child development. The faults of all other forms of child-rearing are combed through in microscopical detail by armies of researchers whilst the damages and stresses caused by the nuclear family are brushed over with soporific functionalist Panglossian, "We live in the best of all possible worlds," explanations.

For example, academic research into orphanages often glosses over the history of the adolescents involved. The young people are overwhelmingly in care precisely because the parent family has not been able or willing to safely look after their child. in the UK it is common for researchers to state that outcomes for young people in residential care are worse than those for their counterparts in foster care. For over fifty years British governments' stated policy for young people in care has been to place them with adults in a family home (i.e. to get them fostered) irrespective of the young person's wishes and irrespective of whether the young person has suffered multiple previous foster placement failures. The consequence, as recognised by successive UK

Parliamentary committees, is that residential care is seen as the place of last resort i.e. for the children seen as the most difficult or 'demanding'.

Yet many adolescents request to be placed in a care home either because they see it as a relief from the continual moving from one foster "home" and or because they do not wish to be in a family setting with non-relatives. Amongst the later are many young people who are not comfortable within the highly intense dynamics of family relationships and need to settle down to developing their own resources. (Bring Back Orphanages – Bring Back Attachments, Frampton, Debate, British Psychological Society, 2012).

It should also be emphasised that residential care in the 21st century UK is not in a traditional orphanage setting. Instead, it commonly involves a small house holding four or five young people, with frequent turnover of staff and even more frequent turnover of residents due to social care services trying to minimise costs by sending the young people back into foster care. At best these establishments, known as residential units, are a long-stay halfway house for "difficult children" rather than a home. The residential care system in Britain, out of design, simply does not offer a stable setting for young people. This is a matter of policy driven by funding, careism and childism, which totally ignores the wishes of the young people concerned and imposes huge additional social stress upon them.

Comparative research regarding the development of children in orphanages often fails to take into account the background circumstances of the children, the differing societal roles of orphanages the financial outlays available, workforce skills and the aims of management. Failure to consider these critical factors renders most research lame and prone to produce societal prejudices.

The world of research regarding social orphans reveals itself as riddled with the prejudices of careism and childism. The young people in orphanages are treated like stillborn objects who will come to life if only they were to be plucked out of the ramshackle institution and planted into the womb of surrogate parents. No thought is given to management practices or combatting society-wide stigmatisation, which are seen as a given. No mention is made of replicating best practice elsewhere – or even replicating aspects of the boarding school model which benefitted many of their country's elite.

The casual observer from another culture might conclude that the world of social research has gone insane, looking for the causes of abusive and damaging practices towards children as being the size of the buildings the young people sleep in. Children being brought up in institutions is bad they declare, omitting to mention the private boarding schools that were home for the universities' professors and much of their country's ruling elite.

The sloppiness of the research and the conclusions espoused reeks of academics lining up behind the drug companies like GlaxoSmithKline, the child traffickers and pimps to earn easy money by preying off the world's orphans.

Much of the Western research is predicated on the prevalent modern Western notion promoted by many governments that child abuse is common to residential care and more so than in the nuclear family and the private homes of carers. Childism and children's lack of voice, isolation and disempowerment within the nuclear family makes this assertion impossible to verify. What is certain is that young people who have emerged from the care of non-family institutions have less psychological ties preventing them from speaking out about their abuse as children. Indeed, it was care-experienced people from orphanages and residential homes that first blew the whistle en masse about widespread child sex abuse in the UK, sparking major prosecutions and government inquiries in the latter years of the 20th century.

Careism and Research
Where child-centred research has taken place into care in the UK, if it does not fit the policy and propaganda then it is cast aside, not only by the government but also its agencies and dependencies such as the national children's charities.

One example comes in the 2001 conclusion of a survey of care-experienced young people over the age of 15, which was conducted by Save The Children. In its report, the major UK children's charity declared that they found that a majority of children in care in Scotland preferred to be in residential care. The report stated:

"Frequent moves between foster homes were seen as the norm, despite the popular myth that foster placements are longer-term arrangements, and the children and young people saw this as detrimental to their stability within a safe and loving environment... Many children felt they could not relax in foster homes, partly because it was somebody else's house, but mainly because they were wary of carers usurping the role their own parents should have been taking. They often felt the foster carer's own children were given preferential treatment, leading to feelings of alienation." (A Sense of Purpose: Care Leavers' Views and Experiences of Growing Up, Save the Children in Scotland, 2001)

The charity did little to follow up these findings or challenge the process of forcing adolescents into foster placements against their will. Instead, 17 years later, Save the Children's, Senior Child Protection Adviser, Rebecca Smith, was using unattributed sources, declaring on the charity's website, that orphanages were bad for young people and quoting dubious research conducted mainly on babies and toddlers from the impoverished countries of Eastern Europe recovering from a Stalinist era in which social work as a profession often had not existed.

The conflation of research on society's abandoned babies and toddlers with the fate of adolescents in care demonstrated that the charity was more interested in propaganda that might appeal to governments, childism and prevailing adult prejudices than supporting the world's 8 million orphans (Orphanages are not the Solution, Rebecca Smith, (https://www.savethechildren.org.uk/blogs/2018/volunteering-in-orphanages-not-solution-save-the-children-uk-blogs).

The adolescents' voices calling to be placed in residential care were buried because, Smith, in a classic example of careism declared: *"There is a substantial body of evidence that made the United Kingdom, United*

States, Australia and many other countries transition from institutional care to family-based care," adding, "and yet we continue to support this antiquated model abroad."

This veiled trumpeting of the notoriously catastrophic fostering-based care systems of the USA, Britain and Australia is both breath-taking and alarming enough in itself.

Nor could Smith have paid much attention to the 2015 research report for the UK government's Department of Education. The Place of Residential Care in the English Child Welfare System, written by Hart, La Valle and Holmes, pointed to the differences between the English language countries referenced above by Smith and mainland Europe. Their report noted:

"English-speaking countries tend to place only a small proportion of their looked after children in residential care compared with mainland Europe (6% in Australia v. 54% in Germany)." (The Place of Residential Care in the English Child Welfare System, Hart, La Valle and Holmes, Department of Education, 2015)

The authors had set themselves the task of reviewing the available research on UK residential care for young people in the care system. Regarding Smith's "substantial body of evidence" that she claimed led to the UK running down its residential care, the researchers' conclusions were damning as to the basis of that "evidence":

"There are big gaps in the English evidence base on residential care, in contrast with the more comprehensive evidence base that has been available to inform policy and practice decisions in other children's policy areas in the past decade."

The report was focussed on analysing the research which had taken place regarding residential care and highlighted major methodological weaknesses and evidence gaps.

Regarding the methodological weaknesses, Hart, La Valle and Holmes pointed to faulty research controls, attributes, contextualisation, focus and the ignoring of the need for service user data:

"The evidence base on outcomes from children's residential care is undermined by a number of methodological weaknesses... including:

• Limited 'controls' to enable one to attribute differences in outcome between children in residential care and their peers in family-based care to their setting rather than to the fact that these two groups are very different.

• Limited contextual information that can help to explain positive or negative outcomes from residential care, such as the quality of provision.

• A focus on a narrow range of mainly negative outcomes from residential care, while we know from research in other children policy areas (e.g. early years) that a wide range of outcomes is needed to understand how policy and practice can effectively intervene to support children's wellbeing and life chances.

• Very limited evidence collected directly from children with experience of residential care and their parents."

The gaps the authors found in the evidence base for the research should be even more concerning, stressing how little or no attention was given to the views of the young people:

"...there are some major gaps in the English evidence base on children's residential care which leave some key questions unanswered, including:

• What are children's experiences and outcomes from children's homes in England?

• What are the broader experiences and outcomes of children in residential care beyond the more typical narrow focus on pathologies and problems?

• *To what extent can we attribute differences in outcome between children in residential care and their peers in family-based care to their setting, rather than to the fact that these two groups are very different?*

• *What are the features of English residential homes that can help to explain positive or negative outcomes from residential care and 'what works' (and does not work)?*

• *Which children are most (or least) likely to benefit from different types of residential placement?*

• *What do children and their families think about residential care?"*

The authors also concluded that the "placement of last resort" approach common to the UK and USA is centred on the service providers' needs rather than the young people's. Regarding such usage, they concluded:

"At the moment, it is predominantly but not exclusively used for older or more troubled children within the care system, three-quarters of whom have a history of failed placements behind them. There are a number of problems with this approach. Firstly, it does not reflect the evidence described earlier that some residential care can achieve positive results in the right circumstances. Secondly, it does not reflect the views of children, some of whom say that the idea of living in someone else's family is uncomfortable for them." (The Place of Residential Care in the English Child Welfare System, Hart, La Valle and Holmes, Department of Education, 2015)

Nevertheless, Save the Children and UNICEF plough on.

The Reality of 'Modern' British Care

"An orphanage is no place for children to grow up," stated Rebecca Smith. For those that are not aware of the realities of the 'modern' model of foster care trumpeted by Save the Children and these governments, the foster care system is an utter nightmare for tens of thousands of children.

The British-based Save the Children declare that ending orphanages will present governments with "a historic chance to really invest in child protection systems" to keep children in the family. Anyone with knowledge of the British care system's experience will be more than surprised as this statement completely conflicts with the British experience. Whilst the number of care homes in England has dramatically declined since the early 1990s, the numbers of children in care have risen from 50,000 in 1994 to 78,000, and rising, by 2019. (Looked After Children statistics, Department for Education, 2019)

As to the impact of the closure of the orphanages and state reliance on the fostering system, the UK Children's Commission produced its 2020 Stability Index for Children in Care outlining the chronic sobering situation for children in the foster care system. With a long running shortage of 10,000 foster carers, the care system can often offer only emergency, temporary or inappropriate (i.e. ill-advised) placements for young people in care. In built into the system are foster carers who only accept children of certain ages meaning those children are forced to move on whether they have settled or not into their new environment.

The lucky children get to only move homo a few times and may get a good family. But Is it enough to callously throw vulnerable children rescued from chronic abuse and neglect into a sink or swim lottery in the hope that they might find a home which meets their care and development needs? The result for the unlucky ones is chronic instability and being passed from one foster "family" to another, living ten or miles away from their communities, changing schools in the middle of the academic year, and losing the friends they had made. The Commission reported its research findings:

- 1 in 10 children in care live in three or more placements each year

- 4% experience four or more placements in each year

- 1 in 6 live in at least four different placements in 3 years

- 1 in 10 under 4-year-olds have at least 3 placements in a year

(Stability Index for Children in Care, Children's Commissioner, 2020)

Notably, these figures cover just one year. By their teenage years many children have suffered a dozen and more moves and I have met young people who have suffered 40 moves and more. The cumulative destructive impact of multiple moves on education, self-esteem and personal relationships during a young person's formative years has nothing to do with care and everything to do with extreme neglect and psychological abuse. Some respond by saying that the child would have been better off with their chronically abusive family but what does that say about society and the "rights of the child"?

Adolescents suffered the most placement moves. This is not surprising since many who have been in the system for many years become so used to be moving around that they cannot settle and those that enter care during adolescence often find it difficult to adjust or simply don't wish to be a part of a stranger's nuclear family. This much was evidenced 20 years previously by the above mentioned Save the Children research which the charity and the government wish to forget. As a result, typically when a family placement breaks down the adolescent is sent into residential care but then 'cost pressures' are cited as the reason why the young person is sent to another family. The intense social and societal stress pressures are left to be borne by the young person and the young person alone. The phrase in care is being 'tossed around like a ragdoll' (hence my childhood memoir's title, The Golly in the Cupboard).

Another phrase for the systematic use of placement moves phrase might be 'psychological torture'. You may recall above how DeWall quoted research showing that for the brain the pain of social rejection is similar to the infliction of physical pain and that: *"a daily dose of acetaminophen…. an over-the-counter analgesic commonly used to treat physical pain was effective in reducing emotional responses and neural correlates of social rejection."* How many beatings do they think a child can take? There should be no surprise that the foster-based system is awash with drug use – to ease the pain.

The Commission's findings revealed that one in five who had entered care as adolescents had lived in at least three placements during the 2018/19 year:

"Older children are more likely to experience multiple placement moves in a year than other children in care.... 11.5% of children aged 12-15 have had two or more placement moves in 2018/19. Rates are highest amongst 12-15 year olds who also entered care aged 12-15, where nearly 1 in 5 of these children experienced multiple placement moves in 2018/19." (Stability Index for Children in Care, Children's Commissioner, 2020)

The Commissioner and many others have reported on the terrible impact both on the young person's mental health and education. It is no surprise that well above average numbers of young people passing through this horror emerge as adolescents with major problems and often end up in mental health units, on the streets or in prison.

Residential Care for the Elderly
To put the pressure to close down orphanages into perspective, it is worth considering the position of elderly people in residential care. The Organisation for Economic Co-operation and Development (OECD) in 2020 estimated that the world's over 80s population will rise from less than 100 million today to over 1 billion by 2050, representing a social explosion which will have a huge impact on the world economy and state funding. (Who Cares? Attracting and Retaining Care Workers for the Elderly, OECD, 2020)

According to the OECD, governments already hand over £200 billion a year just for private sector care and see costs ballooning in the decades to come. The noises from government about ways to cut care costs by placing the care burden back on families and women in particular have already begun.

In 2017, speaking in the UK Parliament, Care Minister, David Mowat declared: *"One of the things that has struck me is no one ever questions that we look after our children – that is obvious. No one says that is a caring responsibility, it is what we do. I think some of that logic and some of the way we think about that in terms the volume of numbers that we are seeing coming down the track will have to impinge on the way that we think about caring for our parents. Because it is a responsibility in terms of our life cycle which is similar."* (The Guardian (UK), January, 2017)

In many Western cultures young people who don't live with their family or relatives are seen as "troubled" and "bad" children. In other less economically prosperous cultures, it is old people living on their own who are seen as bad because, with little or no income, if they are not living with their children then the children, it is assumed, must have rejected them. Yet, if the welfare state, pensions and home ownership continue to get whittled away in the West, this stigmatisation of the non-family dependent elderly may be the prospect especially for the childless in their impoverished old age.

How will elderly people in residential care in the Western world feel about being moved out, placed in the family of strangers and having to abide by those strangers' rules? Of course, they would receive assurances that if their placement didn't work out that they would be moved to another family and could see if that worked out - because "every elderly person should be with a loving family" shouldn't they? Put the prospect held out by the government minister to elderly residents today of the moves, the undermining of their dignity, the uncertainty in the context of declining mental health and expect an outpouring of discontent. It would represent an attack on their human rights to live a dignified life in their latter years and be extremely likely to be injurious to their health. It is not an elderly-centric approach. Nor is that of clearing children out of orphanages child-centric.

Research in Emergent Eastern Europe
Smith went on further to surprise by quoting from the Bucharest Early Intervention research study that began in 2000, to suggest that orphanage care was proven to be seriously deleterious for children: *"On average, for every three months that a child was in an institution, he or she lost one month of development compared to a child in foster care."*

Smith's assertion amused me, implying that when at 17 I passed my university A-Level entrance exams, I was, according to Smith et al, likely to be a full four years behind my parented classmates. On a more sombre note, regarding the foster-care based system, a UK Cabinet Office evidence paper in 2002 reported that in the year to March 2000, 80% of young people with ten or more placement moves in England left care

225

with no educational qualifications at all. In 2005, the government reported that over half of all young people in care left with no qualifications (Department for Education and Skills, 2005).

Alpers, Johnson, Hostetter et al. in 1997 also came up with the conclusion that children in orphanages they studied in the newly emerging former Stalinist world had their growth stunted by 1 month in every 5 months. (Alpers LH, Johnson DE, Hostetter MK, Iverson S, Miller LC. Health of children adopted from the former Soviet Union and Eastern Europe: Comparison with preadoptive medical records. JAMA. 1997).

Yet from my orphanage upbringing I reached five feet 10 inches at 17, played in my school's rugby team and was by no means the tallest of my orphanage peers, even though by Alpers et al.'s reckoning I and my orphanage peers should have been physically almost three years behind our school counterparts.

Applying statistics from impoverished countries known to have been dominated for centuries by oppressive autocratic regimes of one type or another and concluding that the results have implications for modern developed societies which claim to respect young people's rights is a misuse of social science.

Orphanages and Child Labour
There is another side to the call by UNICEF, Save the Children and other organisations to close down orphanages and place the children in families and that is opening more doors to domestic child slavery. It is not twenty years ago that I was still reading and hearing from people who as children were sent by the British governments and children's charities to be 'cared for' by families around the UK, Ireland, Australia and the USA where they were immediately put to work on farms or in the household. The exploitation of orphans by families in Tsarist Russia was precisely the reason why in 1918 the revolutionary Bolsheviks moved to make the practice illegal. State care was to be introduced but the ongoing foreign military invasions created seven million orphans, overwhelming state care. Especially where state supervision of care

placements was weak or compliant around the world, then children in family care effectively became child slaves.

The major Western children's charities, alongside the Christian churches often acted as the soft ideological arm of the state, in sending social orphans and children from impoverished families to the colonies to be set to work for the White settler community. The British government aided by 50 charities transported over 100,000 of its adolescents to populate the corners of the Empire and be used as cheap labour. (Child Migration: Philanthropy, the State and the Empire, Constantine, 2008, Lancaster University)

As with UNICEF and Save the Children today, the charities argued that it was the best solution for destitute children and children in care. In 1906, the Barnardo's charity was claiming:

"For many of our children, emigration cuts the cord that in this country would bind them to degraded relatives and seriously handicap their futures." (From the Streets and Highways, 1906, D236/A1/17/6, Liverpool University Archives)

At our orphanage we were painted glorious pictures of a new life in the Australian sun. I wanted to go but wasn't selected. The Australian government were only keen to have White children, so boosting their notorious 'White Australia' programme. Little did we know the terrible outcomes that would have awaited us. We were lucky.

At first sight it is surprising that UNICEF teams up with a children's charity like Save the Children. The charity was exposed as long as 50 years ago for being an arm of cultural imperialism in a film on the charity's work in Kenya that they commissioned and paid for. The documentary was made by the celebrated progressive film director, Ken Loach, and exposed the charity's oppressive culturally-insensitive practices to such an extent that Save the Children refused to show it. Like the mythological Narcissus, they were captivated by their own self-image. Loach showed the reality for cultures they invaded.

When the film was finally shown ten years ago, the Financial Times (UK) was moved to comment on its continued relevance: *"...the 53-minute film remains pertinent today. Many people continue to feel uneasy about patronage relationships cultivated by philanthropy, the limits of aid and the after-effects of colonialism."* (Ken Loach's Film - Save the Children, Financial Times, April 23, 2012)

Half a century on, Save the Children's website proudly announces that their main sponsor is the British international pharmaceutical drug monopoly, GlaxoSmithKline, which has been cited on many occasions by media around the world for preying on vulnerable young children in care and poverty to use for drug experiments (e.g. UK Firm Tried HIV Drug on Orphans, Barnett, Guardian (UK) Sep 1, 2004).

With the same company cited as testing its drugs out on HIV children in Rumania's orphanages (Romania's AIDS Children: A Lifeline Lost, New York Times, July 1st, 2001), it raises major questions concerning the validity of the much quoted studies regarding outcomes for the victimised children in those orphanages

Today's Western-based global charities mirror the policies of governments unwilling to put financial resources into child protection and eliminating children's exploitation. That scores of national governments have laws against child labour and child slavery but let it take place under their noses while the rich countries continue to profit from the cheap goods made by these children tells one side of the story. The other is that providing non-exploitative supportive residential care for children is considered too expensive by these governments, too much of an affront to the doctrine of the nuclear family and considered too much of a sop to the 'undeserving poor' and their children.

Meanwhile governments allow the charities to run underfunded orphanages, which help, as was the case for hundreds of years, in keeping young children and adolescents off the streets, out of the public eye and exploitative street crime gangs.

The reality is that across the world, the market for child labour remains strong and growing. UNICEF and the International Labour Organisation's estimate of over 160 million child labourers represents a growth of 8.4 million since they reported in 2017. (Child Labour: Global Estimates 2020, Trends and the Road Forward, June 2021, UNICEF/ILO)

The report states that child labour is three times more prevalent in the rural areas away from the gaze of the state as it is in the world's towns and cities. UNICEF and the ILO also estimate that more than three quarters of the growth in using child labourers is accounted for by children in the most hazardous of work, including working down mines and sexual exploitation. Domestic child slavery accounted for an estimated 5.5 million children. Up to a million of them were in India.

For these young people who are, according to Free The Slaves, traded for less than $100 a time, life is far more hazardous: *"Modern slaves are not considered investments worth maintaining... today, when someone in slavery gets sick or injured, they are simply dumped or killed."* (www.freetheslaves.net/our-model-for-freedom/slavery-today)

UNICEF's own representatives in 2002 highlighted the plight of over 150,000 children in Haiti who were sent by their families to work as domestic slaves in a system so common that it has its own name, "restavek".

In 2010, the international news agency, Reuters, quoting UNICEF, reported on the extent of the problem: *"A 2002 study for UNICEF and other organizations by Norway's Fafo Institute for Applied Social Science said there were 173,000 restavek children, more than 8 percent of the population between 5 and 17,"* adding a comment from a former child slave called Cadet who when his mother died young was four years of age when he was given to a wealthy family and put to work. (www.reuters.com/article/us-quake-haiti-restaveks, Jim Loney, 2010)

One year after UNICEF's report on Haitian child slavery, Marta Santos Pais, Director of UNICEF's seemed oblivious to the implications when she wrote in UNICEF's research journal, Innocenti advocating against orphanages:

"There is a growing global consensus that sporadic or isolated efforts to improve individual institutions will not solve the problems of children in residential care, or meet their best interests. .... Placement in residential institutions must be the very last resort." (Marta Santos Pais, Director, UNICEF Innocenti Research Centre, Children in Institutions: The Beginning of The End? UNICEF, 2003)

UNICEF representatives may call for an end to orphanages but orphanages are often the only respite from the children being taken into domestic or industrial slavery or living on the street and privy to being exploited by crime gangs. Having visited several orphanages in India, I am only too aware that many of the children have fled from such situations. I have also spoken to child slaves, watched them at work and listened to their freed peers relieved to be living in orphanages. Closing down orphanages in countries where child labour is still commercially viable will only boost the child labour market.

UNICEF claims that orphanages are the cause of family break ups:

"By volunteering in orphanages, many well-intentioned tourists are supporting an industry that tears families apart and exploits children." (https://www.unicef.org/rosa/what-we-do/child-protection/volunteering-orphanages, May 2021)

Yet by UNICEF's own calculations there are twice as many children working in domestic child slavery as there are in orphanages. UNICEF seems to want people to forget that India alone has 10 million children living on the streets. In comparison the numbers in the country's orphanages are a drop in the ocean. They didn't end up on the street because of the orphanages. Research comparing the lives of ghetto and street children in Trivandrum, India illustrated despite the hardship of living on the city's streets, the street children had generally better outcomes than those living with their parents in the slums where homes were beset by abuse, alcoholism, lack of food and basic care. Many of the children were on the street for that reason (A Study on Street and Slum Children of Thiruvananthapuram City, Don Bosco, 1997). What is driving families apart is poverty created by governments putting profits before people and children in particular.

The UNICEF suggestion is that impoverished parents in developing countries are prepared to hand over their children. Behind this is the Western ruling elites' prejudice that if children's lives and outcomes in care are seen to be too good then the poor will rush to bring them to the doors of the children's homes. Care must be made to be seen as the "last resort" not for the child but for the poor parents. Better to let them be left out on the streets? And this while residential care in the form of private boarding schools is seen as the default option for many of the wealthy whose organisations fund the charities.

Exposing UNICEF's cultural imperialism, they have yet to publicly argue that the orphanages in the UK and the USA were 'tearing families apart and exploiting children' or, for that matter, the current raft of large residential homes in Germany and Denmark. Moreover, UNICEF is not yet to be seen organising similar campaigns to close down private or public boarding schools – residential care for the children of the rich and middle classes.

In the previous chapter of this document, when we considered the situation in private boarding schools, the response, in the UK to their chronic reputation for abusing pupils in their care was: *"It is not like that today...we have changed with the times and are no longer abusive, now we nurture the children ..."* Yet for orphanages there is no room allowed for a rhetoric of positive change from the bad days of institutional abuse and assault. According to UNICEF et al, orphanages are per se bad for children.

It is a strange contrast – the haven of the boarding school and the dystopian hell of residential care. Both involve professional carers. Their narrative resolves down to children who are not protected by private wealth and power being doomed to suffer at the hands of professionals. It tells a terrible story about our civilisation scarcely having risen above barbarism and leaves no room for government, community or charitable intervention.

There is no fundamental difference between a boarding school for the poor and an orphanage. Indeed, there are arguments that a boarding school for the poor is more detrimental for the child than an orphanage where children attend local schools because they are excluded from learning from a wider sphere of their peers and isolated from a well of peer support for which they may need recourse in combatting adult maltreatment in the residence.

Calls to close down orphanages might sound attractive to parented people who instinctively find it almost impossible to imagine a fruitful parentless childhood. However, it is irresponsible of Western governments and charities to fuel then take advantage of careist prejudices to abandon neglected, abused and orphaned children.

Nor should the irony be lost of UNICEF and the global children's charities holding up the nuclear family as the ideal solution when all evidence shows that the nuclear family model is in total crisis in the Western world. The perennial major shortage of foster carers reflects the crisis. The nuclear family cannot even care for all its own members at present let alone others. The size of the nuclear family is not shrinking because of personal whims, it is because of the contradictory pressures of modern capitalist society. Nevertheless, at a time when all around see evidence of the dramatically failing nuclear family model, the global children's charities clinging to cultural imperialism, earn their livings out of demanding that vulnerable children be sacrificed on the altar of the fantasy family.

If these organisations wished to evidence their claims to being child-centred they would put serious funding and effort into putting to the young people the choices of:

- living in the orphanage

- taking the chance of being with either a caring family or being a domestic child slave

- being sold on by a family

- living on the street or homelessness.

For orphan children the real choices are much starker and hazardous than many researchers and governments appear to consider.

Impact of the Closure of UK Residential Homes

Another long running UK children's charity, National Children's Bureau, was brought in by Warwickshire County Council to study the impact on young people's outcomes of the county becoming the first Engish county to close all of its children's homes in 1986. The NCB research not only showed that outcomes had not improved for the young people in care but had also impinged on them negatively, leaving them in a worse situation. The council had, so to speak, sold off the children's 'family silver'.

The Guardian journalist, David Brindle. reported on what childcare writers chillingly described as a corporate attitude of "benign neglect."

"David Berridge, who was then NCB's research director and is now professor of child and family welfare at the University of Bristol, says …'they felt that this was a golden opportunity to ask if we needed residential care, did it serve its purpose and was it value for money.'

"The answers, awkwardly for Warwickshire, were broadly "yes": based on the follow-up of 215 children, the policy change was found to have disadvantaged them, relative to children in care in other parts of the country, by limiting options for their placement, reducing contact with families and friends, and disrupting their education.

"A recent assessment of the findings, published in 1992, by childcare writers Robert Shaw and David Lane goes as far as to say: 'As a result, [Warwickshire's] much-vaunted 'good practice' resulted in more adverse outcomes for children in care than possibly those of authorities where benign neglect was the order of the day.'" (Are children's care homes still needed? David Brindle, www.theguardian.com/social-care-network/2015/jun/02)

As with the Save the Children research in Scotland, the NCB research findings were there for all to access. However, local and national government turned a blind eye as they careered along the path of closing children's homes, avoiding evidence-based research and instead hiding behind the public outrage over widespread tolerance of child abuse by staff at the badly managed homes, which provided a convenient excuse to sell off the homes to fund other services hit by cuts in government funding.

McKenzie's Research on US Orphanage Outcomes

Another significant comparative study regarding children in care, which is generally overlooked is that carried out by Professor Richard B McKenzie. McKenzie is the Walter B. Gerken Professor of Enterprise and Society Emeritus in the Paul Merage School of Business at the University of California. The economics' professor spent much of his childhood in an orphanage during the 1950s and has written extensively of the benefits of orphanages for young people in care:

"No one has thought to ask us orphans, the children who grew up in institutions, what we would prefer. I've spent a lifetime quietly listening to others disparage orphanages as cold and loveless Institutions where every child longs to be adopted. I know that this description is out of date and out of whack, and should have no bearing on the debate of how to help some of the least fortunate children among us. I was there, I grew up in a home with 150 or so other girls and boys in North Carolina in the 1950s-and I'm damn proud of it, and thankful!

"Life in The Home (which is what we called it) was no picnic. When we were young, we got two baths and changes of clothes a week, regardless of whether we needed more.

"We went barefoot to school until late November (which, until it got cold, was a marked advantage). We went to bed in "sleeping porches" that were totally unheated. We worked hard for long hours on the farm and in the shops, and we lacked a lot, not the least of which were the daily hugs other children take for granted and the requisite level of encouragement to read and study.

"Critics of orphanages stress what the children there did not have. Those of us who were there have a different perspective. We were, and remain, able to draw comparisons between what we had at The Home and what we would have had outside it." (An Orphan on Orphanages, Richard B. McKenzie, The Wall Street Journal, 1994)

In order to test out his notions, in 1994/95 McKenzie carried out an in-depth study into outcomes for 1600 people who had been brought up in orphanages in the South and Midwest of the United States prior to 1967.

His study, based largely on respondents' self reporting, concluded that the orphan-experienced adults significantly outperformed their parented counterparts, going against the predominant trend of thinking in social work and academic research:

"The general conclusion from that study was startling and, at the time, stood in sharp contrast with widely held, conventional childcare wisdom: The orphanage alumni, all of whom were white, had outpaced their age category counterparts in the white population by wide margins on all social and economic measures covered by the eight-page survey questionnaire – that is, except for divorce." (The Impact of Orphanages on the Alumni's Lives and Assessments of Their Childhoods. Richard B. McKenzie, 2003)

The professor carried out a second survey of careleavers in 2002, involving five additional orphanages and used the same questions and analytical techniques. Once again, he found the results to be very positive in relation to outcomes:

"The general conclusion to be drawn from this second survey is still very favorable to the life-outcomes of the orphanage alumni. However, the conclusion cannot be as sweeping as was the case for the first study. In this second study, the orphanage alumni have outpaced their age-counterparts in the general population (often with only non-Hispanic whites used as the comparison group) on a substantial majority of the social and economic measures covered, but this also means that they did not measure up as a group on several social and economic measures, with divorce again being the most problematic for the respondents. In general, the two older alumni

groups (those 55-64 years of age and 65 years of age and older) had relative social and economic outcome measures that were superior to the younger alumni (those 45-54 years of age) included in this survey and to their counterparts in the white population."

McKenzie also referenced social workers, Myers and Rittner's much smaller 2001 study of careleavers from a Florida orphanage, Adult Psychosocial Functioning of Children Raised in an Orphanage. Their research produced similarly positive results, leading them to call for more positive attitudes towards 'orphanage care':

"Recently there has been a resurgence of interest among policy-makers regarding the feasibility of using orphanage care for some of society's dependent children. The assumption among many social service providers is that this kind of care poses long and short-term risks to children placed in them. The present study explores the experiences of 94 residents at the Florida United Methodist Children's Home (FUMCH), a traditional orphanage. Residents were surveyed using two standardized instruments and a demographic questionnaire developed for this study.

"Their responses suggest that for many of the residents, the experience was a positive one. Generally, they report average or above average social and economic success. These results call for a more positive reappraisal of the value of orphanage care for dependent youth who cannot remain with their biological families and who are not appropriate for more traditional family-based foster care."

(Adult Psychosocial Functioning of Children Raised in an Orphanage, L. Myers, B. Rittner, Psychology - Residential Treatment for Children & Youth, 2001)

Short-Termism and Residential Care
Back in 2001, as Chair of the UK's newly formed Care Leavers' Association, I sat on the UK government's Social Exclusion Unit's Advisory Committee investigating educational attainment of children in care and the awful truth that the educational achievements of young people leaving care were well below that of their parented peers. The Social Exclusion Unit's research demonstrated that the longer children

spent in care and the more frequent their placement moves the more they fell behind. In this regard, the shortage of residential care placements was considered to be a major problem, destabilising life for many young people in care. Reflecting the impact of the headlong rush to close children's homes the committee concluded: *"Replicating the family model, 'foster care', was not always the best approach for Children in Care (CiC) and that the wholesale closure of local authority homes might need to be reversed in order to provide the range of placement options that were required."*

I put it to the committee officers that large permanent-stay residential homes of a manageable size could bring stability, sibling retention, a socialised childhood, much improved educational results and be more financially efficient. The officers said that they considered my proposal, to create at least one or two such "orphanages" test out its efficacy, as very meritorious but replied that the government's Treasury Department would not consider it because results could not be achieved within a five-year plan.

Since when, one might ask, have children been a five-year plan? The same government was spending billions on military hardware, space exploration, transport and IT projects none of which would bear fruit in even a ten-year plan, but investing so that the 100,000 children who are in and out of care so that they would become productive citizens was dismissed.

As Sir Martin Narey, former Director General of the Prison Service of England and Wales, said in 2007 of the UK care system, when he was Chief Executive Officer of Barnardo's children's charity: *"Our society spends £1.9billion a year on doing a pretty awful job. I think that if we take this opportunity to look afresh at how and where we spend that money, and possibly putting some more of it into a different form of residential care, then I think we can make a big change to the life chances of the children we're talking about."* (Bring Back Orphanages, Channel 4 TV, 2007)

In 2015, at the request of British Prime Minister, David Cameron, and with the aid of a team from the government's Department of Education, Narey conducted an independent review of residential care in England. His focus in his 2016 review, Residential Care in England, was specifically on residential homes (as opposed to other residential care such as the secure units) and these homes overwhelmingly house adolescents.

He concluded: *"Children's homes are often viewed as an anachronism, to be used only as a last resort. That is significantly to underestimate the contribution they can make, the stability they can deliver, and the high-quality care they can extend to children who have had terribly fractured lives. I found the children to whom I spoke to be overwhelmingly positive about life in a children's home. Many have a preference for living in a home rather than being fostered. That was the view of the Children's Commissioner, confirmed by the survey she commissioned to support this review."* (Residential Care in England, Sir Martin Narey's Independent Review of Children's Residential Care, July 2016)

Those who suggest that these young people would be better off placed in the 'right' family forget that many adolescents in care may, for good reason, not thrive in another family. This may be due to family-phobia brought of experience of multiple placement moves, unwillingness to acknowledge the personal 'authority' of any but their birth parents or several other reasons.

Narey's report also made recommendations for major improvements, adding: *"we should no longer see the homes in which they work as institutions to be used only as a last resort."* These residential units are the most basic of accommodation and are too small to provide a stable basis for long term sibling and sibling-like relationships, rendering peer support and nurturing. Indeed, Narey went so far as to comment that some care providers felt larger homes were more suitable for young people in care:

"The Mulberry Bush argued that sometimes, small homes can be too intense for children: 'We increasingly have children referred who are not

238

able to sustain the intensity of living in a small family unit. The larger institution seems to reduce the intensity of the relationships and provides an opportunity to develop the social and emotional skills to live alongside others without spreading overwhelming anxiety into others.'

"Stephen Blunden from Childhood First also argued that larger homes were better for some particularly challenging and damaged children: "A counter-cultural truth is that these children and young people are most effectively or safely looked after in larger units... Our homes typically, and unfashionably, look after 6-18 children, and we look after them in two age ranges – 5-12 years old and 11-18 years old. Up to a point, and varying with age, the larger the group the more effectively the peer dynamics can be orchestrated to keep the children safe and to offer the rich relational environment that they need to be healed.'" (ibid.)

Economic and Social Benefits of Large Orphanages

In Denmark and Germany, I found some large children's homes generating hugely better outcomes for their adolescent residents. In 2006, 2010 and 2019, I made return visits to Kinderhaus (Mark Brandenburg) in East Berlin. Kinderhaus currently houses over 300, mainly local, children, aged 6 months to 18, many of whom reside with their siblings in family group apartments (akin to the past Barnardo's villages). By chance on one occasion, I came across a sibling group of five who'd been there since my visit four years previously – something almost impossible in the UK care system.

German child protection expert, Professor Reinhart Wolff, proudly told me that 100% of Kinderhaus adolescents achieved the German equivalent of 5 A-C GCSE's (Berlin schools were averaging 85%, British care 11%). Moreover, 20% went on to achieve the equivalent of 3 A Levels. The professor explained: *"What we find is important is that you do not sever the links of a child to his or her local environment, so it's fairly important that most of the children, more than 80% living here, come from the area. And they still keep their links to their schools and friends."* (Bring Back Orphanages - Bring Back Attachments, Frampton, Debate, British Psychology Society, 2012)

The stability afforded, he added, also allowed staff to concentrate on the children's development using social pedagogy: *"If the child has an assurance that this situation will not be broken up by the school, or by the child welfare department, then of course the child can settle down and muster his or her resources and develop."*

Larger homes find it easier to have the slack to bring in sibling groups but also to take advantage of economies of scale. The complex had a residential family intervention unit, a mother and baby unit, a child protection assessment unit and a day care centre catering for 200 children. All aspects of the care experience were provided for. Specialist staff based at the project benefitted the local community because they provided services for surrounding areas whilst the young people were at school. Yet Kinderhaus's weekly costs per child were just 700 euros, a stunning 20% of the British average, and less than the minimum charged by British fostering agencies.

The children came from the local community and stayed with the local community. They remained at their local schools and so kept their peer groups and continued to be seen as part of the community. It chimed with my own experience in the orphanage where we children got offered local part-time jobs and often went onto local full-time employment. Corporate care can still be community care as long as the young people are settled, have time to grow into the community and the community cares for its children.

Another crucial advantage was that Kinderhaus children were sufficient in number to elect their own youth council, which had powers to summon and reprimand staff and children and to call for management to act. This is a key factor in both protecting children from abuse and correcting bad management practices. Just before I arrived, a member of staff had been reprimanded by the youth council for levying fines on young people as a form of punishment. The youth council, aware that the carer's actions contravened the rules of the home, reprimanded her and called on the Kinderhaus board of directors to take action. She was sacked.

The children operated as a collective but not only in this regard. Professor Wolff explained that stability allowed the elder children to play a nurturing role with the younger children and, as a result, all ages benefitted. However, in the context of modern society glossing over the role of the child in the home, it is not surprising that this beneficial aspect of child development is neglected. The relatively close bonds of young people facilitated by larger homes also plays an important role in negating the impact of turnover of staff who are peripheral in the 'community of children'.

New residential care staff arriving at our relatively small Southport children's often commented that they considered us "out of control," but we simply had other levels of control which they feared they could not penetrate. They could come and go but we who stayed had to live with each other, relate to each other and in most cases care for each other.

In The Golly in the Cupboard, I narrated an episode in my childhood when I was punished by the staff for hitting another six-year-old as her punishment for 'telling tales' to the staff. I wrote: *"I was sent to my bed early. Alone in the dark, I cried a little. When the other boys came up I told them: 'I got the cane but I didn' cry.'*

"Vengeance was done. Rules were rules. Neverneverland had its own rules. The staff were our crocodiles and set their boundaries.

"You didn't tell tales or else you got punished. That was one of our rules. Hit another child and you get caned. That was one of the crocodiles'."

As with childism, adult-centric careism wrapped up in its own self-centred parameters blinds itself to the realities for children.

Young People-Centred Research into Residential Care
What is lacking in the discourse about orphanages is full consideration of all the anecdotal evidence and voices of young people and investment in genuine comparative research as to how residential care could improve outcomes for these adolescents instead of employing academics to justify the closing of such 'orphanages' without any viable plan to settle them safely elsewhere.

The world bodies should commit to research into how orphanages can deliver the vast improvements in outcomes that orphans, as society's children, deserve.

That so much research revealing the benefits of residential child care is lost in the fanfare for the sanctity of the nuclear family is not surprising if one considers the rising governmental trend to short-termism with accompanying low welfare and minimal investment policies. In the West, the UK led the way in closing down children's homes, many of which were donated by wealthy philanthropists and others built by charities or taken over by local authorities. The sale of these large properties generated billions of pounds for local government and the charities. As the above mentioned Warwickshire County Council research foretold, the young people saw no improvements in outcomes. Instead, the funds generated were spent elsewhere.

Tied into low taxation policies, governments are now reluctant to find the money for impoverished children in care who have no votes, no homes of their own and no Members of Parliament. Consequently, all the government committee, research and service-user and service-provider calls in the world to reverse the trend and bring about modern adequately sized children's homes have not generated a penny of government funding.

Residential care requires investment and the children in the state's care are an investment. However it is much cheaper to present selective funded academic research and the prejudices of careism than to pay for well trained professional care and invest in adequate purpose-built accommodation. They toss the children into the bagatelle of short-term experiences of living in other individual's or dual carers' homes and refer to this as family life. Then they hold out their well-washed hands in gestures of anguish claiming that in the circumstances it is "the best of all possible worlds."

As with residential schools, the search should be on for best practice to secure best outcomes. Professional residential care should produce outcomes at least as good as the average family. That much is demonstrated by the examples of McKenzie, Rittner, Kinderhaus et al. For all its faults, I consider that the orphanage that I grew up in also produced as good a cross range of long-term outcomes as one would expect from a working-class neighbourhood. The practices in these orphanages left huge amounts to be improved with systematic toleration of staff psychologically, physically and sometimes sexually abusing children but this was largely due to poor management involving an absence of child-centred oversight, total lack of staff training, the impact of careism and childism and the stifling of the collective voice of children in care.

Collective Empowerment of Young People in Care

In many orphanages and children's residential care establishments, the abuse was drawn from a management-directed systematic reign of terror. Indeed, I was made aware of an orphanage in Scotland where the children were routinely lined up and beaten with a tawse before breakfast as a supposed warning for the pain that would be inflicted upon them later should the staff decide they warranted it.

For many young people the situation was intolerable. As with the exposure of widespread clerical paedophilia around the globe, governments threw their hands up in horror when the levels of abuse in care hit the headlines. Yet the warning signs had been there.

What starker alert to the despair of young people in some care homes could have been given than the 1947 Standon Farm incident referred to earlier? Sick of their treatment a group of nine teenagers in care at the government-run residential school raided the cadet squad's armoury with the aim of killing the headmaster, stealing money and his car and escaping. When a teacher came across them by accident, they shot him dead and fled. The boys, aged 15 and 16, were all caught and sentenced.

A public enquiry was rapidly convened and concluded that the main nine causes of the murder included: *"the long-standing regime of limited freedom...The collective punishments and the threat of collective fines."* and the boys' belief in the headmaster's *"unfairness"* but pointed the finger at, *"a boy with a very strong personality and a burning sense of grievance."* The inquiry team made cursory visits to other homes but their main conclusion was that no live ammunition should be kept in the schools, which appeared to have been mainly focussed on protecting the staff.

Meanwhile the abuse in the other care homes was allowed to continue and governments turned a blind eye to paedophiles taking advantage of the children in their care.

Dr Barbara Kahan OBE was adviser to the 1983 Parliamentary Select Committee, whose deliberations resulted in the 1989 Children Act. A former Children's Officer, she was a leading figure in the world of child care for many years, from after the war to her death in 2000. She became a senior civil servant, co-authored the famous Staffordshire "Pindown" report on residential care and was Chair of the National Children's Bureau. Her telling analysis of attitudes, even as late as the 1960s, towards abuse of children and the post war changes in care practices were expressed in a speech just before her death:

"Great difficulty was sometimes experienced in getting doctors, police, and lawyers to believe what was happening. ... there was little public discussion about abuse - other than scandals about excessive corporal punishment ... and the occasional knowledge of someone being moved on for sexually inappropriate behaviour to boys or girls.

"We now know from disclosures leading to an immense amount of inquiry work of various kinds that sexual abuse - accompanied by other forms of abuse was widespread in some residential settings. Its incidence in foster care was unknown and is only now beginning to be looked at."
http://www.davidlane.org/children/chukmar/mar2000/bkspeech.htm

I was asked to give evidence to the House of Commons Home Affairs Select Committee inquiry into *"The Conduct of Investigations into Past Cases of Abuse in Children's Homes,"* which sat in 2002. Future Prime Minister, David Cameron, was amongst those MPs on the committee who sat in on the sessions, grilling the witnesses. The committee was called by MPs in response to thousands of young people who had spent time in orphanages and government detention centres coming forward with allegations of abuse, which some police forces finally investigated and brought charges against a few of the abusers. It had taken collective action with the support of some brave social workers and journalists who helped to unearth paedophile rings operating across the country. When the accused included police chiefs and social service directors, the establishment decided enough was enough and began to round on us.

The deliberations of the parliamentary select committee shocked me. Accusations flew around depicting survivors of the care system as at best fantasists but otherwise gold-digging criminal elements and those solicitors that aided us were also accused of fermenting exaggerated claims so that they could professionally profit. The police forces, the Committee concluded, had obviously got it wrong and been "overzealous". The government and establishment put the matter to bed for a decade. Meanwhile notorious paedophiles such as Jimmy Savile, the MP Cyril Smith and Bishop Peter Ball were left at large to continue their preying on children. Only in 2012 after the uproar began following the exposure of Jimmy Savile's widespread abuse of children, young people and those with disabilities was the government forced once more to take the matter more seriously.

Many of the survivors testifying at the UK's government-run 2014-21 Independent Inquiry into Child Sexual Abuse Inquiry were from children's homes. Government records showed that regarding the Forde Park approved school in the south west of England, the government had recorded survivors' individual allegations of brutal sexual or physical abuse of boys against almost 2,000 named members of the home's staff.

As in my own orphanage, the only reason that the widespread abuse of children in care homes was exposed was because some groups of adolescents in residential care got together, organised themselves and protested. The continuation of the abuse had nothing to do with the orphanages as such and everything to do with a rotten social order which at every official level tolerated that abuse.

We told staff about the abuser in our orphanage. We warned the charity managers responsible for the home. Even the police and the government department responsible for the police, were told but they sat on their hands and never brought the abuser to justice. They only acted when the collective of young people forced their hand, and even then, they did the minimum so as not to embarrass the charity with its royal patronage. I would later reflect:

"In all this, my heroes were we, the urchins, hidden in Britain's underbelly. We were the characters required to show fortitude in the midst of rejection and cruelty. You might ask yourself why so many authors contrived with the establishment to paint a picture of the rescued unwanted given a life of bliss by a caring society. The establishment perpetuated a myth. They drew a veil across the suffering of the unwanted in their care." (The Golly in the Cupboard, Frampton, 2004)

We children were the citizens standing up for the laws of society. Only collectively and aggressively were we able to successfully assert our citizenship rights and have them even halfway respected.

The children's charities that fawn before Western governments, drug companies, social media giants, fast food companies and the like, should reflect that the battle is not with buildings but a society that is prepared to exploit children no matter that those young people are its future.

Collectives in Foster Care

The collectivity of the homes gave individual children a voice through others, a voice which is often buried in the family setting. Young people's complaints about treatment in foster care, as with the crimes of fosterers against children, are treated as individual and isolated cases. Only the statistics which governments choose to collect tell a more composite story, and little digging is done beneath.

Democratically organised collective empowerment of young people in care should be welcomed rather than feared and needs to be encouraged as a means of improving outcomes for all. The Kinderhaus elected and empowered Children's Committee model could have led to very different lives for many young children, adolescents and careleavers over the last 50 years. Collective empowerment of young people in any setting is important but particularly settings where young people are away from the public eye.

The idea, reflected in the USA's private "tough love" boot camps, that adolescents benefit from being subjected to a reign of terror is based on the idea that the trauma will bring them down to the reality that they must subject themselves to the will of adults. As media celebrity Paris Hilton and many other "tough love" survivors have commented, it involves a vicious attack on their search for self-esteem and self-identity, often psychologically disorienting them and, as they lose trust in their peers' ability to protect them, deterring them from meaningful communication with others.

Collectively empowering adolescents places them on a more level footing for the negotiations with carers and institutions. Kinderhaus demonstrates that it allows for more reasoned discussions and stresses and strains that are more akin to those that will arrive in adulthood.

While collectively empowering fostered children poses more challenges, it is possible. At the government's 2001, Social Exclusion Unit committee, I proposed that fostered children be brought together on a reasonably regular basis at a venue where they could, amongst other things discuss together the issues that they were facing and propose actions. I was told by some agencies that fostered young people did not like being brought together. I was doubtful. My own conclusion was that any reluctance indicated that when the youth were together, they could not see the benefits accruing to them.

Later, in 2007, I was contacted by an organisation called Dreamwall who invited me to visit their project which involved annually bringing together 100 young people in residential and foster care for a 4-day residential camp and three weekends away. It was funded as part of a proactive respite programme giving carers regular rather than ad hoc reactive breaks from their care duties. I could see from the young people and providers I met that the project was a huge success, a residential respite care scheme that young people in care look forward to and that also immensely improved their self-confidence and educational engagement levels.

"It's been a huge success amongst Councillors, managers, staff and foster carers," Les Valentine, Southampton City Council's Service Manager responsible for children in care told me when I was interviewing him for The Guardian newspaper, *"We have rarely seen such a group of young people with such difficulties enjoying themselves and communicating at such a level. Foster and school placement stability has improved. At reviews, Dreamwall is often spoken about as having a positive impact on the lives of the young people."*

In The Guardian, I highlighted the educational impact of the project:

"Jason Ashley, deputy headteacher at Bitterne Park school in Southampton, says the impact of Dreamwall's work has been improvements in attendance, behaviour and performance. 'Watching some students grow emotionally and mentally, I have seen them become more focused.' A recent Ofsted area review described Dreamwall's work as 'outstanding'." (I Saw I Had Made a DifferenceFrampton, The Guardian, February 12, 2008)

Dreamwall demonstrated that young people in care can welcome coming together and this is the opportunity to collectively empower young people which is being ignored by many care providers. There are UK authorities, which claim to bring young people in care together to discuss their issues and these should be built on and their views acted upon so that giving young people a collective voice becomes a genuine level for empowerment instead of a tick box exercise.

Research & Promoting Best Practice for Orphanages
Rather than Western governments and Western funded global charities demanding the closure of orphanages in developing countries, they should be using their funds to invest in discovering and assisting implementation of best practices at home and abroad, which can potentially improve the lives of children and adolescents everywhere.

Progressing in this research requires a recognition of the societal marginalisation of children that also ignores the active contributory role they play within the household and the family, resulting in children having little or no say in their treatment. There is evidence from the research examples quoted above that society can benefit from studies into young people's nurturing and supporting of siblings and peer groups, and especially the lessons regarding adolescents' capacity as demonstrated by young carers. Residential care and residential schools will benefit from research into best practice in collectively empowering children as a means not only of advancing their development of self-identity and self-esteem but also as a means of mutual advocacy and ensuring a non-exploitative upbringing.

If governments have their financial heads on, they might now take heed that the world is witnessing the beginning of a dramatic change, requiring a new approach. Perhaps the poor treatment of children in care is reflected by the low price of children traded on the black market. However, the legal supply of young people into the regulated labour market is no longer cheap.

A huge countervailing process is taking place with birth rates falling and society ages, threatening the sustainability of market economies as is seen now in Japan. This country which led the post-war world in industrial innovation and for many decades kept its doors closed to mass immigration has for the last five years been recruiting several million interns and immigrants to make up for acute labour shortages. Hungary and Russia are offering large financial incentives for families to have three and more children and China having recently abandoned its one-child stricture is now imploring its families to have three children.

With more women in work and the costs of rearing children rising, women have been delaying having children until a later age when they can be more confident of affording the costs. The OECD in 2019 reported that this has been a developing international trend over the last half century:

"In most OECD countries, the average age at which women give birth now stands at 30 or above ...Most OECD countries have seen the average age of women at childbirth increase in recent decades. Between1970 and 2017, most OECD countries saw the mean age increase by somewhere between 2 and 5 years..." (OECD Family Database, 2019, https://www.oecd.org/els/family/database.htm)

Conclusions Regarding Adolescents and Residential Care

- With productive young people at a premium, it is time to urgently reconsider investment in research that casts aside the social prejudices of childism and careism and is aimed at improving outcomes for all young children and adolescents. That, or society faces increased burdens from filling the hospitals and clinics with mental health patients and the prisons with lifelong repeat offenders.

- Successful contemporary models of residential care allied with systems of young people's collective empowerment such as exist at Kinderhaus in Berlin need to be studied and the lessons applied to restructuring of care systems.

- The voice of adolescents has for too long been infantilised and stigmatised in the care system by careism and those researching the system. Both carers and young people would benefit by centring their studies on the views of care-experienced adolescents as to the type of care setting which will best meet their various needs.

- Facilitating young people's transition to adulthood by ensuring adolescents have domestic stability and can freely engage in collective peer-group settings should be at the heart of research into developing models of care.

- Research funding should be diverted from exporting Westernised atomised models of care to a focus on the realities of child poverty, homelessness and child exploitation.

Ways Forward

Content

In this chapter consideration is given as to moving forward regarding some of the issues raised by the Mystery Wall, Recognition of children's active role in the family and the benefits of parenting skills discussions for adolescents are raised for further debate and research. We highlight some of the issues raised for adults and adolescents to consider and also what teenage and adult action are required for meaningful collective empowerment of young people.

Parenting Skills: Crossing the Wall

We have seen how the siloing of the parented and corporate academic worlds is harmful on many accounts. The teaching staff are left to educate their students without any regard to the socially critical act of parenting, which is one of the most complex of human activities which will engage them for up to half their life time. Instead, adolescent pupils are fed "sex education" and expected to focus their consideration on sexual acts, akin to teaching someone how to sow a seed but denying them the knowledge to nurture the plant to full health.

To illustrate the critical nature of this siloing act, I was drawn to further consider the state's approach to parenting. Few would doubt that the source of many of our society's problems lies in inadequate or damaging parenting. Many adults, especially from comfortable backgrounds, are mistakenly drawn to opine about the responsibilities of parents for developing their children from the perspective of these relatively well-off adults' own experience, Often, even the most caring amongst them imply that poor outcomes for the young people are down to poor parenting, and therefore a fait accompli.

Singling out the failing parents for blame is a useful measure for underperforming governments, who can employ it as a means of pressurising other parents through fear of stigmatisation. However, this is of little benefit to the young person who may justifiably conclude that he or she has not only been failed by parents; but also, by society as a whole because nobody else was prepared to intervene. Hence the young person can drift into becoming an alienated, counterproductive member of society.

In reality the societal approach to parenting is systematically inadequate. Discussions on young people and parenting today need to address the realities. Millions on millions of parents are not living comfortable lives.

Many parents are struggling to bring up their children while pressured into taking two or more poorly paid jobs on zero-hour contracts. There are millions of parents suffering from major disabilities or incapacitated by medically prescribed nerve depressants and by illnesses such as alcoholism or drug abuse. There are armies of single parents working every hour and unable to focus on their children who have to try and survive on sink estates, avoiding the grasp of the pimps and drug dealers. For these parents, considerations about their children's future are often buried in the nightmare of surviving the present.

At the same time, our society treats parenting as instinctively passed on from parent to child, suggesting that we are no different to animals and ignores the complex nature of our communities. Parenting is not a simple matter, yet it is an anachronism that governments place pupils' learning of a foreign language on the national school curriculum rather than parenting.

Parenting is much older than humanity, that much is true. Many parenting approaches may be instilled into our DNA but this should not blind us to the changing circumstances over the millennia and centuries.

The Changing Rationales for Child Rearing

We have for long been in a very different era to when child rearing was directly linked to personal survival and to the rest of one's family. There was a time when children represented not only a domestic and productive workforce but also greater numbers for defence of the family and kinship care in old age. Having children was a necessary act for the family and their social group. The struggle to survive necessitated that children were put to productive activity as soon as they were able.

Anthropological studies of contemporary pre-capitalist societies have reported on cultures where children as young as four begin to fend for themselves and where five-year-olds were proficient enough to gather 50% of their calorie intake from foraging. Childhood as we know it today was brief. In mediaeval Britain, girls could be married off at 12 and boys at 14 whereupon they would prepare to raise their own children. As capitalist production and, along with it, living standards, developed it was no longer hugely profitable to employ children and more important that young people developed at least basic skills of literacy and numeracy, and from this layer would then come those trained for the many additional skills required in industrial production.

In rural societies today, young children remain an asset for the basic tasks involved in farming but in modern capitalist cities there are few avenues offered for the children to be employed productively in the labour market. The more a society insists on the academic education of its children, the more children become a burden. Recent studies have revealed how rapidly birth rates are declining in developing countries where accelerated industrialisation and urbanisation is taking place. The decline is precisely because of the reduced "labour value" of children in urban settings and also, hence of the relative value of producing children.

Growth in per capita incomes has also led to capitalism, either via the state or commercial companies, reserving part of the surplus labour as old age pensions, offering an income to the elderly until death. Children are no longer a material necessary for any part of an adult's life. For the individual's life, children have moved from being a necessity for survival to a luxury, from being born of need cloaked as desire to being born of desire cloaked as need... a process that accelerated rapidly in the 20th century.

The Western world sits on the crude notion that parenting is instinctive or passed on from parents to children. This may have been the case when societal productivity was much lower and children were a necessity but parenting out of desire for offspring that will remain unproductive for 18 years then make no material contribution to one's life brings in a qualitatively different ethos to parenting out of material need.

Modern capitalism also presses parents into working as many hours, as possible, which creates additional pressures for child-rearing.

Earlier in this paper, the Danish socialist historian, Hendrick, was quoted, arguing in his 2016 work "Narcissistic Parenting in an Insecure World" that under-pressure modern society had shifted towards: *"'behavioural', punitive and managerial methods of child rearing..."* and that this trend was: *"symptomatic of the sour, mean-spirited and vindictive social norms found throughout society today, which undermine the better instincts of parents and damage parent-child relations... parents are much more inclined to regard children as a nuisance, a hindrance, a burden..."* (Narcissistic Parenting in an Insecure World: A History of Parenting Culture 1920s to Present, Hendrick 2016)

The growing proportions of women across the workforce has also fuelled the need for capitalism to pay some attention to gender equality. At the same time rapid technological and industrial changes have helped to create an historically rare climate of economic and social uncertainty reflected in "short-termism". The guaranteed jobs for life at the local mines, factories, stores and banks have gone. Automation and new technology have brushed aside the manual jobs previously reserved for the fittest of males. The male can no longer guarantee to offer the income for life, or even its largest part. to the family.

Soviet psychologist, Lev Vygotsky's contention that cultural mediation and interpersonal communication play an important part in the development of the higher psychological functions is today more widely accepted. (Mind in Society, Vygotsky, Harvard University Press, 1978)

If one accepts Vygotsky's observation that the shared knowledge of a culture was passed down, with children internalising that knowledge as with eating an orange or riding a bike, this has major implications for the family and parenting. Given the huge changes which have taken place in the last half century, there is a major question regarding how much of relevance can be passed down and how confident parents are when passing on this information.

In Western societies, patriarchy, at least in the family, is experiencing the overture of its death knell. Centuries on centuries of household patriarchal wisdoms and abuses born of being the dominant gender in society, have been handed down from father to son.

The basis for so many patriarchally passed down behaviours has been critically undermined by capitalism, impacting not only on fathers but also mothers. What are they to tell their children about the way things are between men and women, fathers and mothers, the way they should be and the way things were? How are they expected to renegotiate their roles with each other based on what they learned from their parents whose notions were drawn from a departed era?

Discussing Parenting Skills in the Classroom
I have long advocated the teaching of parenting skills to adolescents and have additionally suggested that the narrower topic of sex education should be part of this framework as one part of the process of reproduction. Currently sex education is doled out as an issue of sexual

health and demystifying a taboo. Yet the real taboo is societal engagement in the issue of parenting skills.

This applies most notably to young people. In an educational setting, the encouragement of adolescents to reflect on all the issues involved in parenting and how they would bring up children of their own age could be of huge benefit. In learning about parenting, adolescents can potentially begin to frame and understand their parents' actions and hence engage in a more meaningful dialogue.

With greater dialogue and understanding adult society may begin to treat teenagers as social adults rather than animals fitted with brains of dangerously combustible chemicals and needing the whip and the leash for their own and others' benefit. If so, with patient dialogue new passages through the Wall between adolescents and their parents, carved by increased mutual understanding and trust could appear.

Discussing parenting skills with adolescents would nevertheless involve the almost rational world of social education invading and threatening to undermine the irrational world of the nuclear family. The prospects of government taking up such a proposal are slim because of the fear that arming young people with rights to openly discuss the rights and wrongs of their own parenting would undermine the social pact of parental authority in return for parental control (or oppression) of their children.

The very idea of adolescents returning home and challenging parental autarchy would doubtless lead to social outrage in various quarters for some time, even if it would mean generations to come would prosper. At the same time many will argue that the "nanny state" is invading the family, a notion which is based on adolescents not being able to reason for themselves, and a notion that will gain currency while society rests on childism and suppresses rather than empowers adolescents. More informed and engaged teenagers will be a barrier to dominance of the state rather than a prop. The state has leaned on childism to justify increasing exploitation of young people. Combatting childism releases the energy and agency of youth to assist parents in their mutual efforts to experience a fulfilled life.

Shrouding parental skills in a secret shrine, a mystical parental soup composed of handed down advice, instinct, role models and parental autarchy, keeps the adolescent at bay so that they cannot have a meaningful say in their own parenting. The parents are left to take them on a journey which even they have no idea where they are going, where they will all end up. Or perhaps that is the point; that society cannot agree what parenting skills are, so is reluctant to allow the adolescent in to see that the shrine is full of groups of high priests accusing each other of hocus pocus, which might also explain the popular references to *"the magic of childhood".*

Recognising Children's Active Role in Child-Rearing
Many modern governments preach empowering of service users, of the people, of giving a voice to service users and (as fundamental to a democracy) a voice to the people. Yet, the adolescent provided with the service of parenting, is, as service-user, denied a meaningful voice by being excluded from the discussion. One important cyclical outcome is that the parents of the future have also little left to guide them when they take on the mantle of reproduction.

The potential gains from involving young people in contemplating and discussing their parenting include not simply more harmonious relations with parents, offering a less traumatic transition through adolescence.

For example, it was earlier pointed out that the role siblings and peer nurturing, scaffolding and mentoring play within child development are often passed over. Many orphanages, where children were often left to their own devices, displayed significant elements of peer nurturing and mentoring. Like most children, outside of the classroom, we learnt more from our peers than from adults, mainly because we spoke the same language, and had the same reference spheres, in contrast to our brief discussions with adults.

As Young-Bruehl argued, by recognising and moving away from childism and the notion that young people lack *"agency or capacity for choice, expression of interest, or reason,"* adults can avoid *"contributing to the difficulties children have in developing their capacities."* (Childism: Confronting Prejudice Against Children, Young-Bruehl, 2012)

With Britain's birth rate in 2019 at 1.6 and expected to have fallen by another 10% in the 2020 lockdown year, it is now only threequarters of the rate required to naturally sustain the population at its current level. Even so, for the last 200 years and more, the majority of the population has grown up with siblings. Yet, psychologists have highlighted that there is a dearth of research data on siblings, their psychology, interactions, peer nurturing and interdependency.

At a time when financial and time pressures on adults is said to be the cause of falling birth rates, one might expect to see an increased role of siblings in peer nurturing. Psychologists have observed that, in families where children suffer parental neglect, then often one or more of the siblings become the primary attachment for the other children. The role of children in under pressure families becomes, as observed in the most impoverished communities, more critical.

Other psychologists and sociologists pour over ways of reforming the roles and attitudes of adults. It is as if they deliberately ignore the most important resource in the room, the children, and prefer to busy themselves changing around the deckchairs on their proverbial Titanic. This is not to suggest that children should have their playtime cut. Play is one of the most important parts of child work. The issue is how sibling can be more respected for their actions and become more conscious of their role in the family. Play is being cut because of a failure to recognise its contribution not because it is considered sacrosanct. The alternative of playing in between observing the angst and tempers of stressed-out parents can't be half as much fun.

Child Work Revisited
We referred previously to Chakrabarti's analysis of child work and how alongside women's housework, child work (in the household) was marginalised (Children's Working World through the Lens of Class, Anjan Chakrabarti, Journal of Social and Economic Development July - Dec. 2007).

There is a strong case for the formal teaching of parenting in high schools enabling young people to become more conscious of the processes going around them and their roles within the home. Involving adolescents in considerations re-parenting skills also opens the door to the possibility of, for example, more conscious sibling mentoring and additional aid for the pressured adults in the household shouldering the tasks of child-rearing. This requires the beginning of a societal shift regarding the attitude towards children's contribution to the family. At the same time, there is an urgent need for professionals to focus on child-centred research regarding sibling relationships, peer mentoring and nurturing, for the benefit of young people, parents and society as a whole.

Moving Forward

Central to this paper is the need for reframing adolescence within the context of the importance of collective empowerment in the development of the self-identity and self-esteem required for productive adult engagement with society. Rather than undermining and threatening adolescent association and collective empowerment, society needs to protect and support adolescent spaces and socialisation. This involves a redefining of the societal relationship with adolescence being recognised as a vital organism of modern civilization.

This also requires combatting childism and recognising that all ages have a role to play in raising a child and that includes young children and adolescents. Parents passively recognise this but male-dominated capitalism, in denying the value of women's labour in the household also glossed over child work and the contribution of children to the family.

There is a need to secure adult recognition of children's role (whether through participation in chores, childcare or nurturing and peer development) and of the fact that this work is carried on in households across the world and needs a context where it is valued rather than buried in exploitative concepts such as 'duty'.

We have considered how anthropologist, Margaret Mead and others have studied scores of cultures in which teenagers do not experience the levels of trauma common to Western civilisation, demonstrating adolescent trauma is a cultural rather than biologically driven phenomenon.

There is a danger that whilst society rests on current prevailing concepts of the nuclear family, the crude isolating of the parenting world from the school world will continue. Each one rests on the other and their owners draw a veil; the rational school world pretending to be blind to the societally constructed irrationality of the parented world, imbibe that irrationality and so contributes to the alienation of their young students who in turn absorb the rigid compartmentalisation of the two worlds.

Each morning as they pass through the school gates, adolescents hide their experiences of their parenting world in their socks so they can be parked for the day, allowing the students to swim in the relative peace and freedom (or confront the bullying nightmare) offered whilst attending to their formal education. The school world turns a blind eye to their parented world and enforces the taboo while muttering under its breath demanding the parents must live up to their part in the charade.

As a result of these fears and divisions, both the child and society pay the huge price of adolescence. In the melee of confusion as to their newfound sense of alienation, millions of teenagers are directed to doubting their self-worth, to self-loathing and many graduate to self-harm and substance abuse. Furthermore, though some may pass through unscathed, for millions this is no passing forgettable episode, it leaves its scars all over the adult impacting on mental health and revealing itself in substance abuse, obesity, anorexia, misogyny, nervous breakdowns, sociopathic and psychopathic disorders and child abuse.

Hundreds of millions of parents recognise that adolescence is, was or will be a difficult time for their children. The gemeinschaft seems to want them to pass through unscathed but the gesellschaft adopt a harsh unrelenting stance portraying adolescents as anti-social threats to communities, to families and one another. We have discussed how governments and media pour out unrelenting propaganda aimed at justifying the oppression of adolescents, not only encouraging parents to turn on their children and their children's peers but also turning adolescents against themselves.

Meanwhile governments encourage an army of academics and social workers to biologize adolescence in the hope that the rest of society will go along with believing that the children they reared were at teenage struck by Original Sin which, after centuries of priests' prayers had in the modern era mischievously avoided appearing in the new born only to reappear later in life in those raging adolescent hormones. In parallel, the same governments employ another army of academics and social workers to patch and mend and patch and mend the damage that the state's attacks on adolescents continue to generate.

Given the attention paid and laws enacted by Western governments to curbing adolescents' perceived anti-social behaviours, one might expect a more studied analytical approach to understanding the underlying causes and the tracking of trends in behaviour trauma etc. Yet the absence of clear data on adolescence, in the UK for example, is striking.

Searches for relevant composite data in the UK at best involve piecing together statistics from varying school and college years. The lack of a serious framework for an evidence-based approach to adolescence raises questions as to whether governments prefer to be guided by the ratings-driven commercial media than by studying the facts and listening to the key stakeholders, namely in this case, young people.

Instead, to those surviving adolescence without being convicted of harming others, society, having near criminalised them throughout their teenage years, then suddenly performs an about turn and issues a general pardon: "*It was not your fault,*" but then adds a rejoinder, "*Nor was it ours. Let's all move on.*" The teenager spends the next 30 years wating for their parents to apologise and the parents spend the rest of their lives hoping their kids will say sorry. And so, the wheel turns and the battered, scarred young adults are invited to be involved in the mauling of the next generation.

The Mystery Wall is just one symptom of the damaging distortions of the family that prevailing property relations have created. If society is to move forward then it needs to find ways of embracing the collectivity and collective empowerment of adolescents rather than continuing the repressive road of mistrust, atomisation and repression. That will mean society re-embracing collectivity but for the 'whole village to raise a child' it will require recognising the key role of the children in the village and may mean challenging not only the government of the day but the social order, its priorities and preferred property relations.

Central to my conclusions regarding the Mystery Wall was the role that collective empowerment plays within the development of adolescents as they prepare to take their place in the world as adults.

Human beings are nothing if they are not collectively organised. The search to succeed without others is meaningless. As the sociologist, Durkheim wrote: *"The individual is not an end sufficient unto himself. When he looks for his purpose within himself, he falls into a state of moral misery which leads him to suicide."* (Emile Durkheim, Moral Education, 1925)

Modern civilisation is based principally on this collectivity. The brutal reality of the 2020 pandemic has highlighted that. The rich and famous were forced to openly pin their very existence on the sacrifices and heroics of lowly paid workers. So many were hit by a blinding light, declaring "we are all in this together", appealing to the forgotten people's good natures, promising them a brighter future and hoping that their treating them with contempt would be forgotten. For one moment the state pleaded with and tried to charm rather than bully its citizens. Nevertheless, as billions suffered economically from the lockdown, governments did not bat an eyelid when it was revealed that the world's billionaires banked trillions of dollars through profiting from the global crisis.

At the same time the lockdowns of whole regions and countries highlighted how important collectivity remains for young people and the family. Countless media reports eventually emerged of young people begging to be reunited with their friends at school. Governments responded that children not attending school was bad for their mental health. Notably there was little government discourse on why so many children's mental health was suffering. Yet there are two factors which stood out. Whilst the vast numbers of families living in cramped inadequate housing conditions was one, the other, most referred to by parents was the children's lack of engagement with their peers, with their collectives.

Human society is collectively organised and the anachronism at the heart of modern society is an economic system that treats people as individual commodities in the production process rather than as human socialised collectives. Consequently, as the productive forces grew, the 'whole village" raising the child was replaced with one father and one mother, and the processes of atomisation at work has, for tens of millions reduced this to a single parent or carer.

In the collective world, the nuclear family has become an isolated atomised unit trying to cling on to socialised elements of collectivity with most of these reduced from caring to cash relationships. The whole village the collective brought up the child to engage in the collectivity of the village. In the nuclear family, the family is the bunker and the child as property of the parent must respond to the parent. Yet outside in the village very different rules apply. At the heart of much of modern society is the contradiction between the assertion of the individual as opposed to the supremacy of the collective. That same tension exists in child-rearing. The cost of drifting away from the tribe, the collective, was often fatal.

Maslow's shift from the collectivity of the Blackfoot tribe's hierarchy of needs to his own world-renowned individualistic hierarchy of needs represented the prevailing Western establishment ideology based on the concept of the atomised individual's contract with society. Sociologists and social psychologists struggled with the dualism of the individual and the collective and some have dismissed this but the two are real. The problem more lies in focussing on one or the other since they exist together in a dialectical relationship ever struggling or embracing each other on different planes. This is what adolescents are faced with getting to grips with after having had most of their own primitive needs as young children met within the nuclear family.

The question that the Mystery Wall enquiry raises is whether society could save itself from a great deal of unnecessary pain and suffering by not only recognising that it is the primary cause of that suffering but also that part of the way forward involves ending the societal oppression of adolescents and supporting their collective empowerment.

Adolescent trauma comes at a huge cost to society as well as those who experience that trauma. We have explored the Mystery Wall, a previously unidentified societal process which takes place in plain sight of parents, adolescents and the education system. The Mystery Wall demonstrated that it was a barrier erected in the mind that siloing one's parental/domestic life from one's corporate social life. We considered it from the point of view of adolescents where it appears to be a much more intense phenomenon.

Pertaining to the life of adolescents, we have identified the components of the Mystery Wall. One component of the Wall manifests itself openly as a creation of adult society, separating children as part parental property and part corporate property in the sense that parents are given free rein to deal with their offspring in the home but cede control to the state or other corporate entities for the duration of their children's academic education.

The other component of the Wall is that created by adolescents to protect their development when faced with the contradictory learning settings of their atomised disempowered parented lives on the one hand and their collectivised peer empowered corporate lives on the other.

In adult society, the Wall operates as a compromise whereby parents are given freedom to control their households in return for handing over their children to be academically educated largely in the manner that the state sees necessary to prepare the young person to play a useful part in the workforce and society as a whole. The academic staff and the state do not interfere in the parented life of the child so long as he or she is returned to school in a condition fit to absorb further corporate education. Equally the parents are not expected to challenge their children's passage through school unless they are returned home, seriously harmed either physically or psychologically or majorly failing to achieve the academic results that the parents expected.

For adolescents the Mystery Wall manifests itself outside the parental home as an unconscious, almost impregnable defensive barrier whereby discussion with those outside the family about one's homelife is a subconscious taboo. This is a taboo, which generally is not manifest in early childhood or in adulthood. On the contrary, society openly encourages adults to "share", if discreetly, their problems in the home with others.

In the parental home the Wall is employed by adolescents as an almost impregnable but slightly more conscious barrier to parental invasion of adolescents' efforts to make sense of all they are accruing from their peer-empowered life in the corporate school world. The most common manifestations are teenage responses to questions about their wellbeing which often involve grunts, one-syllable answers or silence all accompanied by sight of a pair of heels heading to the bedroom.

For adolescents, the principal role of the Mystery Wall is to protect their new found world (whether that be school or friends' circles) of burgeoning personal and collective empowerment which in turn is nurturing their sense of self-identity and sense of self-esteem.

It has also been argued here that the young persons' parented and formal academic worlds, based on property and power relations, generate contradictory and polarised learning frameworks. During their teenage years, young people process these learning frameworks as separated by the Wall. The result for many adolescents is that the existing formal (academic) and informal (parental) education system undermines their sense of wellbeing due to the contradictory messages and experiences emanating from these parallel worlds.

The cornerstone of adolescents' development of a sense of identity is based on engagement and association with their peers. On the road to adulthood, adolescents' sense of identity is developed not from themselves but from the results of their engagements with others and particularly their peers. In the collectivised corporate world of school, they not only have the opportunity for such engagement but also to benefit with their peers from a collective empowerment that is denied them in the parental world. It is in the collectives of engagement and empowerment that much of the adolescent's sense of identity is forged.

In the home, the emerging self-efficacy and empowerment processes generated by adolescents' physical and psychological (e.g. rapidly increasing capacity for abstract thought) development on the road to adulthood emerges while the adolescent is still perceived and legally positioned as a child and the property of the parents.

For the adolescent to secure new freedoms of movement and action often requires a series of negotiations between the adolescent and the parents, which may not necessarily be bilateral but involve both parents and even considerations regarding siblings. The parents have the power of gatekeepers so negotiations can be exceedingly psychologically tense and fraught with errors causing apprehensions and discomfort to all parties. These struggles can themselves cause major damage and setbacks for the young person's self-esteem with every barrier reinforcing a sense of being trapped in a childish serf-like status the consequence of which could also be to undermine their status in their peer group.

For the adolescent, the Wall acts as a cocoon, protecting often delicate emerging senses of identity from the psychological turmoil created by adolescents' changing relationships with their parents.

This siloing of the parented world and the corporate academic world has other consequences both for adolescents, staff and parents. The commodification of the students is met by the commodification of the teaching staff. Both parties only exist in their performances at school. They are half humans, leaving half their lives buried. Neither the students or the teachers care what is taking place in the other half except perhaps when the other implodes. The adolescents can use their collective power to bully or even destroy a teacher and the teacher can use their authorised power to bully or destroy the adolescent.

Furthermore, adolescents by unconsciously hiding their parented worlds from their peers, initially engage with each other on a relatively superficial level, which partially explains the more frequent changes and U-turns in their choices of friends during this period. Most importantly, at a time, when they are reaching out to their peers and engaging in their new more collectively empowered world, they have to hide away from others any tormenting issues they are facing in their parental world. This, after all, is where the Mystery Wall investigation began. I was envied by my middle-class peers because I was 16 years old and living on my own in a bed-sit sharing the bathroom with down and outs. They didn't ask why.

We have argued that the collectively empowered world of adolescents and their physical and intellectual growth offer an exciting time for the world as they reach out and assess the validity of the truths they are handed down as against their experiences and their developing logical skills. The threat to parental and adult autarchy is palpable. The state at best aims to channel this intellectual and physical energy into safe channels promising future rewards for the 'ablest' of young people.

With the increasing marketisation of education directed by the state, schools are in competition as profit and loss enterprises. They must show test results. Practises such as denying enrolment in school to young people in care who are considered likely to be poor performers have crept in necessitating state intervention but reflecting the gross distortion of education.

We have seen how schools have cut down on pupils' association and play time and for adolescents this means reducing the time in peer-group engagement and collective empowerment. What is so valuable for the child is considered valueless by the state. Both the young child and the adolescent must be measured by what the market deems is measurable. The state growls at threats to this process of standardisation and intensified commodification. Bring in the 'rebellious teenager' whose mind is unable to rationalise the socially irrational, except as a plot to bake their brain to produce "Another Brick in the Wall".

The state also stands for the maintenance of the social order, the nuclear family, the parental autarchy, childism and the submission of adolescents as parental or adult property. It bears down on teenagers particularly in their collectives as a threat to society... "out of control" "rampaging" "anti-social behaviour".

A cursory check over the last half century unearths a bizarre list of the groups of adolescents demonised by the British establishment and media as terrorising society: young people with long hair, young people with flowers in their hair, young people with braided hair, young people with no hair, young people covering their heads, young people wearing boots, young men wearing pointed shoes, young people riding scooters, young people standing on street corners, young people dancing in fields, young people with black skin - teenagers.

It is as collectives that young people are empowered against adult autarchy and it is this collective empowerment that the state and the media mainly focus on, using it to bring in measures of oppression specifically directed at young people by preying on parental sensitivities.

We have highlighted how little consideration is given to the impact of the societal attacks on teenagers' self-esteem and collective self-esteem. Adolescents can either receive these messages as a malevolent or misguided attack on their age group or they can absorb them and begin to fear or loathe their peers; a divisive message that corrodes society and undermines adolescents' confidence in others and their own confidence regarding their ability to make the right choices. When adult society signals that one's peers are to be loathed, what is wrong with joining in the attack and exercising one's prejudices with fat-shaming, bullying, sexting, racial and sexual abuse of other adolescents?

The antidote to this and to bullying is adolescent peer-engagement, wearing down prejudices and building the collective empowerment that is an important cocoon for developing sense of identity and helping to build self-esteem. Yet we have seen how adolescent socialisation time has been cut by the schools and colleges as unimportant compared to responding to government and market pressures for exam grades.

It should not be surprising that more adolescents are suffering acute mental distress leading to self-harming, eating disorders and nervous breakdowns. Government and media cynically pour on the petrol, light the fire then point the finger at the teenagers seen tossing round the embers.

The state, keen to develop obedient citizens for the workforce, by its actions makes the adolescent transition to adulthood far more traumatic than it needs to be. Riddled with childism, grudgingly it has retreated on issues such as corporal punishment of children whereby outright physical assaults of children are barred across most of Europe. Hesitantly it ended corporal punishment but in the UK for example, the government is yet to even tentatively recognise that the abolition of the right to attack children may have been a factor in the dramatic 30-year decline in reported youth crime for fear that it will trigger a review of the state's use of other terror technics used for repression.

Residential Settings in Adolescence

This book has highlighted the difficulties posed for adolescents transitioning to adulthood via school and the parental home because of property relations and the sharply contrasting learning settings of the private parented and corporate academic world. The question was also posed as to how adolescents fare when such daily contradictions dominating the school year are taken away. Relevant research is scanty but there is enough on boarding schools to suggest that non-academic outcomes can be better for adolescents in residential schools and that the factors may include greater consistency of learning settings, decreased friction with the parental autarchy and greater experience of peer empowerment and engagement with collectives.

More relevant reliable research has been conducted into boarding schools than care homes, which may be because the former are overwhelming the territory of countries' fee-paying upper and middle classes. There is a case for much greater research across the board in this field. In the modern era especially, residential care is required to be professional and is therefore costly and much more so than leaning on the double exploitation of women in the family.

The Child Poverty Action Group in 2020 estimated that in Britain the cost for a couple to raise one child was over £150,000 (Hirsch, The Cost of a Child in 2020, Child Poverty Action Group). Nevertheless, that is easily topped by the average cost of just eight years at private boarding school costing £260,000 in term time alone, whilst residential care homes will charge governments a minimum of £800,000 and secure care units £1,600,000 over a similar period.

Whilst we have referenced the Berlin Kinderhaus to illustrate that there exists vast room for economies of scale in residential care, it is clear why governments' short-term interests of the state turn them away from funding major research in this field. The above figures may help people to put into perspective why the UK government maintains that residential care is bad for most children yet subsidise with tax-breaks or directly subsidise ten times more places in private boarding schools than the numbers of young people they fund to reside in state residential care, even though there are almost 50% more children in care than there are private boarders.

Government accountants and careism have stripped young people out of the community's care and onto a short-term cash balance sheet which, like a magic carpet, flies children around the country leaving them invisible and governments happy to keep their suffering out of the public eye. Some of the research examples have shown that orphanage care can be community care because it can bring stability to young people's lives.

Yet the cost of prioritising short-term finances and so failing young people in care is carried for a lifetime both by the care experienced and by society. Each lifetime spent in and out of the criminal justice system will alone cost the state millions.

Ways Forward Research
There are several major areas indicated here. One is how the contradictions between the learning settings of the parented world and

the adolescents' academic world could be reduced or eradicated. Another is whether doors or corridors through the Wall could be opened. Use of residential schools for educating adolescents or acting on analysis of the factors that benefit adolescents in residential care settings points to the former, whilst the teaching of parenting skills to adolescents, reviewing siblings' roles in child development and ending the government sponsored societal war on teenagers point to the latter.

Western countries would benefit from half century reviews of their youth crime statistics and the reporting and use of them. This may be difficult because of reporting issues, and changing attitudes to what the court considers as crimes but there are crime and social attitude surveys from 50 years ago which can be replicated as shown by the example given in the text of The People newspaper's longitudinal comparisons. By the same token, research is required into the link between declining pupils' school breaks and adolescent trauma.

The central theme has been to recognise, value, protect and strengthen the adolescent world of collective empowerment. There may be many other ways in which the issue may be approached and may be thrown up by stripping away the trappings of childism and careism and supporting the empowerment of adolescents. What is clear is that despite all the talk of youth empowerment, little has been realised over the last 40 years by focusing on the adolescent as an individual within society. Rather, in line with neo-liberalism, over large swathes of the world, the rights of adolescents have been reduced. This only serves to emphasise the importance of collective empowerment, as the prime route by which youth can assert and advance their position in society.

Nevertheless, there are fundamentals changes that are worth seeking to take young people further along the road to emancipation. We have illustrated how children's exploitation takes place at the expense of society as whole. Market forces ensure that children will continue to be exploited and oppressed whilst they are denied an effective voice. It has been argued that given the processes behind childism, this voice can only have sufficient power if it is collective and collectively organised. It is for adult society to allow this voice to come through and combat attempts to

271

suppress it. At the top line that means supporting young people when they protest, when they strike and when they gather to improve their situation as young people. At bottom it means finding effective ways to encourage that voice and to listen.

Governments should be pressured to hold their hands up, declare an end to the Teen Year War and commit to ending the repression and exploitation of young people. If statues are part of a people's history let them build youth monuments and permanent exhibitions celebrating the role adolescents have played and the sacrifices they have made in the ongoing struggle for a better world.

What is certainly required is an international discussion on childism and adolescent repression which starts from acknowledging the harm caused by that repression and rooting out the structural and political causes and, crucially, which involves adolescents.

A useful starting point would be adoption of an adolescent-centred approach given that they are the inheritors of the productive role in our societies. Adolescents after all are the bedrock of our future comforts. Teenagers possess an energy and dynamism, which may not be blessed with years of experience of the adult world, but certainly have the measure of adults on the adolescent world.

To progress the discussions, requires abandoning the prevailing worship of the flailing nuclear family and lifting the anchor to move away from an academic education system fashioned for the minimal needs of the ruling elites in the 19th century and generally established without democratic consent for the purposes of militarism, popular control and religious indoctrination. This is not to say that family and education must go, only that society needs to look at its failings to deliver the promised wellbeing despite all the productive power and inventions amassed over the centuries and question every aspect shorn of the trappings of tradition and vested corporate interests. Only then can we begin to consider how education can be most productive for adolescents and hence society in the 21st century.

A debate, with adolescents engaged at the centre, must look at encouraging and supporting the collective empowerment and emancipation of young people. Part of this process is to acknowledge the positive contributions that children and young people often play in the family particularly in the nurturing of siblings. Acquainting adolescents with discussions about parenting skills will also assist them finding their place within the family and encourage meaningful discussions with parents.

However, there are some structural political and financial issues which need addressing and which could be considered as emancipatory acts. One of them is the right to vote at 16 (or 15) years of age but this needs to be accompanied by discussions around the creation of democratically elected youth advocates having representation in corporate bodies making decisions which will specifically impact on young people within the organisation.

If a person is mentally aware enough to carry out a serious crime, then they should be considered old enough to make a decision about whom they might wish to represent them in parliament. The age of criminal responsibility in England is ten yet the same young person is not considered fit to vote for another eight years.

Regarding the age of universal suffrage, the case for voting at 16 has generally been won and should be implemented. Voting at 16 is now a right in Argentina, Brazil, Cuba, Ecuador, Nicaragua, Austria, Malta, in Bosnia and Herzegovina (for the employed), in various local and state elections in Germany, local elections in Estonia and for the Scottish and Welsh parliaments. The British Conservative government is holding back on lowering the voting age despite the fact that the party in power allows 16-year-olds to vote for its leader and, in effect, elected Boris Johnson to the post of Prime Minister when his predecessor stood down. They fear the radicalism of youth. In contrast, the UK nations of Scotland, Wales and the crown dependencies of Jersey, Guernsey and the Isle of Man all give the right to vote at 16 for their parliaments and local elections. This should be just a part of the process with high school students encouraged to have debates for each age group as to whether they consider they should have the right to vote and their deliberations and decisions reported back to local and national election monitoring bodies for enactment by the elected parliaments.

Being able to vote every few years for political representatives is only one small part of the road to emancipation. There are a series of other emancipatory acts that governments which are serious about supporting adolescents could introduce. One of the most important of these is a global ban on all corporal punishment of children. Assault should be a crime whatever age the victim is. However, the allowing of "reasonable chastisement" of children as spread from English law is applied in many of the 50 plus countries around the world that have so far banned corporal punishment, still in effect endorses intent to cause harm to a child.

Access to free school, college and university education should be across the board to allow for young people to reach their full potential. At the same time, adolescents at each age group should also be engaged in a comprehensive nationwide debate about the role of the minimum school leaving age, whether it meets the needs of young people and what if any alternative structures would be preferable.

School students in the UK have declared that their school breaks, which have been significantly reduced to meet government pressures, are too short. Discussions should take place amongst school students on what they consider to be the value of the various breaks and what the preferred lengths would be for their school and year groups. Effecting such a plan requires the students to face no barriers in organising collectively and democratically across schools. Education workers' unions should consider offering support and local educational authorities pressed to implement a plan. Governments should be pressed to stipulate minimum times for school breaks.

Most importantly. young people will never be near to full emancipation until the principal of equal remuneration for equal work is established in law and in practice. Rational employers will make their decisions based not on age but on the many factors which directly benefit the workplace. National minimum wages should be set at the same level for all employees and contractors and the same for all trainees, apprentices and interns whatever their age whether it be ten years old or 75. Trade unions that wish to show they respect young members rights as equal members of their organisations should be campaigning and fighting for all employers to pay the full rate of pay at 16 based on equal pay for equal work.

The public sector is a major employer in the modern age. If governments wish to be true to their statements about the living wage and human rights then they should make a start by pledging that the national minimum wage will be the absolute minimum paid to government, and government contractors' employees and all those working for government-subsidised companies.

The discussions on countries piloting basic universal guaranteed income schemes should also include adolescents, with the same level of guaranteed income being available to all from the age of 16, so increasing young people's opportunities to make clearer life choices. Meanwhile as with the national minimum wage unemployment benefits should be available at 16 and at full rates.

Lack of access to free healthcare including mental and sexual health services without parental permission is also a major problem for many young people and makes no sense when domestic child abuse remains so prevalent.

Charting the way through to a better more productive pathway from childhood to adulthood will not be achieved by simply listening to armies of neuro-scientists, psychologists and sociologists. The core voice that needs to be engaged and empower, as Paulo Frere, argued is the service-user, in this case the child, the adolescent, the teenage rebels, the shy nerds, the hoodies and quirky Goths, the young punks, the sports junkies, the little swots, the rap fiends, the young gang members and juvenile delinquents.

Empowerment of young people may only come when the right of every young person, worker, school or college student to form and join a democratically organised students' union and/or trade union and the right of all students, trainees and apprentices to assemble, to protest and to strike has been won, not simply written on paper but demonstrated in action.

One major reason why the oppression of adolescence has been allowed to intensify is because it is a relatively short and transitory part of a young person's life. Their reaction to their oppression can be passed off as a passing affliction like chicken pox.

One of the barriers to considered adolescent-led discourse is that it needs to be developed with a speed and intensity since one's adolescence doesn't last forever and soon one is faced with conducting self advocacy for a self which has gone.

On the other hand, that all people have been young provides a wealth of experience and evidence in all generations – which cannot be said for any other age cohort. And whatever may be lacking in time, the youth have the empathy, energy and collectivity to generate those huge bursts of collective social energy that can combust, producing the work of several years in one day, scorching past ground as it heaves society forward.

Hitherto most youth movements have been around ad hoc issues and often have taken their cue from other organisations. The politically oriented youth organisations that have existed have largely been directed to deliver results for others' rather than for the youth. The world needs independent democratic youth organisations with each as 'a body for itself' not simply a 'body for others', and which at the same time understands the importance of its relationship to other exploited sections of society.

Most peoples in the world aspire to equality or rights and equality of opportunity for all but we are still paying a heavy price for exploitative discriminatory practices such as racism, nationalism and sexism. Only when societies begin to recognise and acknowledge these practices can they make a start on understanding the cost to humanity and see the benefits of eliminating them. The same can be said of childism and adolescent oppression. Societies bear the price of childism because they do not recognise it. As was the case with the other prejudices, the fault is identified in the oppressed rather than the oppressor.

Society can move forward in leaps and bounds but first of all it must begin by acknowledging the oppression and understanding its cost. Collectively empowering young people is a critical part of the process whereby children can take a meaningful place in decision making of society. Adult society needs to do much more than the token gestures of youth parliaments with no power, youth charters with no jobs, youth and youth projects with no prospects.

The Black Lives Matter and Climate Change protests illustrate how young people are prepared to make a positive collective contribution to moving society forward. The scale and breadth of the global events dwarfed the anti-nuclear, anti-racist movements of the 1960s. Whether such energy can be harnessed to making the world a better place, reaching in to scooping out the dark realities of poverty, trauma and depression depends on whether professionals can ally with young people and the professions and society can be won to the notion that it takes a whole community to raise a child and that community includes its children.

Peering behind the Mystery Wall leads us back to the importance of the collectivity in our childhoods and the urgent societal need to embrace and develop the collective empowerment of adolescents.

Appendix

The Mystery Wall – Matters Arising

Content

This discourse has highlighted some of the problems facing adolescents, the family and society as a whole regarding approaches to children and their education. It has been argued that the source of these problems is deeply rooted in the make-up of modern society but that actions can and must be taken to overcome them because society has been brought to a crossroads. The document was written to promote dialogue and, in this chapter, we suggest some of the issues arising from the Mystery Wall discourse for discussion by social workers, professionals, parents and adolescents. Firstly, some suggestions for professionals and parents, then we highlight some issues that adolescents might wish to consider.

Matters Arising: for Social Workers and Professionals
There are many areas regarding practice which social workers, teachers, other professionals and parent groups could fruitfully discuss. Primary amongst these is whether the role and aim of the education system is capable of meeting the educational needs of modern-day adolescents – as defined by a) adolescents and b) educationalists.

The Siloing of the Parental World and the School World
The document has focussed on the impact of the siloing of the young person's parental world and their school/adolescent peer group world. the Parents commonly struggle when faced with the adolescent's Mystery Wall. It creates anxiety and often leads to conflict and misunderstandings. Core questions for professionals should include:

- How should professionals approach the issue of the adolescent's Mystery Wall - as a threat or a benefit?

- How can professionals promote discussion re-the Mystery Wall amongst parents/young people?

- Does the siloing of parental and academic staff's responsibilities benefit or hinder professionals assisting adolescences to become a rounded adult? And, if so, what is to be done to improve the situation?

Empowerment and Collective Empowerment of Young People

This discourse has highlighted the critical importance of collective empowerment and peer groups for adolescents and adults. Critical questions for practitioners to consider include:

- How do and can young people benefit from engagement in collectively empowered settings?

- How should professionals respond to the issue of adolescents in collectively empowered settings?

- How can professionals support collective empowerment of adolescents?

- How should schools view school breaks?

- How can professionals support young people by ensuring they can access and engage with peer groups?

Online Communication

Of all the mediums of adolescent engagement, the ability of young people to engage with their peers and others, social media and online communication creates the most parental and societal apprehension. On the other hand, online communication has given a huge boost for teenagers organising actions which have forced corporate businesses to recognise their racist practices and rein them in, have led to the courts taking more decisive action against racists and led to the removal of many racist symbols for the benefit of billions of people worldwide. Online collective sharing of information has boosted knowledge and understanding, helping to undermine prejudices and discriminatory practices.

- What does collective empowerment mean in the online world?

- Is it any different from collective empowerment in the non-virtual world?

- Are the benefits and opportunities for adolescents any greater?

- Are the threats any greater?

It is acknowledged by many authors that there has been a shortage of research on sibling relationships and the role they play in child and family development. This feeds into misleading and dangerous societal narratives that children play no worthwhile role in family development, the pressure for standardisation of children to meet market rather than family development needs.

Social workers and professionals may benefit by hosting and promoting discussions on:

- The pro-active and re-active roles of young children and adolescents in family development.

- How professionals can encourage and discuss adolescents' views of parenting and of what adolescents consider parents and carers should do to meet the needs of someone their age.

- Whether and how families would benefit from classroom discussions on parenting?

- Does discussing parenting skills in the classroom represent state intrusion into the family and whether and how this might be desirable?

- How prevailing ideological prejudice against adolescents in collectively empowered settings impacts on research findings and social work practice.

- Whether the profession/team is infantilising adolescents as a means of disempowerment/objectivization/taking away their voice?

2. Matters Arising: for Adolescents

This page puts forward some issues arising from the discourse and suggests questions around topics which young people might wish to address.

Young Children and Adolescents' Role in the Family

Young children and adolescents are often perceived as simply receivers of adult nurturing and protection. We have highlighted several important roles that young people play in assisting the family, particularly other siblings. Looking forward to the future:

- What roles do young people play within the family?

- How could young people's role in the family be improved and what actions may be needed to bring this about?

- How would adolescents benefit from classroom discussions on parenting if at all or would it be detrimental?

Combatting Adolescent Trauma and Anxiety

Adolescence and particularly the teenage years are seen as the most turbulent and trying periods of any age group. They are seen as part of the transition to adulthood. Many adolescents face anxiety. In some it reaches an acute form undermining their mental health. Arising out of the Mystery Wall discussion, questions that could be discussed include:

- How could adolescent trauma/anxiety be reduced?

- What individual actions are required by adolescents/parents to bring about change and reduce adolescent trauma and anxiety?

- What collective actions are required by adolescents/parents to bring about change and reduce adolescent trauma and anxiety?

- How could parents and professionals support adolescents to bring about change and societal oppression of young people?

Equal Rights and the Meaning of Adulthood

In Western society, adulthood is generally understood to be mainly a biological phenomenon. However, adult rights and responsibilities are conveyed by society, making adulthood also a social phenomenon and one decided by politicians and rulers. We have pointed to how the age of sexual consent ranges from 13 to 18 across the world, the voting ages for electing politicians range from 16 to 30, the age of criminal responsibility varies from 10 to 16. Young people of the same age can live in the same street and play in the same local football team but if a national or state border runs along it, one may be able to vote and the other not, one may legally have sex but the other not and one may be able to buy beer and one not. Issues that arise from this discourse and are suggested for discussion include:

- What the age of maturity should be and why?

- What the voting age should be and why?

- What the age of criminal responsibility should be and why?

- How adolescents would benefit or be disadvantaged by having a set age such as 15/16/17/18 for all adult "rights" and responsibilities - instead of the current variations from 10 to 23? What is the preferable age?

- Who should be involved in deciding the ages of responsibility and rights and how should this be done?

Collective Empowerment

The Mystery Wall raises the issue of the importance of collective empowerment (i.e. young people coming together and so giving themselves greater power to impact on their world and to level the playing field with adults where they feel they are being discriminated against). Collective empowerment is expressed in nations coming together, in women coming together to win the right to vote, in workers protesting and striking together and dolphins hunting together. Most of all it requires being able to associate together.

School and college breaks and youth clubs

- How should school and college organise breaks or periods to allow young people to freely associate?

- A national survey found a large majority of adolescents calling for longer lunchbreaks. What is the value of school/college breaks?

- Should school/college breaks be lengthened within the school day?

- Should towns and districts have dedicated buildings for young people housing youth clubs and places where they can organise meetings and freely associate or should young people's activities be mainly focused around schools and youth clubs?

Collective empowerment also means protecting the group. Issues that could be discussed include:

- Whether and how young people should take responsibility for the wellbeing of others in their peer group/class/team?

- Whether and how collective peer group action can deal with bullying/abuse?

- What the benefits and drawbacks of collective action by their peer group are - as compared to young people operating on their own? What benefits could be gained by stepping up their collective actions and what the dangers might be?

How does and could applying collective empowerment of young people impact on online communications is an important issue given social media is portrayed as a major threat to young people's mental health. Issues to discuss could include:

- What the benefits of the internet are for adolescents' communications and how these could be improved especially for peer group communications?

- What the threats of the internet are for adolescents and whether and how these could be improved by peer group collective control?

Join IFSW

Anyone can join IFSW as a Friend

IFSW Friends join to show their support for international social work and to become of a world-wide community. As a Friend of IFSW you receive:

- Free online access to the journal: International Social Work (ISW) published by Sage publications. You will be able to access all the articles in the journals dating back to January 1959.
- Advance access to all IFSW publications at reduced cost.
- Discounted conference registration fees (whenever possible)
- The opportunity to create and/or participate in international, regional or local social work or social justice campaigns.
- The IFSW Friend pin and certificate of 'Friends Status' membership

How to Join IFSW as a Friend

Go online: http://ifsw.org/membership/friends/

The costs of joining IFSW friends is:

- US$50 per year for an individual
- US$25 per year for a student
- US$600 as a one-off fee to get Life Membership
- US$1000 per year for organisations

International Federation of Social Workers
Maiengaessli 4
CH-4310 Rheinfelden
Switzerland

General enquiries
global@ifsw.org

Technical support
online@ifsw.org

Notes

Notes

Notes